R

CORONATION OF CHARLEMAGNE

THE
CORONATION OF
CHARLEMAGNE

THE
CORONATION OF
CHARLEMAGNE
25 December 800

Robert Folz

Translated by
J. E. Anderson

Routledge & Kegan Paul
London

English edition first published in 1974
by Routledge & Kegan Paul Ltd
Broadway House, 68–74 Carter Lane,
London EC4V 5EL
Printed in Great Britain by
Butler & Tanner Ltd, Frome and London
Translated from
Le Couronnement impérial de Charlemagne
(Trente journées qui ont fait la France: 25 décembre 800)
© *Éditions Gallimard 1964*
Translation revised, and some appendices translated, by Henry Maas
Copyright © *this translation Routledge & Kegan Paul Ltd 1974*
No part of this book may be reproduced in
any form without permission from the
publisher, except for the quotation of brief
passages in criticism

ISBN 0 7100 7847 1

Contents

Illustrations

vii

Maps

Preface

It is with some hesitation that I publish this book. In the first place, the subject is highly complex. The fact seems so clear; everyone has known since childhood that Charlemagne received the imperial crown on 25 December 800 like a splendid Christmas present; but really it is one of the least understood and most complex events in the whole history of the west. Though we know more or less what took place in Rome on 23 and 25 December 800, the preparations for the crowning of Charlemagne as well as how the event is to be interpreted still present questions that are not easily resolved. Thus anyone giving an account of this history, with all its uncertainties, must pay attention to all the details, many of them trivial enough, that may serve to show us something of the chief participants' thought. His hypotheses must be based upon some probability, and he must beware of any solution which appears to explain everything but turns out in the end to be mere guesswork. Above all, he must never lose sight of the heart of the problem: how it came about that the king of the Franks was raised to a title that had been extinct for more than three centuries, and thus seemed to inherit the position of the Caesars of old.

My hesitation is doubled by the fact that this volume is to form part of a series intended to concentrate attention on a number of decisive days in French history. Intellectual honesty compels me to quote at this point the judgment pronounced not merely on the coronation of Charlemagne, but on the whole Carolingian period, by one of the greatest of French medieval historians, Ferdinand Lot:

> Charlemagne has ceased to belong entirely to us . . . the future France was only part of his realm, and despite the legends this was not the part that claimed the greatest share of his attention. It is the overall importance of the seventy years from 771 to 840 that justifies our treating his career in detail. . . . Had the event of 25 December produced really lasting consequences, it would have meant that there would be no such thing as the history of France. (*Naissance de la France,* p. 339)

It is no part of my task to dispute this view. I merely say that it seems exaggerated. It is true that Charlemagne does not belong to France alone. But did France exist in the eighth century? I am not sure, and am inclined to think that it came into being in 843, with the break-up of the Carolingian empire. But it is also true that the Frankish period, and especially the Carolingian phase of it, laid the foundations on which France was to be built. When the country became aware of its national identity, it recognised Charlemagne both as the chief founder of its greatness and independence, and as the creator of its place in the development of western civilisation.

Thus it is that many have preceded me in attempting to give some account of what Charlemagne's coronation really was. The material here has been divided into three parts. The first aims to give the reader some picture of the Frankish state. The second analyses the imperial coronation by following the converging lines leading us to the subject, though even then it will not be possible to have a really comprehensive understanding of it. There will remain obscure areas, like those on a map where the continuous line representing a road breaks off abruptly into a dotted line. It is to be hoped that the reader will at least see how the empire came into being, and how contemporaries sought to understand it. The third and last part will bring us face to face both with the dissolution of the empire as a fact, and with its survival in the minds of men for whom 'Charles li reis' remained 'nostre emperere magne', and became the pattern and patron of French royalty, upon which his shadow rested. So deep-rooted was this belief, that Joan of Arc could declare that, along with St Louis, 'St Charlemagne' was interceding with God for his successor Charles VII.

Part One

Preliminaries

From Clovis to the accession of the Carolingians: Frankish Gaul at the beginning of the eighth century

Some three centuries elapsed between the baptism of Clovis and the imperial coronation of Charlemagne. In the course of this long period, what were the characteristics of the country that was later to become France? Let us try to gather them into a general picture by placing ourselves at the moment when the Merovingians were on the point of being supplanted by the line to which Charlemagne belonged.

The civilisation of Frankish Gaul was essentially rural. Its setting was in varying types of countryside, whose distinguishing features were of ancient origin, and in certain areas are still perfectly recognisable today. In the centre of the Paris basin, in the east, in Lorraine, in Alsace, in northern Burgundy and the Franche-Comté, long open fields predominated, with small clusters of villages varying in form. The land was usually divided into plots, growing a regular succession of crops. A three-yearly rotation of crops, which, as Marc Bloch conjectured, 'had perhaps originated in the gleaming plains of Central Europe, where we find the earliest evidence of it', was then beginning slowly to win its way in these regions. Ninth-century documents show that it was already established in parts of the Paris region, where one plot was reserved for winter corn, another for spring corn, the third left fallow and providing rough pasture. The fields were usually worked collectively, in accordance with precise rules. None the less we are only at the beginning of the three-course system, the two-yearly rotation is still much the commoner at the moment we have selected. In Atlantic France, the cultivated countryside is totally different: it consists of rough woodland, with fields enclosed by earth banks or lines of trees round their borders, irregular patches of ground cultivated under a two-yearly rotation, the inhabitants being widely dispersed in hamlets, and living a much less developed social life than in the north and east. These two fundamental types of cultivation extend to the south, but 'shade off and change through an infinite number of gradations'.

Whatever the region, the cultivated areas were separated by vast tracts of forest and virgin waste. The land was worked either by small proprietors, whose holdings or *mansi* probably corresponded to the lots distributed to each family when the land was seized in the distant past, or by landed seigneurs, who were the owners of domains or *villae*. These latter had a variety of origins. Some were the old Gallo-Roman *villae* which kept their original territorial holdings or were split up into smaller domains; others were produced by local clearings; others again were formed by the incorporation of villages of free peasants and their lands into the properties of powerful landlords taking advantage of the patronage over the villages they had by custom exercised since the days of the Late Empire. This process of absorption continued during the Carolingian epoch, but it was never completed; free or allodial peasant lands continued to exist on the fringes of both the smaller and larger estates. The working of these had become gradually more uniform, and the land constituting them was divided into two groups: on the one hand, the ground directly under the owner's control, forming the seignorial *mansus* or *indominicat*, based upon a working centre, the *curtis*, or seignorial *casa*; on the other, holdings that were either *mansi* incorporated from former peasant freeholds, or ones carved out by the lord from his own lands, on which he had settled slaves and free peasants as cultivators. Both classes were hereditary tenants of their holdings, and owed the proprietor of the domain various dues, in kind or in money, and especially in services in the form of work on the seignorial lands, called—incorrectly, by the way—*corvées*, and required because of the lack of manpower attached to these lands. Such were the broad lines of the pattern of rural life at the period we are considering; and they continued to change throughout the Carolingian period.

Rising out of this wide expanse of crops and vines, meadows,

4

forests and waste land, were the towns. All of them were ancient Roman cities. In Provence, in the region of Narbonne, and in the Rhône valley where Roman—and therefore urban—settlement had been considerable, they were numerous, and often fairly close together; but further north they were more widely dispersed. They were all small towns, walled and bristling with towers, for in the third and fourth centuries, menaced by barbarian invasion, they had hastily fortified themselves, though without walling in the whole area they had occupied in the prosperous days of the early empire. Only a part of each town was fortified, and it was into these parts that life retreated. The area enclosed was small—20 to 30 hectares at Rheims, some 30 at Bordeaux and Marseille, 11 at Dijon, 8 to 9 in Paris, 6 at Auxerre—and was the home of a comparatively small population. (The 265 hectares at Trier were exceptional, and only to be explained by the part it played in the fourth century as the capital of the Prefecture of Gaul.) There were 10,000 inhabitants in Marseille, perhaps 6,000 at Rheims, 900 at Châlons. What a contrast with the several hundred thousand living in Constantinople or Alexandria! Nevertheless, the inhabitants were closely packed together, for the enclosed towns were full of churches, and parts of the ground were not built over. Some of our documents give us glimpses of houses huddled close together, sometimes two or three storeys high, along streets which were sometimes, but not always, still paved. Since the sixth century, however, a slow transformation had been taking place, linked with the growing part played by the Church, which was represented in the city by the bishop. From Merovingian times onwards, he was the highest moral authority in the town, and often subsequently became its political head. Now the Merovingian bishops were great builders, and close to their towns they founded sanctuaries, which were often abbeys. These foundations soon became centres of new settlements as they opened hospices for travellers and pilgrims, and attracted men to till their soil. And so in the north, centre and west of Gaul—but, by a striking contrast, not in the south—the towns began to look like nebulae: the urban nucleus became surrounded by new centres of population which, especially in the ninth century, were in their turn surrounded by walls and so turned into fortified towns like Saint-Germain-des-Prés, near Paris, Saint-Médard de Soissons, Saint-Remi de Reims, and many others.

This cramped character of the towns is in keeping with the slow pace of life in them at this time. In some of them, there were still craftsmen's workshops, where men made pottery, fashioned cloisonné jewellery and glassware, selling their products outside the town. All the towns had lively markets; and some of our documents mention merchants, like those of Verdun. But the towns of Gaul certainly suffered from the economic depression which had characterised the whole of the west from about the third century onwards. We must not be deceived here by outward appearances. As in Roman times, Gaul had continued since the fifth century to have a gold standard. But the precious metal had become more and more rare, and was hoarded; from the middle of the seventh century, no more gold coinage was struck. It was replaced by silver, in the form of the *denier* or the *sceatta*, a coin of Anglo-Saxon origin, which gives an early indication of the growing importance of exchange with the north. The trade carried on between west and east by way of the Mediterranean still continued. Silks, spices and ivory were unloaded in the ports of Provence to supply the needs of wealthy customers. Olive oil was needed for food and lighting, and Egyptian papyrus was used to write on till the middle of the eighth century. But this was an unbalanced trade, which had to be paid for in gold. Its volume continued to decrease; in any case it could not be called very great. The chief middlemen were foreigners, especially Syrians and Jews, the latter being particularly active in the towns of the south— Marseille, Arles and Narbonne. Alongside this traditional commerce, another kind had grown considerably since the end of the sixth century, that of the Frisians, which spread out from its central depot or *wik* at Duurstede on the Lek in the direction of the Anglo-Saxon and Scandinavian countries. These peddlers of various cheap wares, especially textiles, the *pallia frisonica*, short striped tunics, probably manufactured in the domanial workshops of northern Gaul or England, would carry with them a supply of *sceattas*, as they worked their way up the French rivers and penetrated as far as the Ille and the Vilaine, the Cher, Bordeaux, and even Cimiez near Nice, bringing commercial activity to Rouen, Quentovic (near Étaples), and the towns of the Rhineland. And so, through their influence, Gaul slowly found itself drawn into the circle of trade with the north.

Such was the situation when an event took place that was of vast significance: the arrival of Islam on the shores of the western Mediterranean. The Arabs had been masters of northern Africa since the end of the seventh century. Carthage had fallen in 698, and they made a rapid conquest of Visigothic Spain in 711. For long centuries the Moslem crescent was to hem in the Mediterranean from the Straits of Gibraltar to the Middle East. In his significantly entitled *Mohammed and Charlemagne*, whose publication in 1937 profoundly affected the study of history, the great Belgian historian Henri Pirenne chose this point—about the middle of the eighth century—as the end of ancient civilisation, following the separation of east and west. He portrayed two mutually hostile worlds confronting one another on the borders of the Mediterranean. The Byzantine empire found it impossible to maintain its communications with the west, and the western Mediterranean consequently became more and more stagnant. Its ports began to decline; their formerly flourishing trade dwindled to insignificance; their contacts with the rest of the continent were weakened; gold coins became scarcer; urban life became paralysed; and the centre of gravity of western civilisation shifted from the south to the north. A new world was born which Charlemagne was to organise; in founding the empire, he completed the break between east and west. And apart from its northern and southern shores, this empire was destined to become land-locked, existing with a self-contained economy. In this sense, Pirenne suggested, Mohammed prepared the way for Charlemagne.

What are we to think of this theory? There is no need to involve the reader in the controversy surrounding Pirenne's great book, and it will be enough to say that his claim cannot be fully substantiated. I remarked above that the bonds between the west and the east had been growing weaker since the third century, and that the west was slowly turning its attention northwards. It is thus impossible to speak of a sudden reversal of the situation resulting from the arrival of the Arabs. Besides, Mediterranean trade does not appear to have ceased at this point. No doubt, it was impeded by piracy, as well as by the economic blockade of the Moslem east maintained by the Byzantine fleet. After 716 we hear nothing more of the import of oriental products into Gaul through the ports of Provence, and it certainly seems that at that time they entered on a period of decay. But trade between west and east continued nevertheless; it was only the trade-routes that changed. From that time onwards, silks and spices reached the west via Italy, where they were brought from the great market of Constantinople, or from Moslem Spain, which received them by sea or overland along the African coast route. The Moslem advance into Septimania (Roussillon and Languedoc), and the opposite movement which was to bring the Franks beyond the Pyrenees by the end of the eighth century, certainly had their economic repercussions. By 775, on the other hand, merchants from the abbey of Saint-Denis were going to Italy. Finally, it must not be forgotten that from the ninth century, Moslem expansion required a constant increase in manpower, which meant a great demand for slaves. Henceforward the slave-trade became one of the most thriving activities of certain Frankish merchants and also of the Jewish settlements in the towns of the Rhône valley, in Provence and in Languedoc, through which passed convoys of slaves brought from their homelands in Anglo-Saxon or Slavic countries, often coming by way of Verdun. Far from being the cause of a break in the activities of the Mediterranean countries, Islam was more probably responsible for a revival of their trade, though the effects were slow to make themselves felt. There is no doubt, too, that the northern trade continued to develop through the agency of the Frisians, and then of the Scandinavian Vikings. But it was chiefly the zones on the fringes of Frankish Gaul which benefited from these long-distance exchanges. The foundations of its economy remained rural: the interior of the country was like a great body composed of multiple cells nourished by local and inter-regional exchanges.

Between 500 and 800, Gaul became France. This statement, taken from Ferdinand Lot, needs qualification. Perhaps it would be better to say that Roman Gaul became the kingdom of the Franks. But the latter very quickly spread beyond the frontiers of *Gallia*, and its internal development led to an ever-increasing fragmentation. It may justly be said that the early Carolingians prevented its dissolution.

First, it is as well to remember that at the death of Clovis the kingdom of the Franks did not as yet cover the whole of Gaul. To the aggregate of territory between the Loire and the Rhine there was added, after the battle of Vouillé in 507, the province of Aquitaine. But it certainly does not seem to have fallen all at once, as a single entity, into the hands of the Franks, for they reached the Pyrenees only about 520, and Septimania continued to belong to the Visigoths of Spain until 720. In the south-east, the sons of Clovis conquered the kingdom of Burgundy (534); and three years later they took advantage of the war between Justinian and the Ostrogoths to take Provence from the latter. Thus, a third of the way through the sixth century, the *Regnum Francorum*, apart from a foreign enclave between the lower Rhône and the Pyrenees, was co-extensive with Roman Gaul. But it had also spread beyond the Rhine, and was expanding in Germania. In the south-west, the Alemanni were defeated by Clovis and acknowledged the supremacy of the Franks. North of the Main, Thierry I and Clothair I destroyed the kingdom of the Thuringians, which was not incorporated but remained autonomous under tributary dukes. The valley of the Main was to become a centre of Frankish colonisation under the name of Franconia. In the south-east of Germania, too, the Bavarians came under the rule of the Merovingians at the end of the sixth century. In the north-west, the Saxons between the Rhine and the Elbe, and the Frisians along the North Sea coast, between the lower Weser and the estuary of the Scheldt, were the only Germanic peoples to preserve their independence. Leaving them out of account, and disregarding Italy, one can consider the kingdom of the Franks about the year 600 as foreshadowing that of Charlemagne.

But while continually expanding, the Merovingian state steadily lost its cohesion. The *regnum* gradually came to resemble a personal estate; and in the absence of any law of primogeniture, and under the ancient Germanic belief that all the king's sons shared in his charisma and could therefore reign simultaneously, it was quite natural that Clovis's kingdom came to be divided. In the century following the death of its founder (511–613), it enjoyed unity only exceptionally, for the first time from 558 to 561, during the last three years of Clothair I, the last of the sons of Clovis. There was a further division between Clothair I's four sons; civil war broke out again even more fiercely than in the first half of the century, and ended only when Clothair II successfully eliminated all his rivals, among them the famous Queen Brunhild, and in thus once again becoming master of the realm as a whole (613).

In these circumstances, it is not surprising that the royal power suffered rapid decline, and that a powerful landed and military aristocracy—whose properties, we now have reason to believe, had grown up out of the royal domains—gradually tended to replace it. But this class, which held the great public offices, was itself deeply split into rival groups, which became pervaded with the antagonisms that set different regions of the kingdom against one another. At the beginning of the seventh century, these were so strong that Austrasia (north-eastern Gaul) demanded its own king. Dagobert, the son of Clothair II, who after his father's death in 629 reigned for some years over the whole kingdom, was compelled in 634 to give the Austrasians one of his sons as king. After his death (639), there were in fact two rival, and even enemy, states: Austrasia on the one hand, and Neustria (north-western Gaul), joined by Burgundy (the area of the Saône and Rhône), on the other. The actual rulers of these two parts of the kingdom were no longer the kings, but the Mayors of the Palace, who held the economic life of the court in their hands, and drew their power from their command of the royal guard and the protection of those who had commended themselves to the king, that is to say, placed themselves voluntarily under his protection. The history of Frankish Gaul after 639 consists of the struggle between Austrasia and Neustria, together with the clash between the regional aristocracies and the Mayors who tried to rule them. In the end, it was the Austrasian Mayor of the Palace who emerged victorious from the great conflict; and by his triumph over the Neustrians at Tertry in 687, Pepin of Herstal made himself master of the whole kingdom. He belonged to a powerful line possessing property in the Meuse and Moselle valleys, rich in lands and men, whose rise can be followed from the end of the sixth century, a line named after its most famous member, Charlemagne, the line of the Carolingians. In comparison with the powerful Mayor, the Merovingian king could assert no more than a nominal authority, which in the last analysis rested only on dynastic loyalty.

Thus the end of the seventh century finds us in a position to come to grips with the realities underlying the concept of the *Regnum Francorum*.

In the narrower sense of this term, it could only be applied to the lands between the Loire and the Rhine effectively occupied by the Franks and forming the heart of the kingdom. But we must introduce a further distinction between the north and north-east of this region, and the territories lying in the west, the centre, and the south. Along the left bank of the lower and middle Rhine and the lower course of the Moselle, the Meuse and the Scheldt, where Germanic dialects are still spoken today, the Franks conquered and populated the country, just as along the left bank of the upper Rhine the Alemanni took possession of Alsace. But Germanic dialects hardly extended beyond a line starting between Gravelines and Visé on the Meuse, then bending round Verviers, crossing the Ardennes, passing west of Arlon and running via Longwy to the Moselle, to cross it between Thionville and Metz, and then head for the Vosges across the plateau of Lorraine, following the ridge of the massif as far as the Ballon d'Alsace, and then going almost straight towards the Jura mountains, reaching them to the east of Mont Terrible. West of the line lies the domain of the French. It will then be seen that the Franks who settled in the Paris basin adopted after a certain time, perhaps in the seventh century, the language of the inhabitants with whom their settlers intermingled, that is, vulgar Latin, from which source was derived Romance, and eventually the French language. This adoption of Gallo-Roman speech by the conquerors is the surest indication of the fusion between the two groups to form a people in which every man, provided he was free, had by the eighth century—and perhaps even in the seventh—become recognised as a Frank. Politically, the Frankish zone was divided into two. Austrasia to the north-east, with Rheims and then Metz as the capital, was partly Romance-speaking, but it was dependent on the Germanic lands of the Rhine and beyond. The importance of these increased, while Austrasia in the course of the seventh century lost its territories in Aquitaine and even, about 680, Rheims, Châlons and Laon. The lands to the north-west, corresponding to the first areas colonised by the Salian Franks, the region lying, broadly speaking, between the Somme, the Seine and the Loire, constituted Neustria, and gradually acquired the name of *Francia*, and eventually France. There the Romance element was generally predominant, and Paris fulfilled the role of capital which Clovis had foreseen for it. The division between royal Neustria and Austrasia, the latter being the base for the domination of the Mayors of the Palace, was destined to continue until about the year 740.

Let us now leave the centre of the kingdom, and consider the fringes. In Armorica, the occupation of the country begun as early as the fifth century by the Bretons, who came from the British Isles, continued. They established themselves on the northern coast of the peninsula in Dumnonia and to the west in Cornouailles; they were split up under a number of princes, and worked their way as far as the Vilaine; moving along the southern coast they reached the estuary of the Loire. Up to the middle of the sixth century they were tributaries of the Frankish kings; from then onwards they were in conflict with them, and very inconvenient neighbours for the western parts of Neustria; by the beginning of the eighth century they had become practically independent.

To the south of the Loire, great changes were afoot. Aquitaine, which the Franks had not settled and had been content merely to incorporate as it was into their kingdom, had lost all semblance of unity. Divided among the Merovingians, it became essentially an area for exploitation, or perhaps rather a cultural reserve for Neustria and Austrasia. Moreover, from 580 onwards, the Frankish kings showed themselves completely unable to protect the southern part of the country, the ancient *Novempopulana*, between the Garonne and the Pyrenees, from invasion by the Basques or Gascons coming from beyond the mountains, who gave their name to the region, although they did not establish a permanent footing beyond the Adour. It is well known that their language, possibly derived from the ancient Iberian, has survived down to our own time in certain cantons of the extreme south-west. Against them Dagobert set up a military command centred on Toulouse, and including also the cities of Agen, Périgueux, Cahors and Saintes, entrusting it to his brother Caribert. After his death, this March-land contined in existence, and during the last third of the century passed under the command of a powerful Frankish personality, Duke Lupus, who extended his power as far as the city of Limoges. The return of the Frankish kingdom to unity after the battle of Tertry (687) meant for Aquitaine, previously divided between Neustria and Austrasia, a process of regrouping. This took place round the figure of Eudes, 'Duke of Aquitaine', a Frank by origin, who comes on the scene at the beginning of the eighth century, and whose authority stretched from the Loire to the Garonne, and even to the Pyrenees, for the Gascons were subject to him. It is improbable that Pepin of Herstal made war in those parts in an attempt to subdue him: in fact, the reconstituted Aquitaine stood confronting the Franks face to face.

A similar evolution took place in Provence. Soon after its annexation by the Franks, it felt the repercussions of the partitioning of the kingdom, and became split into a 'Burgundian' part (the territories on the left bank of the Rhône) and an 'Austrasian' part (Viviers, Uzès, Avignon, Aix and half of Marseille). Each of these territorial groups was administered in the king's name by a high official belonging to the regional aristocracy and—as was natural enough in a country of Roman civilisation—having the title of *patricius*. This division lasted till 679, when Dagobert II of Austrasia died. Then Thierry III, already king of Neustria and Burgundy, succeeded, at least nominally, in getting himself re-cognised as king of the whole *Regnum Francorum*. Henceforward, a single *patricius* ruled over Provence, and was effectively master of the country.

Between the Durance, the Cévennes, the Alps, the Jura and the Champagne plateau, we are in Burgundy. The name recalls the Burgundians (*Burgundi*) who settled there in the second half of the fifth century, and it persisted after they had been incorporated into the kingdom of the Franks. This fact alone is enough to show that the countries of the Saône and Rhône basin were distinct from those of *Francia*. The Burgundians had never been very numerous there; groups of Franks had settled in the north and north-west, but the vast majority of the population had remained Gallo-Roman, and were much attached to their separate identity. For them, to be Burgundian meant not to be, and not to become, Franks. After the reappearance of the *Regnum Burgundiae* on the map of Frankish Gaul in the time of one of Clovis's grandson's, Guntram (561–93), who was incidentally king of a realm that was much enlarged to the west by the inclusion of Auxerre, Troyes, and even, briefly, Chartres and Paris, and to the south by Provence, Burgundy first shared the fate of Austrasia, and then, from Clothair II's time, the fate of Neustria. Although Dagobert succeeded in holding the north of the country, complete anarchy broke out after his death. The lay and clerical aristocracy freed themselves from the Mayor of the Palace, and after being harshly suppressed for a short while by Ebroin (676), they threw off all Frankish authority. Local centres of power grew up, such as the duchy of Lyon and the ecclesiastical principalities we shall be considering later on.

Such in broad outline was the general shape of Frankish Gaul during the time that Pepin of Herstal was Mayor. But together with this it must be noted that the long crisis which ruined the royal power and the state also resulted in the emancipation of the

Germanic dependencies, Alemannia, Thuringia and Bavaria. Furthermore, during the second half of the seventh century, the Franks' northern neighbours, the Frisians, crossed the Rhine and advanced as far as Utrecht. Pepin succeeded in thrusting them back across the river and establishing a provisional authority of the Franks over the Alemanni; although this success was only temporary, it foreshadowed the restoration of the kingdom under Charles Martel.

Finally, it is important for us to grasp the essential features of a world that was full of contrasts, namely the Frankish Church.

The Merovingian period saw the christianisation of Gaul completed. The population of the towns had adopted Christianity by the end of the fifth century, but in the country the new religion had not struck deep roots, and traces of paganism—or rather a mixture of Celtic, Roman and Germanic beliefs—survived for many years. This probably is why the term 'pagan' comes from the Latin word *pagenses*, meaning people who live in the country. On the other hand, genuine paganism persisted throughout the sixth century and a part of the seventh in certain parts of northern Gaul, between the Meuse and the Scheldt and in the Rhine and Moselle regions of Austrasia, which had been settled by groups of Franks who remained faithful to their ancestral beliefs long after the conversion of Clovis. The Frankish Church was confronted with a considerable task, which it carried out slowly, and by a variety of means.

In the pagan areas there were what may truly be called missions. They hardly began before the seventh century, and were undertaken by missionaries of Aquitanian origin, such as Amand (d. 675), trained in the Île d'Yeu, an itinerant bishop in northern France and what is now Belgium, particularly in the region of Ghent, Géry (d. 625) in the Valenciennes region, and especially Éloi (d. 660), founder of Solignac Abbey, counsellor to Dagobert, and subsequently bishop of Noyon and Tournai. Yet the most active agents in this task of conversion among the population as a whole were the monks.

Monasteries in Gaul developed in a number of stages. The earliest date from the time of the Roman Empire in the south-west (Ligugé and Marmoutier founded by St Martin at the end of the fourth century), and in Provence (Lérins and Saint-Victor de

Marseille). The second stage begins in the sixth century, when the institution developed in the Rhône valley and in Burgundy (Saint-Bénigne de Dijon), while certain Frankish sovereigns founded monasteries that were to have a brilliant future—Saint-Germain-des-Prés near Paris (Childebert I), Saint-Médard de Soissons (Clothair I), Sainte-Croix de Poitiers (Radegonde, Clothair I's wife), Saint-Martin d'Autun (Brunhild), Saint-Marcel de Chalon (Guntram) and Saint-Denis (Dagobert). This early monasticism was still largely derived from the oriental monastic ideal, and tended to seek individual perfection. To start with, at least, it does not seem to have aimed or to have had the means to influence the world. In point of jurisdiction, the monasteries were under the authority of the diocese; but some of them remained in the possession of their founders and their families. Finally, we should note the great diversity of their rules. For instance, there was the rule of St Caesarius of Arles in the south-east, which embraced a fairly wide circle. In the course of the seventh century, monasticism received a fresh impulse from the Irish monks, in whose eyes the wandering life, the *peregrinatio*, far removed from their homeland, seems to have been the highest ascetic ideal. Coming to Gaul about 590 with a dozen companions, Columbanus had travelled widely in both the east and the west, founding monasteries along the routes he travelled. The most important of these was Luxeuil, from which the new Columban form of monasticism spread out. Considerable moral demands, with a strong emphasis on penance, the practice of which was made a matter of rule, and a tendency to assert monastic independence of the bishops—such were its most original characteristics. But these ascetics did not shut themselves up in their convents: they preached in the towns and especially in the countryside, where they became active and effective missionaries. The impulse given by Columbanus to monasticism reached its height during the seventh century and the first half of the eighth, when religious foundations multiplied, particularly in Brie (Saint-Faron de Meaux, Jouarre and Chelles), in the valleys of the Seine (Jumièges, Saint-Wandrille) and the Loire (Fleury), in the Jura (Moutiers-Grandval, Saint-Ursanne), on both slopes of the Vosges (Remiremont, Moyenmoutier, Saint-Dié, Munster in the Val Saint-Grégoire, Hohenberg, Murbach), in northern Gaul (Lobbes, Sithiu[1]), in the Ardennes

---

[1] Better known as Saint-Bertin.

(Stavelot, Malmédy), and in the Eifel (Prüm). The founders were kings, great lay lords, or bishops; they endowed the monasteries with land but generally kept them within their own property. It is thus possible to mark out the line of the properties belonging to each family by the abbeys belonging to it. The Carolingian patrimony, for instance, comprised among others the monasteries of Oeren and Pfalzel near Trier, those of Prüm, Echternach and Stavelot in the Eifel and the Ardennes, Nivelles south of the forest of Soignes, and Saint-Arnould de Metz. The rules observed by the monks tended towards uniformity. Most often, they were a mixture of the Columban and the Benedictine rule, the latter being observed in its strict form by some abbeys, among which was Fleury. This abbey had prided itself since the last third of the seventh century on possessing the body of St Benedict. The monasteries were both ardent centres of spiritual life and of evangelisation; and from them too there proceeded the work of clearing and settling the waste places in which they established themselves.

The mission and progress of monasticism largely contributed to the spread of Christianity in the countryside; but it should not be forgotten that its establishment was made possible by the foundation of rural parishes, the network of which had steadily extended throughout the Merovingian period. To realise what a novelty this was, we must remember that the early Church had been essentially urban: all religious life had been concentrated round a single church, the cathedral in the chief centre of the city territory, with the countryside loosely attached to it. In short, one could say that for a long time there was really only one parish for each bishopric. In the episcopal territory, however, there were scattered sanctuaries, but worship was conducted there only when the bishop was passing through on his travels, or delegated this duty to the priests of the bishop's college or *presbyterium* in the city. Changes began to come in from the fifth century onwards, and churches were established first of all in the rural settlements (*vici*) or fortified settlements (*castra*) round the city. Thus parochial districts were formed, with an organisation reproducing that of the episcopal church, based on baptismal churches, administered by a college of priests and deacons under the direction of an archpriest, and provided with independent endowments. Then came a second phase, beginning in the sixth century and continuing till the eighth, during which these districts split up once again, and secondary churches thus became parishes. By secondary churches I mean ancient oratories and new churches, and especially private chapels built by landed proprietors in their domains and gradually transformed into parishes by the appointment of a resident priest. A large number of country churches were built in this way and endowed by landowners, who kept them within their own property. By virtue of this they were able to choose the men to serve them from those belonging to their domains. Hence it came about that the bishop's authority over these private churches was extremely weak, if not non-existent. What was more, these churches were considered, along with the lands that had been given them, which served to maintain the priest, as real estate that could be sold or exchanged. And so in the middle of the seventh century there began a real appropriation of the property and functions of the Church by laymen, a prelude to still more serious troubles in the future.

To this sketch of the basic elements in the spiritual life of the Church it will be as well to add some indications of its material foundations. They were essentially rooted in landed property: the Church was in the process of becoming the greatest proprietor in the kingdom. It received land from kings, from great laymen and from humble peasants; the bishops generally handed over their private fortunes to their cathedrals, and the priests did the same for the parish churches. These gifts could be outright, without reservations, or conditional, as when a donor kept the bequeathed land during his lifetime, by virtue of what was known as a precarial (*précaire*) contract. In this way the wealth of the Church, especially of the bishoprics and monasteries, went on steadily increasing throughout the seventh century; and this involved an element of power, inasmuch as the gift of land brought with it the gift of the men who tilled it. The Church thus became the master of a vast body of human servants, made up of slaves, free or servile tenants, *précaristes* or protected freemen, not to mention the poor of all descriptions, who were looked after by the religious establishments. Their lands, and those living on them, were beginning, on the other hand, to escape from the claims of the state through the privileges of immunity which the Merovingian sovereigns had been accustomed to grant since the sixth and especially the seventh century to the bishoprics and abbeys of the kingdom. By virtue of this privilege, the Church's estates were closed to the agents of the state: they became exempt proprietors, kept the taxes they levied and maintained what amounted to private jurisdiction over the inhabitants of their lands. This picture of growth and consolidation in ecclesiastical property must, however, be qualified by certain facts that stand out clearly from the survey of our period. In the first place, this property was burdened with numerous charges: various requisitions (wherever immunity had not been granted), the building and maintenance of churches, assistance for the destitute, the opening of elementary schools to prepare the clergy for their work. Next, donors might always take back what they had given; the Merovingian kings provide frequent examples of this behaviour. Finally, in its anxiety to make the most of its temporal possessions, a church would often hand over a piece of land to a layman for development; in that case the beneficiary of this kind of concession would keep for himself the revenue accruing, and would pay the proprietor only a nominal rent. Contracts of this sort were often made for long periods, so that it frequently proved difficult for the Church to recover land that had been made over in this fashion. In short, this Church property was a prey to much avarice; and its importance, as we shall see, was one of the causes of the Church's decline at the end of the Merovingian period.

Now let us turn for a moment towards the higher ranks of the hierarchy. The Church had inherited the structure that had come down to it from antiquity, and at the end of the seventh century was divided into 120 bishoprics, the holders of which were absolute masters in their dioceses. The office of metropolitan had been very greatly weakened by the successive partitionings of the kingdom; it was now hardly a title at all, and little more than a memory. In the sixth century, the bishops had often met in council. There are reckoned to have been some thirty of these, including five national councils, the most famous of which were at Orléans (511) and Paris (614). In the seventh century, on the other hand, there was a decline in the number and frequency of these assemblies: only thirteen were held between 614 and 696; and from that date onwards the conciliar machinery ceased to function till 743, and this deficiency is by itself indicative of the crisis through which the Church was then passing. It should be added that the bishops had ceased by the seventh century to have any links with Rome.

On the other hand, there had very early on come into existence a system of close collaboration between the throne and the episcopate. By the sixth century the Frankish Church had become a state Church. The Merovingians had heaped favours upon the Church; in return, they imposed upon it an authoritarian protection, intervening in the nomination of bishops, convoking the councils, giving the force of law to their canons, and legislating even in Church affairs. On its side, the Church took over from the crown some of its duties in maintaining public order—one has only to remember the manifold activities of the bishop in his city; and although it was without much influence over kings and their morals it did its best to keep the monarchy from barbarism by setting before kings an ethical ideal based upon justice—in the sense of respect for each man's property—and piety. We stand here at the starting-point of the christianisation of Germanic royalty. The models set before the sovereigns for their imitation were the kings of the old Covenant: Clothair II was the first Frankish king to be compared to David, and the document giving us the picture, a conciliar canon of 614, goes on at once to invite the prince, after the pattern of David, to serve the people of God—the first groping towards the idea of service which was slowly to become linked with the function of king. What was more, the Church prayed publicly for the king, as is testified by some of the oldest texts of the Gallican liturgy (dating from the seventh or early eighth century); just as in the Christian empire prayer was made to God for the emperors, so here there were prayers for peace, concord and godliness among kings, essential conditions for the service of God if the people were to serve him in peace and tranquillity. A form of prayer for the prince contained in the Mass quotes as examples for his imitation Abraham, Moses, Joshua and David, thus comparing the Frankish people to Israel. This early thought on the meaning of royalty was not to bear full fruit till later on, when the Frankish Church had emerged from the crisis into which it had been slowly sinking since the middle of the seventh century.

The Merovingians proved in fact totally incapable of understanding the programme that was put before them. Just as on the political plane they confused private property and public sovereignty, so likewise they considered the Church, whose material power they had helped to build up, as an instrument for their own purposes. Thus they thought it right to distribute bishoprics at their own will, usually to their retainers or servants. They did not hesitate to sell them, or even to leave them vacant and pocket their revenues, as is shown by disturbing gaps in the links of bishops' names in several dioceses. This evil grew with the increasing anarchy of the seventh century and the virtual cessation of royal authority after the death of Dagobert in 639. The Church was dragged into the vortex of civil war between the rival groups of the aristocracy and the Mayors of the Palace. The most significant episode was the 'passion' of St Léger, bishop of Autun, put to death by order of the Mayor of Neustria-Burgundy, whom he had relentlessly opposed (679–80). The crisis grew worse in the fifty years between the battle of Tertry and the death of Charles Martel (687–741). We need mention only the chief features of this crisis, and principally the destruction of the Roman civilisation which had somehow survived throughout the sixth century with Gregory of Tours and Venantius—a subject to which we shall return. Everything was lapsing into barbarism, except perhaps in Aquitaine, where some traces of the ancient culture lingered on. The decay of institutions was just as evident, testifying to the collapse of the ancient fabric of the Church. It could be seen at all levels of the hierarchy. In the diocesan synod of Auxerre (695)— the last one, for a considerable time, as it turned out—arrangements were made for the attendants of the Churches and monasteries in the diocese to take turns in officiating at the cathedral services because at that moment there were no longer any clergy there. The country churches tended to become more and more independent: the authority of the bishop, as well as that of ancient canon law, seems to have been largely confined to the precincts of the episcopal town. In the same way the monasteries, especially those of the Columban type, slipped from the bishops' control and became the centres of little autonomous dioceses. The conciliar machinery ceased to function; the last councils we come across are no more than instruments of the kings or the Mayors, who resorted to them to secure the condemnation of their opponents. The presence at these synods of members of the court and the higher aristocracy transformed them into assemblies that were both ecclesiastical and secular (*concilia permixta*), but even in this form the institution fell into disuse.

Finally, the power embodied in the episcopate explains why the office was coveted by the lay aristocracy. Each political crisis

1   *A Carolingian sovereign, perhaps Charlemagne* (Bulloz, Carnavalet)
A bronze statuette (24 cm high, 17·5 cm long and 9·5 cm broad), for a
long time in the possession of Metz Cathedral, now in the Musée
Carnavalet, Paris. The rider, the saddle, and the sheath on the left side are
all certainly Carolingian workmanship of the ninth century. The horse is
more recent—perhaps sixteenth century—replacing the original mount,
which had become very worn. The sword is nineteenth-century work.

A unique work of its period. The influence of antiquity is obvious and
particularly evident in the orb the rider is holding in his left hand. This is
the picture of a very secular sovereign; and taking into account the
increasing clericalisation of the image from the time of Louis the Pious, it
may well be that the figure here represented is Charlemagne.

2 *A Byzantine emperor of the early Middle Ages: Justinian*
A mosaic in San Vitale at Ravenna, before 547 (from A. Grabar,
Byzantine Painting). The emperor, wearing the long chlamys which leaves
his right arm free, his head crowned and surrounded by a halo, the
ancient symbol of eternity, is about to make his offerings to Christ. On
his right, there are civil dignitaries and soldiers; on his left, Maximian,
bishop of Ravenna, and other ecclesiastics. Imperial splendour, with
Church and state united in the emperor.

brought important changes in the personnel of the bishops. Where their appointment was concerned, the ecclesiastical aspect ceased to play any part: all that mattered was whether they belonged to this or that political faction, whether they could make war, and whether they could count on a solid body of supporters and had reliable connections. Contemporary sources are full of revealing details: the bishopric of Maastricht changed hands according to whether the master of the moment was Ebroin or Pepin of Herstal. Simony and laicisation increased to a formidable degree. Yet the most significant events took place in Aquitaine and Burgundy, where the formation of episcopal principalities can be traced from the end of the seventh century. At Clermont, after the death of Count Genêt, the last of the Merovingian counts of Auvergne, Bishop Saint-Prix (d. 676), remained the sole 'recteur et tuteur de la patrie'. At Lyon, about the year 700, Bishop Godin was independent, and fought against Pepin of Herstal's son Dreu, who bore the title of duke of the Burgundians. At Auxerre, as we learn from the episcopal chronicle, Bishop Savary 'turned aside from the Church and gave himself over to worldly matters more than befits a bishop'. He subjected the counts of Orléans, Nevers, Tonnerre, Avallon and Troyes, and died in an attempt to take possession of Lyon (719). His successor, Ainmar, who had perhaps not been consecrated, went on with his work and extended his power to such a point—the same source tells us—'that he almost reached the territory of the duchy of Burgundy'. These are interesting glimpses, for they bear witness both to the weakness of the state, and to the increasing laicisation of the church.

But the greatest danger that had fallen upon the Church was the secularisation of her propety by the state. This was already proceeding during Pepin of Herstal's rule, and was to reach its climax under Charles Martel. The rise of the Carolingians was thus accompanied by a crisis which shook the structure of the Church to its foundations.

II

The restoration of the state
and the change of dynasty

The death of Pepin of Herstal in 714 set in train a revolution which continued down to the year 721. Before his death, the Mayor appointed as his successor his grandson, a child of six years old, Theudoald (or Thiaud), in whose name his widow Plectrude proposed to govern the state. But the Neustrians seized the opportunity to revolt and installed one of their party, Rainfroi, as Mayor. He then joined with the Frisians and Saxons, invaded Austrasia, and advanced as far as Cologne, where Pepin's widow had her residence. Salvation came from Pepin's bastard son, Charles, later surnamed Martel (the Hammer). Though at first defeated by the Neustrians, he twice succeeded in defeating them in 716-17, on the Amblève, near Malmédy, and then at Vinchy, south of Cambrai, and pursued them as far as Paris. He next turned against the Saxons and drove them back across the Rhine; then against the duke of Aquitaine, Eudes by name, to whom Rainfroi had appealed, and who had advanced to the outskirts of Soissons. Charles Martel forced him to re-cross the Loire (720-1). At that point the only remaining opposition was from Rainfroi; but the resistance offered by him in Anjou ended about 724. Two Merovingian kings had followed in quick succession between 715 and 721, but had been no more than pawns in the rival parties' hands. In 721 Charles Martel proclaimed as king a son of Dagobert III (d. 715), whom he took from the convent at Chelles: this was Thierry IV, together with whom he was to consecrate himself to the restoration of the Frankish state. Like his father, he bore the title of Mayor, adding to it those of duke and prince of the Franks. In fact, he concentrated all power in his own hands and exercised a quasi-royal authority: *subregulus* ('sub-king') was the title given him in a missive from Pope Gregory III; yet it really falls short of the fact.

The first task confronting Charles Martel was the re-establishment of Frankish authority over the Germanic peoples who had asserted their independence since the close of the seventh century. In two campaigns he effected the annexation of north-west Frisia, leaving only the eastern part outside his kingdom. The same fate overtook the Saxons, against whom the Mayor led several expeditions. Further south, he suppressed the duchy of the Alemanni, and incorporated it in the Frankish state. He also subjected the Bavarians in like manner, but, well aware of their strength and cohesion, Charles Martel left them independent under a duke of their own. At the same time the Mayor of the Palace was anxious to bring about the pacification of Germania by the spread of Christianity, and so pressed on with the evangelisation of the country. It had been begun in certain areas as early as the sixth century, but did not make decisive progress till the first half of the eighth. The missionaries were mostly, though not exclusively, Anglo-Saxon monks who completed the work of their Irish, Aquitanian and Frankish predecessors. An Anglo-Saxon called Willibrord worked in Frisia, where the bishopric of Utrecht was established in 695. Pirmin, an Aquitanian, evangelised Alemannia, where a bishopric had already been established at Constance in the first third of the seventh century. In Bavaria, Irish and Frankish missionaries set to work and succeeded, in the first thirty years of the eighth century, in founding four bishoprics. Such is the general background of the life and work of the most famous missionary to Germania, the Anglo-Saxon Boniface. In close contact (*in familiaritate*) with the Apostolic See and under the protection (*in patrocinio*) of Charles Martel, he carried out the evangelisation of Hesse and Thuringia between 722 and 734. Pope Gregory III made him archbishop; and in this capacity he founded several bishoprics in the lands he had conquered for the Christian faith, and introduced Roman practices into Bavaria, though not without meeting active resistance. This work was complete by the time of Charles Martel's death, and constituted the crowning glory of Boniface as the founder, above all others, of the Church in

Germania. In this way their common Christian faith drew the Germanic peoples and the inhabitants of Frankish Gaul closer together than they had been in the past.

In Gaul, Aquitaine and the south-east still absorbed the major part of the prince of the Franks' activities. The situation was all the more serious in that these two regions were directly exposed to the invasion of the Arabs, who had conquered Spain in 711. A few years later, they had taken possession of Septimania, and were launching raids in the direction of Toulouse, towards the Rhône valley, and even as far as Burgundy, reaching Autun and sacking it in 725, and in 731 pushing on to the very gates of Sens. They then proceeded to attack in Aquitaine, where Duke Eudes summoned Charles Martel to his rescue. In 732—or, according to a recent calculation, 733—a Moslem army advanced on Tours by way of Bordeaux, and the prince of the Franks went out against it and crushed it near Poitiers on a Saturday in October. Coming some fifteen years after the defeat of the Arabs at the gates of Constantinople, this victory brought Charles Martel great prestige; and although it did not immediately break the Arab impetus, it slowed down the pace, and in particular confined it to sorties towards the Rhône valley during the next few years.[1] But the truth would seem to be that the west and the Byzantine Empire both owed their salvation to the profound disturbances in the Moslem world about the middle of the eighth century, which were to lead to the fall of the Omayyads in 750. The victory of Poitiers had the definite result of bringing about Eudes of Aquitaine's submission, though when he died (736), Charles Martel was not able to bring the duchy under the one common law, but had to be content with recognising Eudes's son Hunaud as duke, and imposing on him an oath of fealty. Meanwhile, he had undertaken the reconquest of Burgundy. Lyon was subjugated by 733, but three years later a revolt of the leading men in the country entailed a punitive expedition which took Charles as far as Arles and Marseille. The harshness of his intervention, however, provoked a violent reaction on the part of the local aristocracy headed by the patrician Mauront in alliance with the Arabs. Thus it was not till 739 that Charles Martel and his half-brother Childebrand, at the head of a great force in the Rhône valley, contrived to throw back the Saracens and re-establish the authority of the

[1] See J. H. Roy and J. Deviosse, *La Bataille de Poitiers*, Paris.

MAP I The kingdom of the Franks and neighbouring countries about the middle of the eighth century.

Franks over Provence. The local aristocracy were stripped of their functions for the benefit of Charles Martel's Austrasian, Alemannic and Bavarian retainers.

Such then is the balance-sheet of Charles's rule, at least in its broad outlines. We must however add that these signal successes

25

would no doubt never have been achieved if the Mayor of the Palace had not had at his disposal a large, well-armed and entirely devoted army. This army was made up of his personal followers. Adopting as a general policy the process begun by his father, he increased the number of his vassals to whom he distributed land enough to allow them to equip themselves as fully-armed warriors on horseback, and also to provide other fighting men under their orders. Some of these lands may have come from the Carolingian family estates, or the royal demesnes; but the greater part of them was taken from the Church, whose considerable landed property had already been used for similar purposes by the Merovingian kings on previous occasions, though there had never before been such extensive secularisation. This further increased the disorder that was raging in the Frankish Church. A large number of abbeys were confiscated, and bishoprics handed over to Charles's own supporters, who took the place of the local men. Many of them remained laymen, and handed on their positions to their sons. We know of many examples, which tell their own tale. Laymen, for instance, administered the bishoprics of Rennes and Nantes on the borders of Brittany; in Burgundy, the bishops' sees were left vacant and their revenues passed to the vassals of the Mayor; Charles Martel's nephew Hugues, who died in 730, held in plurality the bishoprics of Paris, Bayeux and Rouen, as well as the abbeys of Jumièges and Saint-Wandrille; Milon, a protégé of the prince of the Franks, who was already bishop of Trier where he had succeeded his father Liutwin, was given in addition the church of Rheims. We may therefore see this as a real process of laicisation in the Frankish Church. The whole ecclesiastical organisation was thus put in jeopardy, which explains why, in spite of the brilliant victory at Poitiers which saved it from Islam, the Church of the ninth century condemned the memory of Charlemagne's grandfather.

For twenty years Charles Martel had ruled the kingdom of the Franks as its master. When the Merovingian Thierry IV died in 737, the Mayor did not appoint a successor; yet the sense of legitimacy was still so strong that Charles Martel did not venture to assume the title of king.[1] But he demonstrated on one final occasion

[1] Charles Martel seems to have been far more prudent than Grimoald, a member of the Carolingian family and uncle of Pepin of Herstal (see genealogical table p. 228) who, in the middle of the seventh century, had tried in vain to supplant the traditional dynasty.

that he was in fact sovereign by disposing of the kingdom on his deathbed in favour of his two legitimate sons, the idea of partition being still so dominant in tradition that it once again prevailed. Carloman, the elder son, received Austrasia, Thuringia and Alemannia; Pepin, the younger, Neustria, Burgundy and Provence. These two new Mayors were immediately confronted with revolts in Germania and Aquitaine. Perhaps this was what convinced them of the need to put their power upon a legitimate basis. At all events, in 743 they set Childeric III upon the Merovingian throne, a restoration which appears to have been initiated by Carloman. But it in no way reduced his authority or that of his brother; the two princes were thus able to re-establish the rule of the Franks over the outlying regions of the kingdom and to find a solution to the problem of the confiscated ecclesiastical lands, which had been further increased through secularisations made by Pepin.

Both these princes had received a certain degree of religious education, Carloman perhaps at Echternach Abbey (founded by St Willibrord, and situated in what is now Luxemburg), Pepin certainly at Saint-Denis; and they seem to have had a better understanding than their father of the Church's tragic position after fifty years of anarchy. Boniface was a member of their entourage, especially of Carloman's, and urged them on to a general reform of the Frankish Church. This was difficult to achieve because it affected the private interests of the laicised episcopate, the lords who had usurped ecclesiastical lands, and the vassals in possession of Church property. Some degree of compromise was necessary: the Mayors followed the Anglo-Saxon's advice, yet avoided acting precipitately. Accordingly three councils, held in 743 and 744, in Austrasia and Neustria, tried to deal with the most urgent matters and the gravest abuses. Several canons, promulgated by capitularies from the two Mayors, prescribed the re-establishment of the hierarchy and the diocesan links, as well as the restoration of ecclesiastical discipline. As regards the confiscated property, it was decided that the legal ownership must revert to the Church. The Church, however, was not to recover it at once: the prince (that is to say, the two Mayors) would retain it and let it out in the form of fiefs (*bénéfices*) for the term of one life to those of his vassals who were already occupying it. In recognition of the Church's ownership of these lands, the vassals would pay a token rent, thus becoming temporary tenants (*précaristes*).

But service (in this case, the vassal's military service) was something due only to the prince; so that later on the benefices they held were called *precariae verbo regis*—temporary concessions made by order of the king. This originated the practice of granting fiefs to vassals for the term of one life; the land might come either from Church property—for secularisations continued to take place in the eighth and ninth centuries—or from the personal property belonging to the Mayor of the Palace (and before long of the king). The latter's vassals would then recruit vassals of their own by allotting them fiefs from their own lands. This association of vassalage with *beneficium*—the fief, as it was later called—was thus the origin of a new social class, and the essential basis of the new political regime that was coming to birth.

After his brother Carloman's abdication in 747, Pepin became sole Mayor of the Palace. By about 750, he had succeeded in imposing peace throughout the kingdom by suppressing the constantly recurring revolts. In particular, he had succeeded in firmly attaching Bavaria to the Frankish state by installing as duke his own nephew Tassilo III, and was preparing the way for his own accession to the crown. In order to disarm opposition from supporters of the legitimate Merovingian line, he set out to acquire a new legitimacy. This was the purpose of the question he asked of Pope Zacharias through the mouth of Bishop Burchard of Wurzburg and Chaplain Fulrad, which deserves to be given in the clumsy form in which it has come down to us in the royal annals. The two emissaries questioned the pope 'on the subject of the kings in *Francia* at that time who did not possess royal power, whether it was well or not that things should be as they were.' Zacharias's reply has remained famous: 'It was better to give the name of king to him who possessed the power rather than to him who did not, so that order could be preserved.' The order the pope had in mind here was not the state of peace that prevailed over the Frankish kingdom in 750, but rather the order of the world as defined by St Augustine in the *City of God* (XIX: 13), 'order—that is to say, the arrangement of persons both equal and unequal assigning each his proper place.' In this universal harmony the king's function is defined by his very title: the king is made to govern, as Gregory the Great and Isidore of Seville taught, following St Augustine. In other words, a king who does not govern is unworthy of the royal function and disturbs the normal order of the world. That seems to be the point of Zacharias's reply. In contrast to the ancient Germanic belief in the transmission of royalty through the link of blood, like a magical power, Zacharias stressed the capacity to be a king, or that suitability on which the Church Fathers had insisted. Yet the pontifical opinion was perfectly intelligible to the lay aristocracy, who had to transpose it into their own scheme of thought: was not the change of dynasty that was at the time being prepared the necessary consequence of the transfer of royal 'virtue' to a more fortunate line? The royal name still borne by Childeric III seemed empty of all content, since real power already belonged to the Carolingians. The idea expressed by the pope, whether interpreted literally, or in terms of the mentality of those times, clearly worked in favour of Pepin; and, fortified with the papal recommendation, he was able to have himself elected king by the Frankish Assembly— almost certainly at Soissons—in March 751. As for Childeric III, he was shut away in a convent, where he ended his days in obscurity.

Yet Pepin's election was not the only act constituting the new royal line. It was still necessary to replace the old legitimacy by some symbol conferring legitimacy on the new dynasty: this took the form of consecration, conferred on Pepin by the Frankish bishops some months after his accession. Our source-material on this matter is very slight: it has been thought—though there can be no certainty in the matter—that it fell to St Boniface to spread the holy oil on the new king's hands. Be that as it may, the ancient biblical rite, which had already taken root in Visigothic Spain in the second half of the seventh century, made its appearance in Frankish Gaul in 751. It marked the new king with a sacred character: Pepin became the elect of God, his adopted son. A new legitimacy was thus created, capable of supplanting the old Merovingian charisma.

The intervention of Pope Zacharias in Frankish affairs at Pepin's request, probably on the advice of St Boniface, was the beginning of the alliance between the Carolingians and the Holy See, an alliance which proved to be one of the unchanging factors in the political and religious life of the eighth and ninth centuries. The new king, who was the first to profit by it, almost immediately had occasion to render a service to the pope in his turn. Stephen II, Zacharias's successor, found himself directly threatened by the progress of the Lombards, who under the command of their king

Aistulf had captured Ravenna and were advancing towards the duchy of Rome.[1] Not being able to count on help from his natural protector, the master of Rome, Emperor Constantine V, Stephen II went to Frankish Gaul to meet Pepin at his palace at Ponthion on 6 January 754.

The discussions that began at once and were continued at Saint-Denis had results of considerable importance. Historians have spent much time discussing the nature of the links that were established between the pope and the king. What seems certain is that Stephen II did not 'commend himself' to the protection of Pepin, and that the two men did not conclude a formal pact of alliance. On the contrary, Pepin swore a solemn oath of fealty to St Peter, to Stephen II and to his successors, in his own name and on behalf of his sons, modelled on the oath of friendship, in which he undertook to give assistance to the Roman Church. In return, the pope consecrated Pepin a second time and likewise anointed his two sons Charles and Carloman as kings of the Franks and patricians of the Romans. He thus became in a sense the spiritual father of the two young Frankish princes, and thus Pepin's 'compère'. Subsequent letters of the popes often allude to this bond of 'compaternity'. As regards the title of *patricius*, originally an honorary Roman title, and later Byzantine, it was borne by high imperial officials—among others the Byzantine governor-general in Italy, the Exarch of Ravenna. By conferring this title on his own authority, and by giving it a specific geographical reference, Stephen II was making Pepin and his two sons the protectors of the city and the people of Rome, of which the pope had assumed charge since the beginning of the eighth century. Moreover, the very precise document which records the ceremony of Pepin's second consecration tells us that Stephen II at this time forbade the Franks to elect a king from outside the posterity of the man he had just consecrated, thus extending Pepin's personal charisma to all his family in the direct line.

The king of the Franks, for his part, succeeded in convincing his people's representatives of the need to help the pope against

[1] We may recall, for the sake of clarity, that in the middle of the eighth century Italy was divided into two zones: Lombard Italy (the kingdom, properly speaking, with Pavia as capital, the duchies of Spoleto and Benevento); and Byzantine Italy (Venetia, the Exarchate of Ravenna, the duchies of Rome, Naples, Apulia, Calabria and Sicily).

the Lombards, though only with great difficulty, it seems, for the two nations had been living in amity since the seventh century. It was because he intended to remain faithful to the traditional alliance, and because he had been helped by the Lombards against

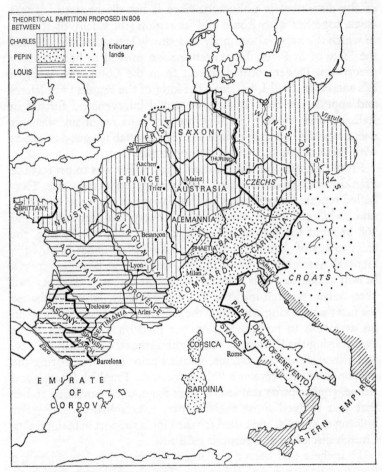

MAP 2 The empire of Charlemagne about the year 800.

the Moslems in Provence, that Charles Martel had fifteen years previously evaded a request from pope Gregory III for his intervention in Italy. In two expeditions into Italy, in 754 or 755 and in 756, Pepin succeeded in defeating the Lombards and compelling them to cede twenty-two towns in the Exarchate, the Pentapolis and Emilia, passing them on not to the Byzantine emperor, their lawful owner, but to the pope. This was in conformity with the privilege called 'the promise of donation' which Pepin had arranged with Stephen II while he was staying in France. (The exact tenor of the document is unknown, since it has disappeared.) These cities, together with Rome and its region (the duchy of Rome), in which the imperial authority was slowly losing its hold, formed the State of St Peter. Its existence soon proved to be extremely precarious. Under constant threat from the Lombards, Stephen II's successor, Paul I, besieged the king of the Franks with letters and appeals for help. But Pepin would intervene no further in Italian affairs, merely inviting the pope to negotiate with his enemies while he himself did his best to re-establish good relations with them, as well as with Constantinople.

From that time on, the essence of his policy was to protect the Frankish state from its enemies and strengthen its structure. Thus he led repeated expeditions against Saxony in response to enemy raids, while arduous campaigns nearly every year between 759 and 768 brought the reconquest of Septimania and, one by one, the chief towns of Aquitaine. In 759 he took Narbonne; in 767, the General Assembly of the kingdom was held at Bourges; in 768 he was at Saintes. This shows that a great extent of territory had been reincorporated into the kingdom. Finally, let us emphasise the fact that the king continued the reform of the Church begun on his accession to power. St Boniface died on 5 June 755 while evangelising the Frisians in the neighbourhood of the Zuider Zee, and although his programme, with its prior aim of restoring the metropolitans to serve as a link between the Frankish Church and Rome, could not be realised, at least the council convened at Ver that year revived some ancient laws, re-established the regular holding of synods, and called for the king's support in maintaining Church discipline and resolving disputes.

Thus there had been a settlement on several points when the first Carolingian king died in 768. The Frankish state had been restored to unity, and the royal power, based upon a strong foundation of vassal service, considerably reinforced. The Church was slowly moving in the direction of reform. Through the king as intermediary, in close alliance with the pope, it had remade some of its links with Rome. A new world was coming to birth; it fell to Charlemagne to give it shape.

III

The kingdom of the Franks
under Charlemagne

The most important part of Charlemagne's reign, which lasted from 768 to 814, falls in the period before the imperial coronation. The successes of the new king of the Franks and the expansion of the kingdom as a result of his efforts are at least a partial explanation of the event of 25 December 800. It will therefore be advisable to make a brief survey of the last third of the eighth century in order to see how the kingdom was extended, and to see the main features of Charlemagne's administration and of his thoughts.

The first years of the reign were far from glorious. In accordance with custom, Pepin had divided Francia between his two sons. The share of the younger son, Carloman, was Alemannia, Alsace, Burgundy, inland Aquitaine, Septimania and Provence. The territories given to his elder brother, Charles, surrounded the others like the arc of a circle, and comprised Austrasia in the north-east, Neustria up to the mouth of the Loire, and the coast of Aquitaine. The two kings, who lived at some distance from one another (Charles at Noyon, and Carloman at Soissons), were not on good terms; and this became obvious when an Aquitanian lord, Hunaud by name, in conjunction with Lupus, duke of the Gascons, started a rebellion against Frankish authority. Carloman refused to join his brother and Charles conducted a quick campaign in Aquitaine on his own and succeeded in putting down the revolt. At the same time, under the influence of his mother, Queen Bertha, Charles adopted a policy of conciliation, continuing the methods pursued by Pepin in the last part of his reign.

He made terms with Tassilo, duke of Bavaria, recognising his independence, and married a daughter of Desiderius, king of the Lombards. This situation, however, did not continue for long. Carloman died in 771; and instead of upholding his nephews' rights, Charles immediately took possession of their inheritance and thus extended his authority over the whole of Francia. The only course open to Carloman's widow was to flee with her children and one of her faithful retainers, Duke Autcharius—the future Ogier of the *chansons de geste*—to the court of the king of the Lombards. Charles then directed his policy along lines entirely different from those he had so far followed. In particular, he broke off the entente with the Lombards and dispatched the princess he had married to Pavia. It was as though he were reverting to his father's early policy: he revived it with new vigour, and made it yield greater results.

In 772 he began his campaigns against the Saxons, who had preserved both their paganism and their complete independence. They had proved dangerous neighbours on the Frankish borders, posing a continuous threat to the Rhineland, Hesse and Thuringia. Charles Martel and Pepin III had done no more than launch punitive raids against them; Charlemagne's first expedition against the Saxons kept this character; but as the years went on, his purpose of protecting the Frankish kingdom and its dependencies against invasion by establishing a March between the Lippe and the Diemel became increasingly clear. His plan was to set up a strongly fortified military zone capable of stopping invaders and providing, if need be, outposts for deeper penetration into their territory.

In 773, however, Charlemagne was distracted from these operations in Saxony by an appeal from Pope Hadrian I to come to his help in Italy. King Desiderius had resumed his advance on Rome, retaking Ravenna and several towns in the Pentapolis and Umbria, and bringing with him Carloman's sons in order to have them anointed by the Roman pontiff. After a fruitless summons to the Lombard king to evacuate his conquests, the Frankish army crossed into Italy by the Val d'Aosta and Mont Cenis, and besieged Pavia. The town resisted for nine months (October 773 to June 774). Meanwhile the king of the Franks went to Rome to celebrate the festival of Easter. Hadrian I received him according to the ceremonial traditionally used for the visit of the Exarch (the former Byzantine viceroy), and Charlemagne confirmed to the pope the donation previously made to him by Pepin. Despite the implications of Hadrian's biographer to the contrary, the tenor of this donation does not seem to have gone beyond the concessions already made to the Holy See. What we know for certain is that the pope was quick to realise that this new patrician of Rome would exercise a much stronger authority over the city of the Apostles than his father had done. In June 774 King Desiderius capitulated, and Charlemagne, having received the submission of all the regions of the kingdom, proclaimed himself king of the Lombards. This was the first instance of a personal union of two kingdoms. At first, Lombardy kept its institutions and administrative personnel. It was not till two years later, after an attempted insurrection by Hruodgaud, duke of Friuli, that the Frankish administrative machinery was introduced into the kingdom of Lombardy. Thereafter, the king of the Franks made his presence felt in the peninsula through his counts, his *missi* and his vassals, and even the Papal State did not escape their control.

In 777 the military operations that had continued without a break in Saxony, along with the construction of castles occupied by permanent garrisons, seemed to open up brilliant prospects. The Frankish March had held out in the face of repeated attacks; and several of the Saxon aristocracy, especially in the eastern parts, had made their submission and declared their intention of being converted to Christianity. The assembly held that year at Paderborn was in fact marked by the first mass baptism of Saxons, an occasion which also marked the first steps in establishing the Church in Westphalia. Perhaps it was then that the king of the Franks became fully conscious of his task of promoting Christianity in pagan lands. Another indication would certainly suggest as much. There appeared before the assembly at Paderborn the *vali* (or governor) of Saragossa, who came to beg for Charlemagne's help in his conflict with the emir of Cordova. The Frankish king, under the illusion that his intervention could wrest part of Spain from Islam, crossed the Pyrenees in the following year. While one army corps was taking Gerona and Barcelona, he himself pushed through Navarre as far as the gates of Saragossa. But meanwhile a loyal *vali* had taken the place of the one who had begged for his intervention; and this fact, together with the approach of the emir of Cordova, made Charlemagne decide to withdraw. In crossing one of the passes in the Lower Pyrenees—probably at Roncevalles—

his rearguard was crushed by the mountain Basques. Roland, prefect of the March of Brittany, Seneschal Eggihard and Anselme, Count of the Palace, were among the slain (15 August 778). The battle of Roncevalles made a deep impression on contemporaries, and later acquired such a permanent place in the collective memory, that it was the origin of the most famous *chanson de geste*, the *Chanson de Roland*. We can perhaps better explain the long persistence of this evil memory by bearing in mind that the year 778 was one of the most difficult in the whole reign. It was a year of numerous crises, all stemming from the reverse suffered by Charlemagne: there were revolts in Gascony and Aquitaine, intrigues in northern Italy hatched by the Byzantine governor of Sicily and the Lombard duke of Benevento, and attacks on the Westphalian March and Hesse by the Saxons, whose chief, Widukind, now wielding ducal power, was henceforward to carry on an implacable war against the Frankish king.

Charlemagne, who was approaching his forties, now began to show his full qualities as a statesman. F. Ganshof, the most eminent of the historians who have made a special study of this great reign, has effectively demonstrated how Charlemagne's actions, which till this point had continued his father's tradition, began from 779 onwards to show a much more personal tendency both at home and abroad. We have only to collate our documents to be convinced of this. First there was a change in his Saxon policy. As an independent country, Saxony was too great a danger to the Frankish state, and from now onwards a policy of conquest seemed imperative, all the more so as it appeared the only way of assuring the triumph of Christianity in northern Germania. At this point there began a series of cruel, relentless annual expeditions (the massacre of Verden, 782). In 785 Widukind finally surrendered, and his submission meant that of Saxony as far as the Elbe. It was incorporated into the Frankish kingdom, and the Church was organised in an atmosphere of terror—witness the famous capitulary *de partibus Saxoniae* threatening the death penalty for any attempt at revolt, any attack against Churchmen, and any maintenance of paganism. The same fate overtook eastern Frisia. A few years later, following the removal of the last independent duke of Bavaria, Tassilo III (788), the whole of Germania passed to the Franks. There is another important transformation to be noted in the southern zone of Charlemagne's domain. Realising the individual character of Aquitaine and Italy, their impatience of Frankish domination, and their aspirations towards autonomy, Charlemagne made them both into sub-kingdoms. At the head of the former kingdom of Lombardy he placed his son Pepin, the second of his sons by his wife Hildegard. The third son, Louis (the future Louis the Pious), became king of Aquitaine; the two young princes received royal unction from the hands of Pope Hadrian I in Rome in the year 781, and each was installed in his kingdom with a court and Frankish assistants. Charles of course reserved to himself the general oversight of both kingdoms. It was on his initiative that the conquest of the Spanish March on the southern side of the Pyrenees was undertaken from 785 onwards. As Ramon d'Abadal has demonstrated,[1] this conquest was in line with the wishes of the Christian population of the towns, which, like Gerona in 785, submitted of their own accord to Frankish domination. During his stay in Italy in 787, Charles took action to counter the manœuvres of the duke of Benevento, who was intriguing with the ex-king of Lombardy's son, Adalgis, a refugee in Constantinople, and Irene, the Byzantine empress. An expedition to Benevento soon reduced the duke to submission. Parallel with these great military and political successes, all through the years 779–99 we may note considerable efforts by the king of the Franks to knit the state together more closely within and strengthen the royal authority; we shall return to this later.

The impetus that marked this decisive and fertile period was, however, interrupted in the years that followed 790, when there was a second succession of crises. First there was an internal crisis. In 792 a conspiracy centring on a royal bastard, Pepin the Hunchback, showed up the discontent of a section of the aristocracy at a government that was proving more and more authoritarian, and perhaps also at the heavy burden of continual wars. This plot led Charlemagne to revive the ancient custom of a general oath of allegiance administered to his subjects. We know that this was carried out in 793, and that it strengthened the bond between the sovereign and his peoples. That same year a violent Saracen counter-offensive overwhelmed the territories already conquered south of the Pyrenees and reached the gates of Narbonne, where it was checked just in time by Count Guillaume de

---

[1] 'La Domination carolingienne en Catalogne', *Revue historique*, 225 (1961), 319–40.

Toulouse.[1] When the alarm was over, the Franks continued their methodical occupation of the March. Finally, in the north-east of the kingdom, there was a general insurrection in Saxony, no doubt caused by the excessive rigour of the Frankish administration; and it was four years (793–7) before the area was reconquered. This outcome was probably assisted by the suspension of the reign of terror begun by the capitulary *de partibus Saxoniae*, and by the inauguration of a more moderate regime. The districts of Wihmode (between the mouths of the Weser and the Elbe) and Nordalbingia (to the north-east of the lower Elbe) were the only ones to continue resistance to the Frankish armies, which were not finally victorious till 804. Thus it was that Charlemagne succeeded in restoring a situation that had looked most precarious at the opening of the last decade of the century. But while reconquering the lost ground, the king also succeeded in a far-reaching extension of the Frankish state's boundaries towards the south-east.

The annexation of Bavaria had in fact brought it into contact with the kingdom of the Avars, a people of Turkish race, originating from central Asia, and since the seventh century installed in the centre of the Danube basin, from the river Tisza to Carinthia. Their king, or *Khagan*, who had no doubt been Tassilo's ally in 788, had raided the frontiers of Bavaria and Friuli. Charlemagne, having attempted in vain to negotiate with him, began a war of conquest in 791. After a brilliant campaign that year which took the Franks as far as western Hungary, the invasion was interrupted in the two following years as a result of the internal disturbances we have analysed; but it was vigorously resumed in 795, when a Frankish army from Italy commanded by Pepin succeeded in capturing the enemy's main camp, the famous *Ring*, situated between the Tisza and the Danube, and again in 796, when the Avars were thrown back across the Tisza. As a result, important territory fell into Charlemagne's hands, which he divided into three groups: the lands along the Danube between the Traun (the Bavarian boundary) and the forest of Vienna, corresponding to present-day Upper and Lower Austria, were annexed to Bavaria; those between the forest of Vienna, the Danube and the lower Drave he made into the March of Pannonia (thus reviving the

[1] Founder of a monastery at Gellone near Lodève, Saint-Guilhelm-du-Désert, called after him.

ancient Roman name of the province); the territories lying south of the Drave, corresponding to lower Styria, Carniola and northern Croatia, were given to the duchy of Friuli, and so joined to the kingdom of Italy. Christianity was introduced into all these regions from the end of the eighth century onwards, but with less violence than in Saxony. These lands were predominantly inhabited by Slavs, who had accompanied the Avars in the course of their westward progress in the two previous centuries.

Our story has taken us, then, almost up to the year 800. We have seen a remarkable increase in the size of the Frankish kingdom. From the March of Spain to that of Pannonia, from the North Sea to the centre of Italy, it covered the greater part of western Europe. In this vast area there were a variety of very different peoples living side by side, each under its own laws. But they had a common bond, the king and the administrative machinery of the Franks; and above all, there was a spiritual bond, the Christian religion. These two aspects are really indivisible; but, for the purposes of our discussion, it will be convenient to treat them separately.

Let us start by considering how the state worked, and what were its principal institutions. In the first place, the change of dynasty did not mean any organic transformation of the kingdom. Charlemagne considered himself the true successor of the Merovingians, invested like them with the royal *ban*, that is, with the right to command, punish and prohibit, and so possessing pre-eminent authority over men as their administrator, judge and supreme lawgiver. It was much more a rule over men than over territory, as is shown by the royal title, which remained *rex Francorum*: king of the Franks (and not king of *Francia*). Charlemagne's Merovingian predecessors had compelled the Franks to bind themselves to them personally by an oath of fealty; but this practice had fallen into disuse, and, as I have already noted, Charlemagne revived it in 789, and again in 793. All the inhabitants of the kingdom of twelve years old and over had to take the oath, which was intended to counteract the administrative defects of the Frankish state, of which the king was fully aware.

He tried, however, to improve the practical administration, and in the first place to solve the fundamental problem of the relations between the crown and the aristocracy. It was a long-standing problem; in the Germanic concept, the aristocracy was much less subject to the king than associated with him in the government and development of the state. Here the experience of the Merovingians had proved disastrous. The 'great men' (*potentes*) gave the king very poor service, and pursued only their own advantage. Moreover, in their efforts to acquire supporters among grasping barbarians, the successors of Clovis had almost ruined themselves. By multiplying their gifts of land in full ownership in order to buy the loyalty of the powerful, whom they at the same time created counts and dukes, they had impoverished their inheritance, the royal domains, which consisted originally of all the land that under the Romans had been state-owned, and had become theirs by conquest. Herein lies the most notable difference between the Merovingian regime and that of their successors.

As we have seen, the assumption of power by the Carolingians was made possible by the considerable following the Mayor had at his disposal, a following of faithful vassals rewarded by Church property, which was—at least from 743 onwards—given to them on a temporary basis. Now henceforward the institution of vassalage, which had up to 751 been private, became publicly recognised, particularly under Charlemagne. In other words, it was incorporated into the state and became, in the king's judgment, its firmest bulwark. So we see Charles multiplying the number of his own vassals, the *vassi dominici*, many of whom were grouped in military colonies in the newly conquered territories. Furthermore, he compelled the agents of public authority, drawn in large numbers from the aristocracy of Austrasia and Alemannia, the counts, marquises and dukes, as well as the Church dignitaries, the bishops and royal abbots, to become his personal vassals. In this way the service these great men owed the sovereign in virtue of their offices was reinforced by the fealty to which they were bound as vassals of their liege lord. Finally Charlemagne encouraged his personal vassals to imitate his example in the same fashion, and to use the bonds of homage and fealty to attach as many men as possible to their own persons. Thus there was forged a chain of fealty which extended through every class of society up to the king.

The system of vassalage, however, did not aim solely at incorporating men in a framework of loyalty. As envisaged by Pepin and Charlemagne, it was also an important economy for the state.

The first two Carolingians, who did in fact partly succeed in re-constituting the royal estates by what they recovered, by clearing land, and above all by conquest, were very chary of parting with any of their territory. On the other hand, by encouraging free men to enter into a vassal relationship with powerful persons, 'for our own advantage', as the edict plainly puts it, he mobilised the for-tune of the landed aristocracy; for it was from their own property that the great men had to set apart the fiefs (benefices) with which to reward the vassals they had to hold at the king's disposal, thus enabling him to avoid the expense of maintaining an army. As for the men of power who participated in the government of the state by the exercise of their responsible administrative offices, they reaped their reward in various ways, particularly by the revenue from lands attached to their offices (*pertinentia de comitatu*).

Such then, in broad outline, was Charlemagne's administrative system. Though logical and coherent, it nevertheless had serious defects, the most important of which was probably its use of land as a means of remuneration. In spite of all the corrective measures applied to Merovingian customs, the land, even when only tem-porarily conceded, tended in practice to be no longer at the king's free disposal. Edict after edict protests against the attempts made by the holders of land to appropriate it; and it required all Charle-magne's power and prestige to keep his vassals faithful and con-strain them to give the service they owed him. The continual wars were a sufficient source of wealth to ensure the obedience of the king's men to himself: one has only to recall the treasure seized from the Saxons in 772, or the enormous booty captured in the Avar *Ring* in 795. But as soon as the campaigns stopped, or royal control over the vassals was relaxed, the situation could rapidly deteriorate, as Louis the Pious was soon to discover, to his own tragic cost. In a word, through the lack of a body of salaried officials appointed for specific tasks, as in the Byzantine and Moslem empires where a monetary economy prevailed, the Caro-lingian administration was rudimentary and diffuse, and the in-stitutions were still those of the Merovingian period. The most that can be said is that they were reinvigorated and completed according to the king's personal ideas, or in response to new needs produced by changing circumstances.

The Palace remained the centre of government. It included the royal family and the great ecclesiastics and laymen chosen by the king for personal valour or high position in state or Church. It was from among these Paladins that Charlemagne recruited his Council, which he convened whenever he thought fit. He would listen to its opinion, but make his decisions alone. This 'secret council' was enlarged on certain occasions. For example, when it was necessary to modify existing laws, Charlemagne would call in jurists expert in secular and canon law. When there were important decisions to be made, especially in military or diplomatic affairs, all the great men of the Palace were called to the Council. Alongside this very fluid body, there were various high officials round Charlemagne. We note in the first place a high-ranking Churchman, an abbot (Fulrad of Saint-Denis), or a bishop (Angilram of Metz, Hildebald of Cologne), head of the Chapel Royal, that is, of the court clergy, called by this name because it housed the Franks' most precious relic, the *chape* (cope) of St Martin. But this 'arch-chaplain' might also be compared to a kind of 'Minister for Worship', since he was responsible for everything to do with the hierarchy and ecclesiastical discipline. He was also in control—indirectly, at any rate—of the chancery, for the staff of notaries was more often than not recruited from among the clerics of the chapel. Their work was directed by the Chancellor or proto-notary, and consisted essentially of drawing up the public or private acts proceeding from the royal will, a task which became increasingly important in view of Charlemagne's legislative and juridical activity. Alongside these clerks were a certain number of lay coadjutors serving the king in such offices as Chamberlain (in charge of the treasury), Seneschal (managing the administration of the Palace and controlling the exploitation of the royal estates), Butler (royal cellars and vineyards), Constable (managing the royal stables), all of them the king's private officers, but often also invested with some public service or mission. The chief lay assistant, however, was the *Comte du Palais*, to whom the exercise of the king's justice was delegated. The king was equally a judge in the first instance and on appeal, and he could always require cases to appear before himself; in addition, he would decide cases brought before him by litigants claiming to have been denied justice. A considerable number of cases came before the king's court in this way, and it was the duty of the *Comte* to sift them, submitting the cases involving great men to the king, and judging the others himself with the help of assessors recruited from the Palace. In spite of the precautions taken to ensure that the litigants should not abuse their right to appear before the king, the Palace, especially towards the end of Charlemagne's reign, was constantly 'resounding with the clamour of litigants'.[1]

Local administration was essentially the responsibility of the Count, who was supposed—in principle, at least—to be the executant of the king's orders. His jurisdiction was over an area that had developed from the decay of the Gallo-Roman city, and was called the *pagus* (which has given us the French word *pays*). At the end of the reign there were some three hundred of these in Frankish Gaul, where the *pagus* and the *comté* were roughly equivalent; but this was not so in the newly incorporated Germanic regions, where there was no such thing as a continuous network of counties, but a survival of ancient administrative institutions, under the more or less distant control of the Count—if there was one. In this case, his authority seems to have been based on a grouping of royal domains, and supported by 'king's freemen' (*Königsfreie*), who were half-peasant, half-soldier. In the west, on the other hand, the *pagus*, which, F. Lot suggests, was similar to the old French *arrondissement*, but larger by about 50 per cent, was fairly firmly established; it comprised subdivisions called, according to the region, either *vigueries* or *centaines*, which were comparable with French cantons.

The Count, who was nominated by the king and could be dismissed by him, had a great variety of powers. He administered the oath of loyalty to freemen, and published the royal edicts in his district; as recruiter of the royal army, he had to raise the levy of freemen and bring them to the main body of troops; he had financial responsibilities as well, for he superintended the payment of the dues and fines owing to the king, one-third of which he kept for himself. But above all the Count was responsible for justice: the title of *judex* (judge) given him in numerous documents defines the essence of his powers. He did not administer this justice, either civil or criminal, by himself, but always from the centre of an assembly of freemen, the *plaid* or *mall*, which met in the chief place of each of the county's subdivisions. About the year 780 an extremely important judicial reform reduced the number of *plaids* that the count could assemble each year, without previous sessions of the assistant judges, to a maximum of three in each *centaine* or

---

[1] As noted by the emperor in one of his last capitularies.

viguerie. These were general courts; but alongside them others continued to hear cases once a fortnight in every *centaine*, and these were attended only by the judges, witnesses and litigants. From this time onwards, the rather vaguely defined competence of these two categories of court becomes distinctly clearer. The principal cases (those that concerned the freedom and property of individuals, or involved the death penalty) were reserved for the general court presided over by the Count; the others were the province of the local courts presided over by the *centenier* or the *viguier*. Moreover, whereas in the Merovingian period cases were decided by jurors chosen at the *mall* at the beginning of each session, the reduction in the number of sessions under Charlemagne necessitated the creation of a body of professional judges well versed in law. These were the *scabini*, appointed by the *missi* in consultation with the count and nominated for life, probably to the number of twelve for each county. They decided cases as a matter of course in the local courts, where they alone were the judges. In the general courts, they proposed the sentence, and the Count merely announced it. This judicial reform, which was one of the greatest achievements of the reign, was inspired by the desire to assure a better system of justice to all the king's subjects, and it attracted widespread attention. The distinction between the competence of the Count and that of the *centenier* was to reappear in the Middle Ages as the distinction between high and low justice; and the *scabini* appointed for life formed a local aristocracy which played a considerable part in the towns of northern France in the period before the communes. In this period, however, the transformations outlined produced only partial results. Charlemagne was constantly at pains to get them applied, and his edicts never ceased to remind the counts, *scabini*, *centeniers* and *viguiers* of their duties. The king could not altogether put his trust in men.

The structure just analysed was modified in the frontier regions, where we come across the institution of the March. This was a military district corresponding to a group of counties under a senior count called the count of the March (marquis or margrave) or duke, who concentrated within his own hands all power in the territory under his control, and particularly all military authority. It is very difficult to describe the exact procedure, for these frontier regions seem to have been largely experimental and the form of administration frequently changed.

Finally, Charlemagne attached great importance to the maintenance of as many contacts as possible with the local administrators, and contrived to supervise them and more particularly to ensure that their management of affairs was effective on the spot.

Contact was assured through the general assembly of the Frankish people, an institution that seems to derive from two earlier practices. On the one hand, there was the mobilisation and review of the army before starting on a campaign. This very ancient Germanic custom had disappeared by the sixth century in Neustria and Burgundy; but it survived in Austrasia, and was actually strengthened under the Mayors of the Palace of Pepin's line. Pepin II in particular restored the institution, and is known to have presided over assemblies at which he represented the king and carried out his functions. From 755 onwards, the assembly that during the first half of the eighth century had met in March (*campus martius*) was called together by King Pepin the Short in the month of May (*campus madius*). It was attended by the leading men of the kingdom with their vassals and the armed freemen. But about the same time it lost its previous purely military character, and took its pattern from the Church councils, which were proving of great importance, and which seem to have been the other source from which the institution sprang. A meeting of bishops at Verneuil in 755 did indeed decide that two councils should be held every year. One should be in March, in the king's presence, wherever he should see fit to convene it; this council therefore coincided with the Marchfield—or, more precisely, since its transfer to a few months later had been decided in 755, with the Mayfield. The other was to be held in October, at a place to be fixed by the bishops during the spring meeting.

It is quite possible that from this time onwards it became customary, as a result of these two councils, to hold two assemblies. The spring one was convened in May or even later at the place where the army was assembled, often in one of the eastern towns (Thionville, Düren or Worms), sometimes even within a recently conquered zone (as at Paderborn in 777 or 799); and, from the end of the eighth century, especially in Aachen. It was a representative assembly of the Frankish people, and consisted essentially of the great men of the kingdom, lay and ecclesiastical, dukes and counts, bishops and abbots, and royal vassals not invested with public office, along with the under-vassals brought by both parties to the assembly. The army proper was present only in the background to receive notice of the decisions taken during the deliberations. The autumn or winter assembly was much more restricted. It was open only to the notables, and worked out with the king the programme to be submitted to the more general meeting of the following spring or summer. Thus the assembly and the council overlapped, while remaining otherwise distinct. It is to be noted, however, that the terminology was fairly fluid: the great assembly, ordinarily called the *placitum generale* or *conventus generalis*, could also be called by the names *concilium* or *synodus*, which usually signify ecclesiastical assemblies.

One can imagine the way the great assembly was conducted. It was divided into two groups, laymen and Churchmen, deliberating together or separately on the programme worked out by the king or his council. They had either to reply to questions put before them, or to discuss the whole of a proposed edict presented to them by the sovereign or his chancellor. Both groups would express their 'consent', that is, they recognised (as Ganshof explains it), that 'what was laid before them was in accordance with the law'.[1] Certain points in the procedure are a good illustration of the double tradition lying behind the *placitum generale*. It was convened and dismissed by the king according to the custom of the ancient assemblies; and those present were restricted to discussing the questions placed before them by the king, and had no initiative of their own—a feature deriving from the conciliar tradition.

The edicts giving force to the decisions taken bore the name of capitularies, because they were divided, in accordance with the assembly's manner of deliberation, into articles (*capitula*). These documents were not the work of the chancery, but of secretaries who had been present at the discussions or had a written schedule placed before them. They are therefore of an extremely composite character, and promulgate in the most confused fashion a variety of diverse administrative and legislative arrangements (moral, religious, civil, penal, political and economic) as well as various articles dealing with the needs of the moment. In fact, as Ganshof's recent researches have shown, the term capitulary covers three different kinds of acts. One kind, in the form of additions to the institutions of common law, is the text of acts in the formulation

[1] *Recherches sur les Capitulaires*, p. 31.

of which legal experts had co-operated in joint session. Others consist of instructions given by Charlemagne to the *missi*, and are concerned with the greatest variety of subjects. Only the capitularies *per se scribenda*, that is, having their own *raison d'être*, deserve to be considered as capitularies in the strict sense of the term. While this triple distinction originated formally in the time of Louis the Pious, it already makes its appearance, though not systematically, in Charlemagne's reign. It was only gradually that the distinction became clear between purely ecclesiastical and lay capitularies. Originally they were a mixture, as were the assemblies to which Charlemagne submitted them for consideration.

It then remained to publish these capitularies throughout the state, and see that they were applied. This was the primary task of inspectors sent out from the palace, the *missi dominici* (envoys of the lord), who gradually came also to undertake the supervision of the administrative work of the counts and the ecclesiastics, the conduct of clerics and laymen, the general control of the administration of the royal estates, and the detection and suppression of abuses. They went about their work in pairs, a layman of high rank together with a Churchman (either abbot or bishop). This machinery had its predecents in Merovingian times, but it was not fully in action until after the year 800. The empire was divided into large districts called *missatica*, of which we can get a glimpse in a document of 802: one corresponded to the northern part of the ecclesiastical province of Sens, and another, roughly, to that of Rouen, though it included the bishopric of Le Mans; a third stretched from Orléans to Besançon by way of Troyes and Langres, and back to the Loire via Autun, thus taking in three ecclesiastical provinces. It was Charlemagne who urged on the *missi* as they completed three or four circuits a year in their districts, holding their sessions in the county *mall*; they thus became a true reflection of the sovereign's determination to achieve unified governmental control. But the institution lost its effectiveness after the death of the man who had created, or at any rate perfected, it.

Thus year by year throughout Charlemagne's reign there had been an immense effort to bind the state together into greater cohesion; and the king had made it his concern to give the constantly growing administrative machinery the impulse necessary to its proper functioning. This happened gradually, and not without checks and passive or overt resistance, for instance in the conspiracy of 792; and yet it was still not enough. Charlemagne, as we have seen, was well aware of the gaps and failings in the administrative machinery. And therefore, in order to make up for the deficiencies in the political structure, it was his policy to rely upon a strong Church and make it serve the state. Furthermore, his legislation aimed to establish a Christian civilisation under the monarchy, and to turn its subjects into a single Christian nation in spite of their ethnic and cultural diversity. In this task the Church had an essential part to play, both as the auxiliary and as the beneficiary of the state. This conception, stemming from Charlemagne's political intuition as well as from his personal piety, comes into the open after the imperial coronation; but it was already in existence long before 800, developing continuously throughout the reign, influenced by many currents, and first and foremost by the alliance between Church and state forged under the Merovingians. It would seem that we must add to this the example of the close union between the spiritual and the temporal which had been effected among the Anglo-Saxons soon after their conversion; and this programme had been explained to the Mayors of the Palace by St Boniface, who had been responsible for the first reforms of the Frankish Church. Nor must we forget that the Carolingian dynasty had been legitimised by the Church, and especially by the papacy; and the two partners had since 754 been linked together in a 'pact of love' and 'compaternity'. Finally, it seems fairly certain that Charlemagne's ecclesiastical policy was based on the precedent of the Old Testament, and that we can interpret it only by bearing in mind the biblical background of his reign. In the capitulary of 789 intended for Churchmen, the famous *Admonitio generalis*, the king of the Franks compared himself to King Josiah in his absolute authority over the religious life of the kingdom of Judah. It will be as well to look first at some examples of the position occupied by the Church in the Frankish state and the considerable efforts made by Charlemagne to raise the level of its life. The general interpretation of this policy will be kept for a later chapter.

In a general way it may be said that the relations between Church and state represented an interpenetration of the spiritual and the temporal. The Church was incorporated into the state and put at the service of the crown. Entry into the ranks of the clergy was

48

subject to the prince's consent, and all clerics had to take the oath of allegiance; the bishops and abbots led their vassals and the freemen from their estates to the royal army. Moreover, the higher clergy played an active part in political life. The positions occupied by the arch-chaplain and the chancellor in the palace were of primary importance; both were Churchmen. In the cities, the bishop and the count exercised joint control, and the capitularies were promulgated by them together. One of the *missi* was always a bishop or an abbot, and seems always to have had the greater prestige and to have commanded confidence as a Churchman. As we have already noted, bishops and abbots took part in elaborating the law in the general assemblies, where they sat either with the great laymen, or separately when purely ecclesiastical affairs were discussed. It is difficult to distinguish between these 'mixed' assemblies and the autonomous councils, such as the Council of Frankfurt (794) undoubtedly was, although there sat alongside it an assembly of laymen. There were others too, as at Aachen in 800; and in 813 five councils sat simultaneously in five towns of the empire.

All the same, the help of a council was not necessarily required for the king to be able to legislate in Church matters. More often than not, he legislated under the conditions described in the previous paragraph. But in either case, the legislative instrument was the capitulary; and it will be recalled that, though some of them were specifically ecclesiastical, the majority were mixed in character. But what was the source of this legislation? Naturally enough, the papacy exercised an influence in favour of adopting a canonical pattern worked out under its aegis. Thus in 774 Charlemagne received from Hadrian I a copy of the collection of conciliar canons and decretals compiled in the sixth century by a monk called Dionysius Exiguus, subsequently enlarged, and called after the customary style at Rome *Dionysio-Hadriana*. Now it is remarkable to note that this collection was not officially promulgated: Charlemagne was content simply to draw largely upon it for his own legislation; thus indirectly was the Roman order established in the Frankish kingdom and Church law unified.

Having thus become the Church's supreme law-giver, Charlemagne likewise took its administration in hand. It was he who nominated the bishops, with very rare exceptions, and, incidentally, he chose wisely. Among the monastic Orders, he generally had the abbots elected by the monks in their monasteries; yet he would sometimes intervene himself and insist on laymen being appointed to an abbacy (for instance, Angilbert at Saint-Riquier), though this was very rare in his reign. As for Church possessions, they came under a regime which assimilated them very closely to the royal domains. They were placed under the protection of the royal *ban*, and anyone who attacked them was subject to the same fine (sixty *solidi*) as those who infringed royal commands. Charlemagne also extended the privilege of immunity, which had first made its appearance in the Merovingian epoch, but he contrived both to regulate it and bring it under state control by creating the institution of the advocacy, the holder of which was nominated directly by the king or by the *missi*, or elected in the count's presence, and was then responsible for the administration of justice in the immune territory, and answerable to the state for its implementation. Finally, the king took good care that the churches should always be ready to come to the state's assistance with their landed possessions, and he invited them to make an inventory of their property and keep regular accounts of their income. In the last analysis, the bishoprics and abbeys held their lands at the disposal of the king. Although the Church did not experience any massive secularisation as in the time of Charles Martel or Pepin I, Charlemagne continued all the same to give some Church property as fiefs, and often invited its owners to 'house' vassals. If we add to the royal powers of legislation and administration the king's supreme jurisdiction over the Church, and if we further take into account that various misdemeanours against the Church came within the royal sphere of justice, and that, conversely, disobedience to the laws of the state was punishable by ecclesiastical penalties, it becomes clear that we must now consider what advantages the Church reaped from this regime.

First and foremost, there was the restoration of its structure. True, the re-establishment of metropolitan sees was only slowly achieved. It went against not only the wishes of the king, who considered himself sole head of the Church, but also the intentions of the bishops, each of whom aspired to be independent in his own diocese; and it was only at the very end of the reign that the metropolitans reappeared. In Charlemagne's will, twenty-one of them are mentioned for the empire as a whole. Within the diocese, the bishop's authority was strengthened. From now onwards, the bishop had the right of visitation in all the country churches and even over the 'peculiars', and incumbents could not be appointed without his consent. The monasteries too, with very few exceptions, came under his jurisdiction. Diocesan synods strengthened the links between the bishop and his clergy and worked out the statutes, which also became one of the sources of Frankish ecclesiastical law. On the other hand, just as the king considered the fortune of the great churches to be at the disposal of the state, he took good care that the rural churches, which often had insufficient landed endowments, should be protected against hardship. It was perhaps with them in mind that he made the tithe regular and compulsory. We are in the dark about the circumstances of its introduction, though it was undoubtedly connected with the ancient biblical institution. The Merovingian bishops had laid claim to it, but there are no means of knowing to what extent it was effectively levied in their times. In Ireland, on the other hand, it had appeared very early on, and spread from there to the Anglo-Saxon kingdoms. Boniface had imposed it, with the sanction of Rome, upon the peoples he converted. With the coming of the Carolingians, a new feature appears—the imposition of tithe by public authorities—in Gaul perhaps in the year 755, in Bavaria in 756. None the less, the first law imposing tithe on the whole kingdom was the capitulary of 779,[1] followed by a whole series of edicts prescribing the regular payment of these dues, and instituting severe penalties against offenders. All property, including the royal lands, was subject to it, and the income—except for the quarter allocated to the bishop—was reserved for the rural churches. Such, at least, is the classical interpretation put upon a much-debated chapter in the history of the Frankish Church; yet the further history of tithe, which more often than not passed into lay hands, makes it doubtful what its precise significance really was.

Side by side with this consolidation of the Church's structure went the promotion of religious life among the clergy and their people; and here we touch upon Charlemagne's special work, constituting one of his outstanding claims to fame. We catch a

---

[1] The same capitulary prescribed in addition for vassals 'housed' on land taken from churches that they should pay to them, over and above the nominal rent fixed by the council of 743 and the tithe proper, a second tithe or *none*.

glimpse of this as early as the *Admonitio generalis* of 789, and henceforward this programme of spiritual and moral improvement was continually being extended, especially after the year 800. The sovereign also became the preacher, teaching 'what should be proclaimed to the people of God in order that they may be led towards the heavenly pastures'. He constantly enjoins prayer, the demands of morality and the law of love, and invites his people to join with contemplation in the Church's worship—exhortations which give certain passages in the capitularies the character of regular sermons.

In order to realise this programme Charlemagne recommended that parents should themselves undertake the religious education of their children, or, failing the parents, the godfather and godmother. The demands and duties of Sunday were to be rigorously observed, especially the duty of preaching. Bishops and priests were to preach on all Sundays and feast-days in the vernacular, and, not content with giving this order, he had a collection of sermons made by Paul the Deacon. By a capitulary he officially commanded its use throughout the Frankish Church. Realising quite clearly that worship was a means of disseminating a higher level of Christian life among the people, he took measures to ensure that divine service should be reverently and punctually held, and followed up the work of unifying the liturgy begun by his father. In 785 Pope Hadrian sent him the Gregorian Sacramentary; but as this book was originally composed for the pope's use only and did not include all the masses and offices, Charlemagne directed Alcuin to complete it. Alcuin made use of an older sacramentary, the Gelasian, and in this way a large number of Gallican versions were included in the service-books. Finally, two years later, the Roman method of chanting (*cantilena romana*) was made compulsory for the whole kingdom by the *Admonitio generalis* of 789.

Since the raising of the Christian level of life among people depended ultimately on a higher level of spiritual and moral life among their pastors, Charlemagne worked unceasingly to effect this object. He not only revived the ancient canons prescribing how the clergy ought to live, but he also encouraged the principle of communal life among the clergy serving the cathedrals and the large churches. Thus Charlemagne's reign saw the rise and development of the institution of canonical bodies. Above all, however, he laboured to improve clerical education, convinced, as he

3–4 *Charlemagne's seal* (Bibliothèque nationale)
(From P. E. Schramm, *Die deutschen Kaiser und Könige in Bildern ihrer Zeit.*)
A Roman gem of the second century: profile of an emperor's or
philosopher's head, and round it the inscription: 'Christ, protect Charles,
king of the Franks.'
Carolingian chancery bull (below)
In use from 768 to 800; in lead, then in gold, and attached to the diploma
by a cord. We have only this one specimen, in a very poor state of
preservation (Bibl. nat., Cabinet des Médailles, no. 996). The
reproduction (from Schramm, *op. cit.*) is a reconstruction from a 1729
drawing.

The missing words (in minuscule) are borrowed from a bull of Charles
the Bald, which is of the same type.

5 *David and Charles*
Vivian's Bible, the work of the
School of Tours, mid-ninth
century (Bibl. nat., Lat. 1, f. 1ᵛ;
cf. no. 17 below).

The text of this page is divided
into two columns. It is in gold
capitals on a purple ground. There
are two medallions of the greatest
interest. The lower one represents
Charles the Bald (*Karolus Rex
Francor.*), to whom the dedicatory
poem refers, beginning with the
line: 'Blessed king, may this book
please you, Charles.' The upper
one bears the inscription *David
Rex Imp.* (David king and
emperor). This is Charlemagne,
king and emperor, represented as
David king of Israel.

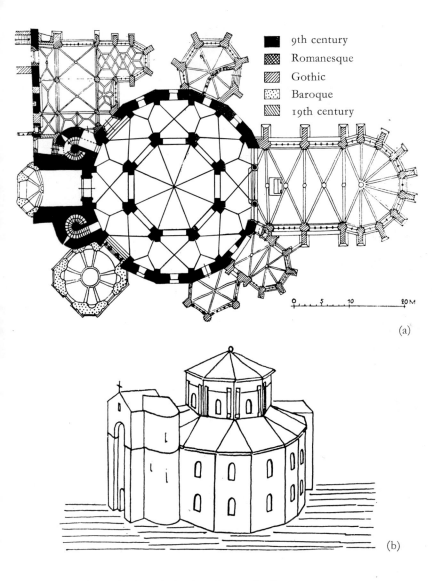

9th century
Romanesque
Gothic
Baroque
19th century

(a)

(b)

6 *The Palatine chapel at Aachen* (see also overleaf)
The plans and figures a, b, c are taken from *Mémorial d'un voyage d'études de
la Société des Antiquaires de France en Rhénanie*, 1951.

  Figures b and c show the skill of the construction—an octagonal cupola,
buttressed by transverse wagon vaults going along above the galleries;
the aisles have groin-vaulting, and the arches are alternately rectangular
in the two storeys.

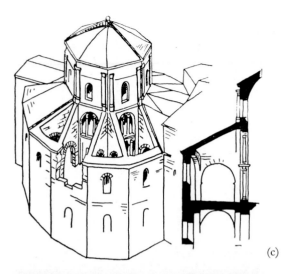

(c)

The Palatine chapel at Aachen
6d (left) gives some idea of
the splendour of the
building, with its wide
openings divided by two
rows of superimposed
columns, whose capitals are
richly decorated (twenty-
five of the forty columns
are ancient). The bronze
doors are of the period, but
the mosaics modern. Left
foreground, the steps
leading up to Charlemagne's
throne (see no. 7).

himself said, that 'knowledge must come before the desire to do good'. This primary intent lies at the foundation of the great intellectual movement beginning at the close of the eighth century and illuminating the ninth, the Carolingian Renaissance, the chief features of which we must now go on to explore.

◈ IV ◈

The Carolingian Renaissance

This Renaissance was first and foremost an intellectual revival perceptible in the field of literary activity. It began modestly but from the last decade of the eighth century onwards its impulse was to prove irresistible. There was the rediscovery of certain aspects of classical antiquity, and the handing on of a certain number of its works. Fertilised by the legacy of the past, it encouraged a constantly growing number of writers. Its chief promoter was Charlemagne. The problems raised by it are manifold, and we must now attempt to get some grasp of the chief ones.

First of all, was it part of a continuous cultural growth, or did it spring up suddenly in a desert? It would seem that our answer to this question should fall somewhere between the two extremes.

After the end of the ancient world, classical culture had suffered a notable impoverishment. The use of Greek vanished in general from the western world in the fourth and fifth centuries, and the sciences fell into decay. The two facts are related since science was essentially Hellenic. Throughout the Middle ages, the west felt the effect of the disappearance of Greek before Greek science had been assimilated into Latin civilisation. Philosophy was an exception: the last genuine western philosopher was Boethius, but he died in 526 before completing the task he had undertaken, to translate into Latin the whole of Aristotle and Plato's works. He managed in fact to translate only a few treatises by the former. In these circumstances, Latin culture was of an entirely literary character at the time the barbarians were taking possession of the empire. It was essentially based upon grammar and rhetoric, it aimed especially at perfection of form—a perfection that degenerated more often than not into mannerism—and at erudition; one has only to read the works of Sidonius Apollinaris (who died *c*. 480) to be convinced of this. But in spite of its faults and stilted style, the prestige of this culture was still intact. It was the preserve of the Roman aristocracy, and became an object of envy to the Germanic kings, some of whom tried to make it their own. We have only to remember the last Vandal kings, and especially Theodoric. But we must now turn to Gaul, and try to get a glimpse of the evolution of its cultural life between the sixth and the eighth centuries.

A number of subtle distinctions will have to be made, in time no less than in distance. First there is the contrast—on either side of a line running from Nantes to Geneva by way of Orléans and Autun—between southern and northern Gaul. South of this line, in Aquitaine, Burgundy and Provence, classical culture survived until the middle of the seventh century. This was Roman Gaul, where the written word persisted, where Latin inscriptions were still plentiful, where the towns still kept a certain degree of administrative life, and all the influence belonged to the Gallo-Roman senatorial aristocracy, who supplied the Germanic kings with their assistants, their officials and their bishops. True, the Roman public schools disappeared at the end of the fifth or the beginning of the sixth century, with the disappearance of the municipal institutions to which they had been traditionally attached; yet the aristocracy contrived, at any rate for a certain while, to mitigate this situation by educating their children themselves, or having tutors at home to teach them. So the culture thus acquired continued for a long time to be the secular culture of the classical epoch; its language, the language of poetry, the oratory, and the epigrams of the period, still did its best to be that of literary Latin and remained for all these aristocrats the clearest hallmark of distinction between themselves and the barbarians.

North of this Roman Gaul stretched Frankish Gaul proper; but it is important to remind ourselves here of the distinctions we drew above from a political point of view. The north-west (Neustria) had very imperfectly been germanised, and the Frankish settlements south of the linguistic frontier were very few and far between. This region, which had only very superficially been romanised and christianised, relapsed into barbarism. The north-eastern regions (Austrasia), on the other hand, were largely germanised, though islands of Romance culture long continued to exist, especially in the region of Trier. Nevertheless the Merovingians seem to have looked upon the south as a kind of cultural reserve. Each of the successors of Clovis was intent upon acquiring a share in it, as though that would by itself initiate him into Roman administrative practice and the culture of antiquity. And in fact it was from these southern regions that, from the sixth century onwards, these influences did slowly radiate towards the north. Although one must not exaggerate the intensity of this radiation, it may be noted that certain Merovingians were men of letters, such as Theodebert and Theodebald of the Austrasian line, or Chilperic, who, barbarian as he was, used to compose poems, and even proposed to reform the alphabet. The most enlightened kings and laymen were gradually won over to the use of written documents, and some of them saw that their children were provided with a minimum of intellectual education. The part played by the Palace as an educational centre for the future official ranks of the kingdom must not be minimised, at least till one third of the way through the seventh century, whatever may be our opinion of the often deplorable morals that prevailed in its environment.

None the less this culture was very fragile everywhere, even in southern Gaul. As generation after generation went by, knowledge inevitably deteriorated, through lack of regular educational institutions, and through the ever-increasing preponderance of barbarism. In the last third of the sixth century, Gregory of Tours's *Historia Francorum* already reveals many serious signs of the decline in ancient culture; and the same is true at the beginning of the seventh century of Venantius Fortunatus, who after a fashion maintained the traditions of ancient classical poetry. 'Woe betide us!' exclaims the former in his preface, 'for the study of letters is perishing among us.' The second admits to never having read Hilary and Augustine, let alone Plato and Aristotle. Was this dislike, or lack of curiosity? To these probable causes of decline must be added the distrust some felt for a literature steeped in pagan tradition. In the course of the seventh century the situation grew even worse. We have only to turn to the Frankish chroniclers—

among them the one known as Pseudo-Fredegarius, a continuator of Gregory of Tours—to be aware of the crudity of their expression. These writings show us, as well as the lack of culture of their authors, the profound change that was taking place in the Latin language, namely the divorce between the spoken and the written word. The latter had for some time been undergoing modifications of morphology and syntax in a Romance direction, whilst the former remained unchanged. The absence of schools explains why knowledge diminished and why Gaul gradually lost touch with the ancient world.

Over against the ruin of ancient learning, we must record the slow emergence of a Christian culture. Its instruments were scholastic institutions of a new type, whose creation can be noted from the sixth century onwards: schools entirely devoted to the religious life, such as the monastic schools for the teaching of Holy Writ, where the monks spent most of their time in study and meditation upon it; or the episcopal schools, where future priests were gathered round their bishops for instruction; or the priestly schools, a kind of extension of the latter, as the network of rural parishes developed. The teaching level in these various establishments was very humble: reading, writing, singing and arithmetic, a summary knowledge of the Bible, a few rudiments of canon law and liturgy—this constituted the ordinary intellectual equipment of the clergy. This was therefore a purely religious education: we do not know of any bishop who arranged instruction in secular literature, except Didier of Vienne, who was scandalised by the surrounding ignorance, and decided to teach grammar and write commentaries on certain poems. But he incurred the violent reproaches of Gregory the Great, and no one else followed his example. Incidentally, we know very little about these schools. But the glimpses we catch here and there show that they were not at first at all widespread. In the seventh century we come across episcopal schools in only about twenty towns in Gaul; information about the priestly schools, however, is scanty, and it is doubtful that they existed throughout the realm. On the other hand, it is probable that, though these schools were intended for future clerics, they opened their doors here and there to children whose future lay in the secular world, and whose parents were keen to have them educated. But here too we have no precise information. Yet it is certain that education remained for a long time most rudimentary, and that these schools only very gradually became centres of sacred study.

This development began gradually to take shape in certain monasteries during the seventh century, and must be set down to the influence of the Irish and Anglo-Saxon monks who implanted their own intellectual tradition in the regions they visited or the monasteries they founded, such as Luxeuil, Péronne, Corbie and Echternach. Nor must we forget the increasing exchanges towards the end of the seventh century between the Mediterranean world and the north. Besides this, we see the monasteries gradually admitting literary studies—particularly grammar—as a means of acquiring a more perfect knowledge of the Bible.

But all this progress was again brought to a halt by the great crisis that shook the Frankish Church and state in the time of Charles Martel. Not only were these ecclesiastical institutions seriously jeopardised by the secularisations, but southern Gaul was ruined as a result of the reconquest of these regions by the Mayor of the Palace. More serious still, the society that emerged from this crisis had undergone a complete upheaval, in which a new nobility, held together by the bonds of vassalage, finally replaced the old Gallo-Frankish aristocracy. It entirely neglected education, and became, with few exceptions, totally illiterate. This is the point at which laymen ceased to be able to write, and were replaced by clerics in the administrative machinery of the state.

In the midst of the surrounding barbarism, we can see only a few glimmers of light. One such centre of light was the Carolingian court, inhabited by the sons of Charles Martel, Carloman and Pepin, surrounded by Frankish, Irish and Anglo-Saxon clerics and monks of some education, pre-eminent among whom was St Boniface. A few signs enable us to measure the ever-growing interest shown by the Palace in culture, signs such as the improvement of the Latin used in the chancery, or the despatch of an important consignment of books sent to the king of the Franks by Pope Paul I.

But it was above all certain monasteries that succeeded in maintaining the traditions of study rediscovered in the seventh century. The plates in the Chatelain Album (*Paléographie des manuscrits latins*) show us the manuscripts that came from their 'writing-shops' (*scriptoria*) and display their efforts to achieve a more correct and regular style of writing. The libraries contained especially works of a religious character—which makes it all the more interesting to note that in some abbeys they gradually began to copy the works of antiquity. At Saint-Wandrille the oldest catalogue of books (about 740–80) contains a treatise on arithmetic; and at Lyon there is a manuscript of the second half of the eighth century which brings together the writings of Porphyrius, Aristotle, Boethius and Apuleius. At Corbie, although the oldest manuscripts are Christian, the monks were copying Livy and Columella about the year 800; and at Saint-Martin de Tours there is a Livy belonging to the period just before the abbacy of Alcuin.

These, then, were the broad lines of cultural and educational development in Frankish Gaul before the time of Charlemagne. Analysis of the facts certainly seems to suggest that the picture of a 'cultural desert' into which the spirit of the Carolingian Renaissance was to breathe new life should after all be rejected. True, the ancient culture was dead, but a new one was coming to birth which picked up some of the threads of the old. There cannot be any question of a uniform 'night' in which Merovingian Gaul perished utterly. It none the less remains true that the period when the Carolingian dynasty came to the throne had been a peculiarly disturbed one, in which the greater part of the clergy, and the whole of the laity, were without any culture. Reform was clearly imperative: it was planned and set in train by Charlemagne.

How did Charlemagne manage to conceive this programme? What was his level of culture, and how did he acquire it? Of his childhood and early years we know nothing; but with a father who had relations with churchmen like St Boniface and St Chrodegang, who restored the singing of the liturgy at Metz, one may suppose that the prince received not only a military education but also some rudiments of humane learning. His biographer Einhard tells us that 'he set about learning to write and was in the habit of placing under the pillows of his bed writing-tablets and sheets of parchment, in order that he might use his leisure moments to practise making the letters; but he took to it too late in life, and the results were disappointing.' Yet it is quite possible, as has been recently suggested, that this refers rather to attempts at calligraphy than to the ordinary use of the alphabet. Einhard also assures us that Charlemagne spoke Latin so well that he would use it as readily as his mother tongue. He understood Greek, too, but did not speak it. His thirst for knowledge was tremendous: he was curious to know and understand everything. His political genius likewise enabled him to see the need for promoting culture if his kingdom was to acquire the splendour and prestige of the ancient world. But in order to raise his people's intellectual level at a time when the laity had ceased to be able to write, he needed to train a clergy able to cope with its tasks. He needed to educate them, to revive the old schools or create new ones, to interest the bishops in this work and get them to find masters to teach in them. This vast undertaking is well summed up in two anecdotes related a century later by the monk of St Gall in his collection, *Histories of Charlemagne*. We see the king inspecting the schools, reproving lazy pupils and congratulating the diligent; we see him watching carefully over the way the clergy in his chapel pronounced and sang their Latin. These stories are very probably based on fact, and are confirmed by certain official texts of the reign testifying that one of the king's greatest concerns was to overcome the negligence or lack of cultural interest in those whom he intended to be the educators of the people.

Let us look at one of the most significant of these instructions. Here, for instance, is the *Admonitio generalis* of 789.[1] We read in Chapter LXXII: 'Let there be in every bishopric and every monastery the teaching of the psalms, musical notation, singing, the Church calendar and grammar, and let there be books that have been carefully corrected.' And in Chapter LXXX: 'To all the clergy: it is important that the clergy should be well versed in singing the Roman Office and that all its rules should be observed both in the morning and in the evening Office.' Between 786 and 800 a capitulary was issued calling attention to the decay of knowledge and the errors that had crept into the Bible text, insisting upon the need to correct the singing in Church and the imperfections in the sacred texts; and the king goes on to say that this work is under way, in continuation of what his father had already begun. Here is another capitulary, of uncertain date, but somewhere between 780 and 800, from which this is an extract:

It has seemed to us pre-eminently useful that the bishoprics and monasteries which the Lord Christ has vouchsafed to

[1] It has recently been shown that Alcuin had a hand in this most important document.

entrust to our governance should not be satisfied with living a regular and pious life, but should also perform the service of teaching. . . . It is no doubt better to act well than to have great learning, but knowledge is required even to do rightly.

The most famous text is still the circular *De litteris colendis* addressed to Abbot Baugulf of Fulda, drawn up by Alcuin (probably between 794 and 800) and couched in the form of a royal directive. In it Charlemagne expresses his desire to see those who devote themselves to the monastic life feel themselves equally bound to study 'so that those who endeavour to please God by living a righteous life do not neglect also to please him by right relations with him'; for study and knowledge are required for the interpretation of Holy Scripture. But the examination of certain writings emanating from monasteries has made the king realise that many monks are incapable of expressing themselves correctly; so he exhorts them to give themselves zealously to the study of letters 'in order to be able to enter more easily and accurately into the divine mysteries of Scripture. Let there then be appointed for this purpose men who have the will and the capacity to learn, and above all the desire to teach others.' The same letter was sent, with a few variations, to the bishops and to all the abbeys of the realm. Finally, in a capitulary of 798, Charlemagne addressed not only the prelates, but also the country clergy, and directed them to open schools for the children.

All these instructions, coming from a man of realistic and practical mind, are a clear expression of the royal will. In each cathedral and each monastery, a school was to be opened; and, as far as possible, in every rural parish too.

As is always the case, the realisation of this programme depended on the good will of the men to whom it was addressed. There were prelates who showed no particular haste to comply with it; the king lectured them severely and shook them out of their inertia, as we see from a letter addressed by him to an unknown archbishop, perhaps Lull of Mainz. Many others understood Charlemagne's wishes and carried them out—such men as Leidrade of Lyon or Theodulf of Orléans, who set up free schools in the towns and villages of his diocese. At all events the work was well under way, and was to be carried on by Charlemagne's successors.

We must now try to form an idea of the teaching that was given in these revived schools. The documents just quoted leave us in no doubt about the general picture. Charlemagne's first thought was for his elementary schools, whose programme comprised reading and writing, arithmetic, singing, and no doubt some summary instruction in the Bible. This education was compulsory for future clerks and monks, but was not refused to laymen, though it is a striking fact that these latter showed no interest in education. Charlemagne was unable, in short, to make what we should call primary education general.

In other spheres, however, he had more success. By the end of the eighth century some cathedral and monastic schools had advanced beyond the first stages and had begun to study the liberal arts. This, too, was in line with the king's wishes. In a general circular addressed to the clergy he wrote as follows: 'We invite you, by your own example and by the example of all we can influence, to learn the liberal arts.' This was the name given to the literature and sciences whose study since Hellenistic times had been considered the preparatory step towards the acquisition of superior culture. There were seven disciplines, divided into two cycles: the *Trivium* (comprising grammar, that is to say, the theoretical study of the Latin language along with the reading of certain great authors; rhetoric or the technique of oratory; dialectic, or the art of reasoning) and the *Quadrivium* (consisting of arithmetic or the theory of numbers; geometry, or the study of ideal figures, plane or solid; astronomy, the science of the motion of the stars; and music, which was quite independent of music as an art, and was mainly concerned with the theoretical knowledge of the laws governing melody). Since the establishment by St Augustine of a programme of advanced Christian education, these two cycles were considered steps towards the full understanding of Holy Scripture. But the practice of the liberal arts also meant the assimilation, in part at least, of the heritage of the ancient world as summed up and classified by generations of philosophers, scholars and encyclopedists. Among these stand out some great names, such as the Italians Boethius (mentioned above) and Cassiodorus (sixth century), and the Spaniard Isidore of Seville (seventh century). This culture had also been introduced into the Irish and Anglo-Saxon schools by the end of the seventh century; it will be enough to mention the outstanding scholar, the Ven-

erable Bede. Now the example of Charlemagne, who (his biographer Einhard tells us) 'passionately cultivated the liberal arts
and heaped honours upon those who taught them', together with
his powerful encouragement, had the effect of not only stirring up
some cathedral and monastic schools to study the seven arts, but
even of stimulating certain laymen to acquire a liberal grounding.
This they did by preference at court, where there was, if not a
proper school, at least 'an intellectual centre', a kind of teaching
establishment for general culture dispensed by the Palace scholars
to those who desired it, in the first place to selected young men
such as Einhard, who came from the abbey school of Fulda, and
others sent to the Palace by the bishops and abbots throughout
the realm, and supported by Charlemagne at his own expense.

The government's main concern was to find masters. Gaul no
longer possessed any, so Charlemagne recruited them from countries where the study of the liberal arts was still held in honour—
Italy, Ireland and England in particular. These men, once installed
in France, became Charlemagne's teachers and, by virtue of the
treatises they wrote, the teachers of the whole country. Let us
see if we can make the acquaintance of the chief men among
them.

One group were natives of Italy, where there were still traces
of the ancient culture, if not in Rome, at least in certain of the
formerly Byzantine towns such as Ravenna, in Lombard cities
such as Pavia, Verona and Benevento, and in some abbeys like
Bobbio, which had been founded by St Columbanus. As early as
774, when he returned from his first Italian expedition, Charlemagne brought back the grammarian, Peter of Pisa, whom he
intended to appoint as his tutor. We still have some of his letters
written in verse, a grammar in question-and-answer form and a
dialogue on St Jerome's commentary on the Book of Daniel. It
was he who revived the teaching of Latin in the Palace. Under his
direction Charlemagne and his entourage set themselves to study
the language and even its poetry, as we can see from the lines
addressed by Peter of Pisa to Paul the Deacon in the name of the
king, who could not compose them himself. Paul the Deacon (so
called because of the rank he held in the Church), whose real name
was Paul Warnefried, had previously been highly regarded at the
court of King Desiderius; he is a good illustration of the way
an intellectual Lombard could join Charlemagne. We see him in

the king's entourage from 782 to 787; and when at this point he returned to the monastery at Monte Cassino where he entered the religious life, he still kept up close links with the king of the Franks. He too was a grammarian, who taught the king Greek, revived Latin poetry two centuries after the death of Venantius Fortunatus, and composed the homily alluded to above. But he stands out above all as a talented historian, the author of a history of the Lombards and a history of the bishops of Metz, in which he made a particular study of the origins of the Carolingian dynasty, perhaps in order to legitimise their accession and to show that the sanctity of its ancestor, Bishop Arnulf of Metz, had conferred on him a genuine charisma. He also exalts Charlemagne's dominance over Rome, 'which was once mistress of the world'. Last, there was Paulinus of Aquileia, so called because he was elevated to this patriarchal see in 787; he came in touch with the Frankish court in 776 as a teacher of grammar. He then turned his talents to theology, and took part in the great religious controversies that marked the end of the century.

Then, alongside the Italians, there were the Irishmen, who stood a little apart from the other learned men of the court, and were sometimes ridiculed by them; but protected by the king, who held them in great admiration. Among them was the great anonymous figure called the Exile from Hibernia (the ancient name for Ireland), a lively poet, author, among other works, of an epic celebrating Charlemagne's triumph over Tassilo; Dungal, monk of Saint-Denis from 784, sometimes identified with the Exile, who taught Charlemagne about darkness and eclipses, and made use of the works of antiquity; and Dicuil, author of a work on geography and astronomy. From all this we are left with the general impression that the Irish at court were chiefly abridgers and specialists in calculation and computation.

Mention should also be made of the Spaniards who had emigrated from their own country, such as Theodulf, an able theologian and capable poet, at home in satire, the ode and the fable, who no doubt was not a teacher, but rather one of Charlemagne's most influential counsellors before his promotion in 798 to the bishopric of Orléans, where his pastoral activity was outstanding. Another ecclesiastic coming from Spain was Agobard, who became bishop of Lyon in 816 and acquired fame as a theoretician of the Christian empire.

But the king's most valuable collaborator, in the stricter sense of the term was his indispensable teacher, the Anglo-Saxon Alcuin. He was a typical representative of his island culture, and was able to put at the disposal of the Carolingian Renaissance all that had been created by his great forerunners, Aldhelm and Bede. Since the end of the seventh century the cathedral and monastic schools of England—Canterbury, Jarrow, York, Malmesbury—had become brilliant centres of study in the liberal arts. In their libraries were to be found side by side pagan authors and the Fathers of the Latin and Frankish Church; and their *scriptoria* produced remarkable illuminated manuscripts, which enjoyed great renown. Born in Northumbria, Alcuin was educated in the school of York, and became its head in 767. He composed some famous lines in praise of his school, and one wonders whether they were perhaps known to the Frankish court. If so, this intense centre of activity may well have seemed to the king an example of what could be done, and a pattern to be imitated. It was in 781 that Alcuin came into contact with Charlemagne, and five years later he joined his court. From 786 onwards, except for two brief stays in England, he remained domiciled in Francia, first at the Palace, then at the abbey of Saint-Martin de Tours, which Charlemagne offered him in 796. This more retired life, however, in no way prevented him from taking an active part in national politics up till his death in 804. The part that he played in Charlemagne's circle was complex. For the moment, we will leave aside his role in the religious policy of the last decade of the century, as well as in the immediate and more distant preparation for the empire. Let us glance at him first as the professor, for that was what he was first and foremost: Charlemagne's tutor, and through the person of the king, the teacher of the whole of Frankish Gaul (*praeceptor Galliae*). An attractive figure, revealing himself to us in his abundant correspondence; a faithful friend, in love with joy and with life, fond of irony; a brilliant mind, though not always original, possessed of a vast and encyclopedic culture, with now and again a touch of pedantry. He was a teacher who received constant admiration as he held forth in the Palace before a select audience which included the king and his family, paladins such as Angilbert, clerics, monks, most of them Anglo-Saxon, whom he would then advance to bishoprics and to the great abbeys, to the great benefit of the educational renaissance—men such as Ricbod, who was to become archbishop of Trier, and Riculf, the future archbishop of Mainz, both sons of great laymen. Alcuin's teaching included the liberal arts, and the little books written by him are so many testimonies to his teaching. Such, for instance was a treatise on dialects in the form of a dialogue between Charlemagne and himself; or a treatise on rhetoric composed between 800 and 804, which is certainly more than a school textbook, since it has quite recently been hailed as a treatise in morals, an exhortation to Charlemagne to follow the 'royal way', setting forth above all the path of moderation. This is the first specimen of a kind of writing that was to have a brilliant future, the 'Mirrors of Princes', written in order to remind rulers of their responsibilities. Nor should we forget a treatise on Latin orthography addressed to Charlemagne, or a Latin grammar in the form of a dialogue between a young Frank and an Anglo-Saxon. Alcuin's scientific teachings are brought to life for us in some of his letters, where he holds converse with certain of his correspondents—and in particular the king—on mathematics (conceived especially as the symbolism of numbers), and on astronomy, as well as in his 'propositions intended to spur on young people', which give solutions to problems in geometry and arithmetic. All these writings draw upon the authors of antiquity, from Cicero to St Augustine, by way of Pliny the Elder and the grammarians of the late empire. Boethius, Isidore of Seville and the Venerable Bede are among his more recent sources. The distinguishing mark of Alcuin's personal teaching was the pre-eminence he gave to grammar, complemented by the study of the great models from the past—not Christian writers but those of antiquity—who in Alcuin's eyes were the sole linguistic authorities. An impulse was thus given to a great movement for the transcription of Latin authors, to which numerous *scriptoria* were to devote their labours.

Yet the liberal arts were not an end in themselves for Alcuin, but simply a means—the way to rise to the knowledge of Holy Scripture, and through this to the wisdom that leads to God. This aim throws light upon another aspect of his activity, his revision of the Bible text, his drawing up of the sacramentary for the Frankish Church, and above all his composition of manuals in which we get a glimpse of his methods of instruction in Holy Scripture beyond the elementary stages and the cycle of the liberal arts, at the dawn of the Carolingian Renaissance. First there was a short introduction to both Testaments (a specimen of which still exists in the *De disputatione puerorum*, by Alcuin or one of his disciples); then some specific books were studied (preferably Genesis and the Psalms, St Matthew and the epistles of St Paul). The explanations given by the teacher consisted sometimes of short grammatical, historical or theological glosses, sometimes of a chain (*catena*) of references, collecting round a particular text the interpretations given by commentators of the past. It was the allegorical sense of the text that was particularly favoured. Once the explanation had been given, these scholars were prepared to venture upon systematic expositions of revealed doctrine on a particular point, or upon the didactic presentation of a particular holy book. The *De fide Trinitatis* and the *Interrogationes in Genesim* are examples of Alcuin's efforts along both these lines.

Finally, it is impossible to separate the name of Alcuin from one of the court's most lively institutions, the Palace Academy. By this name—which incidentally does not occur elsewhere in this period—we must understand the gathering of cultivated men around Charlemagne, the scholars he brought to his court either temporarily or permanently for his own instruction and that of his family and entourage. It was a literary society, essentially a collection of friends who chose names, in accordance with Anglo-Saxon tradition, to match their literary or artistic tastes. Charlemagne was regularly known as David, and we shall see presently the full import of this name; Alcuin called himself Flaccus (that is, Horace), Angilbert Homer, Modoin Naso (Ovid), Einhard—Charlemagne's future biographer—Bezaleel, by reason of his interest in the arts. All these men were bent upon learning and mutual intercourse, and fostered the desire for knowledge. They were always writing and discussing, always in a free spirit, in one of the Palace rooms, at table or in the baths. It is impossible to exaggerate the importance of this Academy, which served as an instrument for spreading the revival of culture arising from a return to the double tradition, Christian and classical, of a synthesis between profane and sacred learning in the service of the Christian religion.

We must now attempt to sum up. Thanks to the strong desire of the sovereign, Charlemagne's reign saw a revival of learning which led to a general renaissance in the course of the ninth century. It will be as well to reflect a few moments on the term

'Carolingian Renaissance', which was launched on the world by Jean-Jacques Ampère[1] in 1840.

There is irrefutable proof that this revival of study almost immediately took on the character of a return to ancient literature, namely the immense interest that was then produced in classical books. These books were obtained in Italy or in England, and they were eagerly recopied in the elegant Carolingian minuscule. From the beginning of the ninth century we find accordingly in the library at Corbie Caesar's *Gallic War*, Sallust's *Jugurtha* and *Catiline*, Statius' and Lucan's poems, and Columella's treatise on agriculture. At Tours there were several books of Livy and Cicero's *De senectute*; at Saint-Denis, the comedies of Terence. The work begun under Charlemagne was continued under his successors; and it may be granted that it ensured the preservation of the great majority of the Latin texts which were to be rediscovered by the first humanists in the fourteenth and fifteenth centuries. Moreover, to judge by some of the declarations of the literary figures in this period whose abilities had been sharpened by the study of the *Trivium* and *Quadrivium*, they almost instinctively compared their period with the glorious days of Athens and Rome, and thought that classical culture was in a fair way towards revival by a return to its authentic sources. In the words of Modoin: 'Golden Rome, once more renewed, is reborn to this world.' As early as 799, Alcuin wrote to Charlemagne:

> If many people became imbued with your ideas, a new
> Athens would be established in Francia—nay, an Athens
> fairer than the Athens of old, for it would be ennobled by
> the teachings of Christ, and ours would surpass all the widsom
> of the ancient Academy. For this had only for its
> instruction the disciples of Plato; yet, moulded by the seven
> liberal arts, it shone with constant spendour. But ours
> would be endowed as well with the sevenfold fullness of the
> Spirit, and would surpass all secular wisdom in dignity . . .

It is impossible not to feel some emotion as we read words of this kind expressing such powerful humanist aspirations and showing such confident and optimistic enthusiasm for the task to be accomplished.

[1] *Histoire littéraire de la France jusqu'au XIIe siècle*, vol. 3, pp. 32-5.

Was there really a Carolingian Renaissance? Our answer must be both yes and no. Let us first remember that in Charlemagne's time this was only thought of as the beginning of a revival. When the revival was at its height after the great emperor's death, did it really take on the character of a renaissance, a return to antiquity, a reaction against the nascent spirit of the Middle Ages, as the humanists of the Renaissance understood it? Surely not. If the chief aspects of the movement can be sketched in a few words, one might say that it was the continuation and expansion of the efforts made a century earlier by the Anglo-Saxons, the fruition of what had hitherto been sporadic attempts to assimilate part of the heritage of antiquity, a generalised attempt to utilise the legacy of the ancient world for the benefit of Christianity. This was dimly foreseen by the most learned of Charlemagne's contemporaries, and was gradually fulfilled in the years ahead. But it remains certain that if a more genuine Renaissance became possible in the twelfth century, as a prelude to further conquests of the human spirit, it was only because of the creation of educational establishments by the wish of Charlemagne, centres of active study, whose work was to make possible the expansion of later days. The men of the thirteenth century were not wrong in attributing the foundation of Paris University to Charlemagne.

For our purposes it was necessary to describe the Carolingian Renaissance at this point, for it cannot be separated from the movement which revived the empire in the west.

Part Two

The Empire of Charlemagne

Preparation, accomplishment
and interpretation

❖ V ❖

The excellence of Frankish royalty

We are now coming closer to the essential aim of this book: to explain the transition from the Frankish kingdom, expanded and brought under control by Charlemagne, to the empire of the year 800. Our sources do not provide any direct answer to this question. The only documents at our disposal, which we shall have to study in due course, are those which attempt to give us information about the conditions in which Charlemagne was made emperor. From the outset of our enquiries, however, we may conjecture that this supremely important event was not fortuitous, but the sequel of a long time of preparation, whether conscious or not. Perhaps we may best come to grips with the question by entering straight away the world of ideas which the numerous documents still enable us to trace. But these ideas are very diverse, complex, often highly involved and difficult to interpret. It is therefore necessary to separate them from one another in order to follow them better, for reality can often only be approached along a series of parallel lines. The first of our explorations will remind us what the empire was, and show us how the Frankish monarchy, confronting the traditional idea of the empire, gained considerable intellectual and religious power and thus made it possible for the king of the Franks to rival the Byzantine emperor.

At the end of the period of antiquity, the Roman empire was envisaged as the framework and centre for a great cultural unity. It corresponded in fact with the domain of Greco-Latin civilisation, considered as the attribute of all humanity worthy of the name. On this view, it was universal. This primary conception was reinforced and elevated by Christianity, which likewise aimed at universality. After having been in opposition, these two universalities eventually fused after the peace concluded between the empire and the Church in the fourth century. Thereafter, 'Roman' and 'Christian' were synonymous terms, used of both institutions, as is shown for instance by some of the oldest prayers in the sacramentaries, where God is called upon as protector of the empire to uphold Roman peace, freedom, safety, and devotion—in other words, to preserve for Christians the qualities they enjoyed as members of the Roman empire.

This first interpretation of the empire as Roman, Christian and universal was modified by events. The Roman empire collapsed in the west in 476 under the barbarian attacks that had been going on for more than a century. It withdrew to the *pars orientis,* where it survived for a further thousand years. In spite of its transformations, it never ceased to proclaim itself Roman, and to hold aloft the ancient ideal in the form of a universality of principles. Confronted by the Germanic kings whose States covered what had formerly been Roman provinces, the emperors residing at Constantinople (the former Byzantium) claimed to exercise over them at least a nominal supremacy. We see the Byzantine chancery elaborating a learned hierarchy among these kings with the emperor at its head, and investing them with the title of sons or friends of the prince. The theory, then, was of an imperial dominion over these lesser kings, an interpretation familiar enough to the west, and reflected in an interesting treatise on public functions composed in Italy or Gaul in the eighth century. It states that the empire holds the first position (*praecellit in toto orbe*), and places the kingdoms on a lower plane (*et sub eo reges aliorum regnorum*).

The most clearly visible aspect of the imperial quality, however, was the sacred character of the monarchy and of its head. In former times the emperor had been worshipped as a god upon earth; since the end of paganism, the emperor had been considered a sort of intermediary between God and men, the Vicar of Christ triumphant, 'the beginning and the end of the empire and its destiny'. He was held to be like the apostles (*isapostolos*); he was even called the thirteenth apostle (*triskaidekatos apostolos*), the new Paul, as he was proclaimed by the Council of Chalcedon in

451. But it went even further than this. Within the Christian scheme, the imperial ideology was linked up with the Old Testament. Moses and David were thought of as prefiguring the emperor, and the title *Novus David* took its place among the imperial predicates, along with that of the New Constantine, thus perpetuating the presence of the Christian empire's founder. This incomparable prestige of the sovereign, rooted likewise in his prerogative as the living law (*nomos empsychos*), found its expression in the extravagant ceremonial of the great palace at Constantinople, which had taken the place of the old imperial worship. One of its most significant features was the rite of proscynesis, in which the emperor was 'adored' by his subjects, and even—on certain occasions at least—by the dignitaries of the Church, including the pope, as we can see in the visit paid by Pope John I to the Emperor Justin I in the year 525. In the same way as the empire was deemed to be part of the divine scheme of things, and destined to last till the end of the world, so the emperor was also held to be sacred, that is, consecrated to God and so protected by the Deity, as the Greek epithet *theophylaktos* proclaims; and the same quality was attributed to everything closely or remotely concerning the prince. It is easy to see from this that the Christian emperor, like his pagan predecessors, very soon became the religious head of the empire. Since Constantine's day he had ruled the Church through the general councils; he had been both lawgiver and judge, and he had intervened authoritatively in controversies over doctrine. This system of Church government by the emperor is generally known by the clumsy and inadequate name of caesaro-papism: it would perhaps be better to call it imperial theocracy, a condition in which the state is governed by the emperor both on the spiritual and on the temporal side, and represents as it were the antechamber of the Kingdom of God.

If these were the most characteristic features of the imperial concept soon after the great invasions, it must nevertheless be noted that the west was not slow to abandon it. True, the empire continued for a long time to be considered as the political expression of Christian universality, the *Imperium christianum*, the *Sancta Respublica* for which public prayer was offered, especially before the Cross on Good Friday. All the same, men's minds were turning towards views very different from those which held sway in Constantinople. This distinction was not due simply to the difference in the way the two parts of the ancient Roman empire had evolved historically; it was certainly an integral element in the western mental outlook. The Latin conception of the empire was not exactly that of the Greeks and orientals; and one has only to turn to imperial historiography to see how the republican tradition had kept its vitality. Moreover, the Latin Church seems to have been permeated quite early with the principle of autonomy for the spiritual sphere, far more than in the east. This was the teaching of some of its most famous writers. St Ambrose, for instance, does not place the emperor above the Church, but rather within it. St Augustine, on the other hand, in his *City of God,* warns of the danger of too close a connection between Church and empire, and shows the possibility for each of these institutions to develop along its own lines. Treating human history as the history of Christ's mystical body, and humanity as the organism whose function is to bring forth not earthly empires but the society of saints constituting 'the City of God', the great doctor sets forth a number of concepts destined to become the fundamental ideas of the Christian state: order, as mentioned above, corresponding to natural and supernatural order, the latter tending to absorb the former; peace, in the sense of harmony between all creatures based upon charity, resulting from the order established by God; justice, that is to say respect for, and realisation of, this order by the power responsible for earthly society. These ideas continued to be repeated, discussed and simplified till they pervaded the political outlook of the early Middle Ages.

After St Augustine, Leo the Great joined the idea of the autonomy of the spiritual realm to the theory, just then taking shape, of the primacy of the papacy and of Rome in the vision of a Church transcending the empire. It was he who laid the foundations of the distinction between two powers formulated at the end of the fifth century by Pope Gelasius I, in a famous text, according to which there were two comparable great powers face to face in this world, 'the sacred authority of the pontiffs, and the royal (or imperial) power'. They had become distinct after the time of Christ, who had united them in his own person, and they each had their own particular attributes; yet the papal authority was the weightier, since the spiritual power was responsible for the salvation of princes.

The fortunes of this Gelasian doctrine were very varied. The impossibility of its being imposed upon the empire is proved beyond all doubt by the history of the papacy itself under the domination of Justinian and his successors (from the middle of the sixth to the beginning of the eighth century). But the case was different with the new states in the west. From the moment when they had adopted Catholicism, the popes (in particular Gregory the Great), and the regional churches especially, strove to christianise the monarchies by turning their attention to the services they owed the Church. There thus developed what has been called the ministerial conception of royalty, derived ultimately from a simplification of the Augustinian ideas set out above, which were brought home to the Christian sovereigns by Fathers such as Gregory I and Isidore of Seville. The kingdom where the first results of this 'political Augustinianism' became evident was the Hispano-Gothic monarchy before its collapse in 711, where the king became the first servant of the Church, and the political order was absorbed in the spiritual order. In Frankish Gaul the atmosphere was different: it was the king who had taken the Church in hand, and the Church had striven—without great success, as we have seen—to map out an ethical and religious programme for the Merovingians. Nevertheless, there did exist a tradition of alliance between the crown and the Church. It had accompanied the rise of the Carolingians from the time of St Arnulf of Metz and Pepin of Landen, it burst into full vigour in 751, and it took firm hold during the reigns of Pepin the Short and Charlemagne, under whom the Frankish monarchy was greatly enriched.

When we come to appreciate the triumph of the Frankish crown during the second half of the eighth century, we shall have a better understanding of Charlemagne's ecclesiastical policy, the bare facts of which we analysed above. We shall also get a glimpse of how Charlemagne very soon ceased to be one king among others and rose to a level not far below the emperor's. It is therefore important for us to trace the themes that went to the making of this rise in status, and search out the men responsible for promoting it.

From Merovingian times, as we have seen, the great figures of the Old Testament had been set before the kings as models to be imitated. The historiography of the early Carolingians recalls this in linking the memory of those distant figures with Charles Martel, who was especially compared with Joshua. Let us remember too the *Missa pro principe*—would this prince have been the famous Mayor or one of his sons?—in the Bobbio missal, full of the idea of the holy war against the pagans, and appealing to the examples of Abraham, Moses, Joshua and David. If this theme belongs substantially to the seventh century, it was Charles Martel's victories over the pagans, and above all over the Arabs, that gave these ancient symbols a contemporary reality. Then came the year 751: a son of the new Joshua was made king with the pope's consent. Three years later, an alliance was concluded between Pepin and Stephen II, with very important consequences for the papacy. It would have been strange, indeed, if the services rendered by the king to his 'spiritual compeer', together with the hope nourished by the latter's successors of reaping still further benefits, had not caused the Lateran court to hymn the new Carolingian dynasty, and in so doing strengthen its prestige. The collection of correspondence between Rome and the Frankish Court, known as the *Codex Carolinus* because it was compiled at Charlemagne's command, is full of indications to this effect.

On several occasions Pepin is called the New Moses and the New David. For instance, in a letter written by Pope Paul I between 762 and 767, the comparison of the Frankish king with the lawgiver of Israel is used to emphasise that 'as Moses exterminated the abominations of the heathen and the worship of demons, so you, the Most Christian King, have rejected the schism of heretics and those who impiously falsify doctrine'. The impious dogma then in question was that of iconoclasm, which Pepin had occasion to reject under circumstances to be related in the following chapter. The papacy could hardly fail to compare the king who freed Rome from the Lombards with the leader who put an end to the foreign oppression under which his people had been suffering. Even more striking was the comparison of Pepin with David. It seemed to be completely justified, for was he not the holy king to whom the psalmist's lines surely applied: 'I have found my servant in David, and have anointed him with holy oil'? And again: 'As David in former days danced before the Lord in front of the ark of the covenant rescued from his enemies, so the helper and redeemer of the Holy Church has every right to overflow with joy, for he knows that an eternal reward is laid up for him in Heaven.' But Paul I went even further, and applied to Pepin the promise made in former times to David: 'God has given him the kingdom so that he and his seed may possess it in glory for ever.' Nothing could better express the character of the Frankish nation as the people of the New Covenant, 'a holy nation, a royal priesthood, a chosen people', as the pope called it, using the same terms as Leo the Great to designate the Romans. This was tantamount to equating the Franks with the Romans, without putting it in so many words, and commissioning them to fight the barbarians, that is to say the pagans, as the term had come to be understood. This was a mission that Charlemagne did his utmost to fulfil throughout his reign. But, strangely enough, Pope Hadrian avoided giving him the name of David: did he perhaps consider it inopportune to repeat a term which inevitably suggested the picture of the priest-king? Yet Charlemagne assumed the magic name in his turn, in a context of thought which we shall be examining later.

The glorification of Frankish royalty through allusions to the Old Testament was carried still further through the titles and honorific epithets applied by the popes to Pepin and his son. These titles proclaimed their excellence (*rex praecelsus* or *excellentissimus*), their glory (*gloriosus rex*), their sublimity, or simply their greatness. *Magnus* was thus attributed to Pepin for the first time by Pope Constantine I, then so frequently to Charles by Hadrian I that in the end the epithet became a permanent part of his name (*Carolus Magnus*, or Charles the Great). Now *magnus* was an imperial epithet, used in particular in Byzantine acclamations; so this is the first indication of the transfer of epithets hitherto reserved for the emperor to the person of the Frankish king. The same is true of the title of conqueror (*victor* or *invictissimus*), which appears in the addresses of Stephen II and Hadrian I. More important still, however, were the epithets of a religious nature lavished by the bishops of Rome on their protectors: Most Christian, Protected, Instituted, Inspired by God. Such formulas were also borrowed from the imperial language; and the same is true of the title *Orthodoxus*, which was only once applied to Pepin, in 767, but was taken up again after 790 by Charlemagne and used with very precise intent. We may therefore sum this matter up by saying that although these appellations did not in general endow the

king of the Franks with specifically imperial titles, they did underline the exceptional character of the prince who figured, in the
words of Paul I, as the *fundamentum et caput omnium Christianorum*.
The same formula was extended to cover the kingdom, which
thus found itself called upon to assume the perpetual leadership
of Christendom.

In the same way, we must ask how the popes who decked royalty in such brilliant colours envisaged the problem of relations
between the spiritual and the temporal spheres in the kingdom of
the Franks. As early as 747 Zacharias was instructing Pepin on
the separation of the two powers, and the need for co-operation
between them. Stephen II had held similar principles, but his
brother and successor, Paul I, spoke quite a different language.
His urgent need for the king's intervention against his Lombard
enemies seems to have made him lose all sense of proportion. He
spoke of Pepin as one predestined, of the Church as placed under
royal control; he equated the king's victory with that of God; and
all these passionate utterances finally culminated in the idea of
such an intimate union between the two powers that they came to
constitute a single whole in the hands of the king. 'Your welfare
is, next to God, our defence,' writes Paul I, for instance; and
again: 'Your welfare is the exaltation of your mother, the Holy
Church; your prosperity, as all men know, is our joy.' Pepin is
proclaimed 'Redeemer of the Holy Church'; as an intermediary
between God and his Vicar, he became thereby superior to the
pope. His mission became in the final analysis a mission of salvation, to establish peace over the Church and over the whole of
the Christian world.

Paul I's outlook was shared by his successor, Stephen III; but
Hadrian I's was a complete reversal, perhaps because of the continually growing power of the Frankish monarchy under Charlemagne. He certainly saw the royal authority as divine in origin
(*a Deo institute magne rex*),[1] but drew from this notion the double
conclusion that the king was dependent upon God (through his
will expressed by the priesthood), and that he was responsible for
the tasks which fell upon him as defender of the Church. In a
general way, the king's power was inferior in quality to that of the

[1] He also used the expressions *potestas divinitus praeordinata* (a power predestined according to the divine plan), and a royalty created by God according
to his heart (*secundum cor suum*).

pope and the bishop. Although distinct from one another, how-ever, the two powers were pursuing parallel aims, the clergy see-ing to the peace of men's souls, the king keeping social peace among them. And so, as we read the letters of the *Codex Carolinus,* we can form some idea of what their influence must have been at the Carolingian court. There can be no doubt that they contributed to the political education of princes; and their themes crop up again in the relationships that came into being between the mon-archy, the papacy and the Church.

But the first point to realise is that the tide of titles and com-parisons that flowed from Rome to the Carolingian kings from the year 754 onwards was a powerful influence in making the Franks aware of their destiny and the exalted status of their sovereign. This awareness had begun earlier. More than a century before, the anonymous writer Pseudo-Fredegarius had advanced the thesis that the Franks were of Trojan origin—a learned legend which attested a strong desire to equate the Franks with the Romans and to give them a place in the development of universal history. In Pepin's day, this comparison had not been forgotten, but it was treated differently. If we re-read the long prologue to the Salic Law composed in the royal chancery about the year 763–4, we shall see that it is an enthusiastic eulogy of

the illustrious nation of the Franks, founded by God the Creator, valiant in arms, firm in its alliances, profound in council, noble in body, intact and pure, of perfect physique, bold, strong and indomitable and recently converted to the Catholic faith. It is a nation which, when still practising paganism, nevertheless, under divine inspiration, sought the keys of knowledge, and according to its lights strove for justice and lived a godly life.

It would be impossible to suggest more strongly that the Franks were predestined to greatness, seeing that even before they be-came Christians they were doing their best to follow the ideals set out in the *City of God.* And the text ends with the following prayer:

All honour to Christ who loves the Franks! May He preserve their kingdom, fill their leaders with the light of His grace, and give them the stronghold of faith. May the joys of peace and happy days be granted them by the King of Kings, the Lord Jesus Christ, in all godly piety. For this is a strong and valorous people. They fought and threw off from their shoulders the heavy yoke of the Romans, and after the knowledge given them by baptism, they clothed in gold and precious stones the bodies of the holy martyrs whom the Romans had put to death by fire, sword, and wild beasts.

Nothing could be more significant than these declarations by which the Franks dissociated themselves from pagan Rome and aligned themselves with the Rome of the apostles and their successors, the Rome that was served by Pepin and Charlemagne.

Next to the nation's destiny came the excellence of her king. The source that gives us knowledge of it may perhaps be considered the masterpiece of the Franco-Gallic liturgy. This is the famous *Laudes regiae,* the Royal *Laudes* which date, in the two oldest formularies that have come down to us, from the end of the eighth century.[1] But they must have been composed considerably earlier than this, and were perhaps in existence by the end of Pepin's reign, and certainly in 774, since in that year Pope Hadrian had them sung for Charlemagne during his stay in Rome. Their origin is complex. They are connected with the acclamations that had formed part of the emperor-worship of pagan Rome and continued in Christianised form in the imperial Byzantine liturgy; and partly too with the litanies of the saints introduced on the continent by the Irish and Anglo-Saxon monks. They began with the tricolon: 'Christus vincit, Christus regnat, Christus imperat', 'Christ the Victor, Christ the Ruler, Christ the Commander', and contained four acclamations addressed respectively to the pope, to the king, to the royal house, and to the Frankish counts and army: Long live the pope, and the prince's family, long life and victory to the king, his officials and his men of war. Each person and each group is placed under the protection of the heavenly powers. Only in the case of the pope and the king is a preliminary reference made to the Saviour in person. Then comes the invocation of the saints: prayers for the pope, three apostles (Peter, Paul, Andrew) and two Roman bishops (Sixtus, Clement); for the king, the Virgin, the three archangels, John the

1 See p. 231 below

Baptist and Stephen—these last two associated with the blessed spirits in heaven because the eastern liturgy accorded them an angelic character; for the counts and the army, two Frankish confessors (Hilary and Martin) and five martyrs who were very popular in the realm—Maurice, Denis, Crispin, Crispinian and Gereon. It may be noted in passing that the three groups of angels, apostles and martyrs were considered in the Hispano-Gothic liturgy to be companions of the Three Persons of the Trinity. But this trinitarian scheme is here replaced by the double appeal to the Saviour, the association of two confessors with the martyrs, and especially by the insertion, between the invocations on behalf of the king, the army and the counts, of prayers for the royal family (*nobilissima regalis proles*). This leads on to a new group of saints, also fairly composite in character: the Virgin, a pope (Silvester), three martyrs (Lawrence, Pancratius and Nazaire), and three women saints (Anastasia, Genevieve and Colomba). In the more recent of the two formularies in question (about 795–800) these invocations are followed by a series of acclamations addressed to Christ Triumphant, supreme protector of the kingdom and the Frankish people ('our glory, our strength, our invincible weapon and our impregnable wall of defence'). After this, the text rises in conclusion to a triple doxology, new appeals to Christ and hopes for happiness, prosperous days and long years of life addressed to all who have handed themselves over to God's protection, and particularly to the protection of the king. In short, we have not only supplications, but wishes and shouts of joy raised to the sovereign of the new chosen people. The place he occupies in the world is one of considerable importance. Although coming second in the acclamations, he is associated with saints of much greater standing than those who surround the pope. Above all, he figures as the living image of Christ, Christ triumphant and Lord of the World. These *Laudes* were sung before the king on the great religious festivals, and they testify most vividly to the hopes placed by the Frankish Church in the Carolingian dynasty, which was both holy, Davidic and 'Christocentric'.

Thus the popes and the Frankish Church had invested the Carolingian line with exceptional prestige; and we must now indicate the pattern adopted by Charlemagne for the performance of this high office. He viewed it as a divine institution, as we can see from the title 'king by the grace (or mercy) of God', which he adopted in the first of his diplomas. The Church, whose 'devoted defender and helper in all circumstances' he intends to be, occupies first place in his concern; and the picture we have sketched of his activities in this field shows the number of problems he was bound, as a devout believer, to confront. Moreover, the king envisaged peace as it had been defined by St Augustine. He proclaimed in the *Admonitio generalis* of 789: 'Let peace, concord and a single mind prevail among all Christian people, between the bishops and the abbots, the counts and the judges, all persons great and small, for without peace nothing is well pleasing to God, not even an offering laid upon the altar.' In the same document we hear him appealing to the law of charity, denouncing envy, cupidity, vengeance and brigandage, and calling upon the counts to fight these scourges. Thus the defence of the Church and order in the state tended to merge into a single spiritual preoccupation. Nothing could better express this truth than a form of words originally used in a diploma for Saint-Denis issued in 755, and repeated by Charlemagne in two grants issued in 799. It includes in a single category the 'faithful followers of God and the king'. This idea, treating believers as the vassals of God, likewise invests fealty to the king with a religious character, and unites in one single obligation both the service of the Most High and the service of the sovereign; it illustrates in striking and original fashion the process of mutual interpenetration of the political and the religious spheres in Frankish Gaul during early Carolingian times. Nevertheless, it was especially the religious character of Charlemagne's sovereignty that struck his contemporaries: in the eyes of Paulinus of Aquileia, Charlemagne is 'king and priest and most wise ruler of Christians'. Alcuin extols him as the *pontifex in praedicatione,* thus recognising in him a mission to teach the bishops. We should be careful however not to overemphasise this point. Charlemagne never took it upon himself expressly to direct the Church; never did this 'most devoted son of the Church', as he liked to style himself, presume to call himself its ruler. One has only to examine his methods of intervention in the most important problems affecting the life of the Church, its theological controversies. It is clear that he placed the issues before a commission of competent theologians and took note of the general opinion emerging from their debates. He then made this opinion his own by promulgating it and seeing

7 *Charlemagne's throne*
(From P. E. Schramm, *Herrschaftszeichen und Staatssymbolik*, I, no. 44.) An
imitation of Solomon's throne, as described in I Kings 10, 18–19. It was
put under the protection of the saints, and relics were placed beneath the
seat and in the capitals of the two near-by columns. This was the scene for
the enthronement of the kings of the Romans after 936.

8 *The Emperor Constantine*

A mosaic in the south vestibule of the Church of Hagia Sophia, Constantinople, from the end of the tenth or beginning of the eleventh century (from A. Grabar, *Byzantine Painting*).

The Emperor, wearing the diadem surmounted by the cross, the symbol of victory, offers the city he has founded to the Virgin.

9   *A pope of the early Middle Ages: Pascal I*
A mosaic in Santa Prassede, Rome, ninth century (from A. Grabar and
C. Nordenfalk, *Early Medieval Painting*, New York, 1957).
    Pope Pascal I reigned from 817 to 824. He is represented here
bareheaded, robed in a chasuble with a *pallium* thrown over it, and carrying
a model of the church. Beside him are St Prassede and an apostle.

10 *A mosaic in the Lateran Triclinium:* general view and detail
(From P. E. Schramm, *Die deutschen Kaiser und Könige.*) Restored in the seventeenth century by Cardinal Barberini, this famous mosaic was taken from its original place by Pope Clement XII (1730–40), and the only remains of it are some fragments in the Vatican Museum. The present mosaic, on one side of the Scala Sancta, was carried out during the pontificate of Benedict XIV (1740–58) from old drawings.

that it was duly applied. If one looks at the matter in detail, one gets the impression that the king was careful not to place himself at the head of the Church; and for this reason it seems that we should avoid the expression 'sacerdotal kingship' as a description of Charlemagne's power. The king stood beside the Church, rather than at its head; none the less, he claimed *potestas* and *dispensatio* 'over the Churches of God, in order that they may be well governed by worthy pastors'. In theory, at any rate, there was no attempt by Charlemagne to assume spiritual power. Alcuin kept the latter distinct from the temporal power, though without establishing any intermediate points between them; on the contrary, he assigned them a common programme 'in order that the flock may be led by Christ, who is the chief shepherd'.

The fact remains, however, that although Charlemagne wished only to be the Church's protector, he was in effect an authoritarian protector. His authority was to increase in emphasis during the last ten years of the century, to such an extent that we may well ask at the end of this chapter if his proclamation as emperor did not *also* take place in order to give a juridical and legal basis for the quasi-imperial power which the king of the Franks was already in fact exercising over the western Church.

VI

Charlemagne and Constantinople

Charlemagne's quasi-imperial power, we have just called it in the last chapter. Our second line of approach will take us nearer to this idea, which begins to stand out by the end of the eighth century from the manifold data that go to make up the problematic relationship between the king of the Franks and the emperor at Constantinople. Let us then proceed to look at these relationships and the consequences flowing from them.

The relations between the Frankish kingdom and the Roman empire of the east had passed through various phases since Pepin's reign. To start with, these were chiefly concerned with the religious policy of the Isaurian emperors. Iconoclasm—that is to say, the condemnation of sacred images, soon extending to the proscription of the cult of the Virgin and the saints—had had serious consequences in the west, beginning with Italy. The edict issued against icons by the Emperor Leo III in 730 led to his excommunication by Pope Gregory III and the revolt of the peoples of Italy. Imperial power for a time barely survived in the peninsula, and only thanks to the loyalty of the pope, who needed his protector's help against the Lombards. A quarter of a century later, Constantine V, the son and successor of Leo, renewed and strengthened the measures taken by his father against the image-worshippers, with the support of a council which sat in the imperial palace at Hieria in 754. This is a date to note with particular

86

attention,[1] for it was in that same year that Stephen II, under direct threat in Rome from the Lombards who had taken Ravenna in 750, came to Francia to solicit the King of the Franks' support. As he had had an interview with the imperial envoys before crossing the Alps, it may be assumed that he took this step with the consent of the government in Constantinople. It is quite certain, however, that in Francia he acted entirely on his own initiative; for it was solely to him that Pepin and his sons owed the Roman patriciate, which, as we have seen, was very different in character and content from the court titles the Byzantine sovereigns customarily conferred on their senior officials. The most important result of this journey was the close alliance which from then on bound the Frankish royal house to the papacy. It led to Pepin's intervention in Italy, with two victories over the Lombards, the seizure from them of the Exarchate of Ravenna, and its cession to the pope, who was already in fact the master of Rome. As protector of this whole area, the king of the Franks must have seemed to Constantinople to be acting as the agent of the pope. It is a striking fact, however, that the Byzantine government, although this operation had meant the loss of its leading position in Italy, did not react strongly, but sought to win over Pepin by diplomacy. It seems that Constantine V, immersed in his heterodox and radical religious policy, was hoping to gain Charlemagne's support and persuade him in his turn to condemn the cult of sacred images. Between 756 and 769 there were no less than three embassies from the emperor to the Frankish court. In 767, a Frankish council sitting at Gentilly under the presidency of Pepin had to concern itself with the question of iconoclasm. Unfortunately we do not know what it decided, but we do know that its decisions were approved by Rome, which had warm praise for the orthodoxy of the Frankish king. All the same it may be conjectured, in view of the Frankish Church's ancient tradition that 'one can be a good Christian without possessing images or venerating them', that the conciliar decrees adopted a moderate attitude, steering between the extremes of the two rival parties— an attitude that was to stand out clearly at the close of the century.

In Italy, however, the situation of the empire grew steadily worse. Rome was slowly emancipating itself from the authority

[1] The Council met on 10 February 754, and held its final session at Constantinople on 8 August.

of the emperor. Gregory III (731–41) was the last pope to announce his election to the emperor and ask him to ratify it. Paul I informed the king of the Franks of his accession without, however, asking for its confirmation. It fell to his successor, Constantine II, to put this request in precise terms, treating it as a *debitum honoris* paid to a prince with whom there was a close alliance. Even more significant were the events that marked Hadrian I's pontificate. The year 772 brought to an end the practice of dating the papal chancery's acts by the years of the emperor's reign. Unfortunately there are no surviving documents from the subsequent nine years, and when the series begins again in 781, the form of dating has completely changed. The one now used—'under the rule of Our Lord God and Saviour Jesus Christ, God the Father Almighty and the Holy Spirit throughout all ages'—shows that at some indeterminate date the pope made use of liturgical formulae and replaced the name of the emperor by that of Christ himself. It should likewise be noted that Hadrian also began to strike coins in his own name, a further sign that he was detaching himself from the empire by ignoring it officially.

Meanwhile the Lombard kingdom had been conquered by Charlemagne. A political power infinitely more formidable than the Lombards now threatened the last Byzantine territories in the Italian peninsula—Istria and Venetia, Naples and its coastline, Calabria and Otranto. Would the empire come to terms with it? This time too it played a waiting game. The first adversaries encountered by the Franks were the local powers, such as the Byzantine governor of Sicily, whose dependencies included the imperial possessions in the south-west of the peninsula, and especially Arichis, duke of Benevento, who was master of an important territory in the centre of southern Italy, a Lombard duchy which had remained independent of the kingdom, and was not subject to the authority of the Franks. Duke Arichis, who was the son-in-law of Desiderius, the last of the Lombard kings, assumed the title of prince, and did his best to dominate the whole of southern Italy. With or without help from the duke of Sicily, he proceeded to harass the Papal States. Hadrian's correspondence with Charlemagne constantly denounces his intrigues and his inroads on the Church's patrimony in the Campagna. As far as the imperial court was concerned, it had welcomed Desiderius's son, Adalgis, and made him a patrician, which suggests that it thought of using him as an instrument against the Franks. Perhaps there was some idea of organising an expedition to bring the prince back to Italy; but the momentary lack of a fleet forced the government to postpone this project for the time being. Besides, it was not long before new circumstances served to give a different inclination to the Byzantine attitude towards Charlemagne.

These were circumstances connected with the transformation of the empire's religious policy. Constantine V had died in 775, and his successor Leo IV adopted a more moderate attitude in the iconoclastic dispute. When he too died in 780, leaving as his successor a ten-year-old child, Constantine VI, the regency was held by his widow Irene, a convinced image-worshipper, who slowly prepared a reversal of policy. She thought it as well, with this end in view, to cover her western flank, and as early as 781 sent an embassy to Charlemagne asking the hand of his daughter Rotrud for the young Constantine. The Frankish king was delighted to seize this chance of linking his house with the empire, which enjoyed great prestige in his eyes. No doubt he also saw this step as a prelude to the recognition by the court of Constantinople of a certain equality between the king of the Franks and the *basileus* (the emperor's official title). Alliance with Constantinople, moreover, meant that Charlemagne could have a free hand in dealing with Benevento. These various reasons explain why the king gave his consent to the marriage: vows were exchanged and Rotrud was entrusted to the care of Byzantine officials in order to be instructed 'in the Greek language and letters and the customs of the Roman empire'.

This Franco-Byzantine alliance lasted six years. In 787 a dangerous turn of events forced Charlemagne to make radical changes in his policy. He was in Italy, where, after an expedition penetrating as far as Capua, he had just compelled Duke Arichis of Benevento to submit, when he was taken unawares by a sudden change in the policy of the imperial Regent. Angered by the Frankish intervention in southern Italy, and anxious to recover her influence in the peninsula, Irene made an alliance with Arichis by which she ceded Naples and conferred the patriciate upon him. It was further agreed that Adalgis should land in Italy and raise his father's former kingdom in revolt; and by the summer these plans were already under way. Then Arichis died, and his successor designate, Grimoald, found himself in effect a hostage in the hands of the Frankish king, who at once sent *missi* to ensure that the inhabitants would be faithful to him. But they were unable to fulfil their mission, for meanwhile Adalgis had landed in Calabria and stirred up agitation as far afield as the Pentapolis; and early in 788 the widow of Arichis received Greek ambassadors, who renewed the former imperial treaty. But there was worse to come. For some years Irene had been making preparations to convene a council to condemn iconoclasm. She had sounded Pope Hadrian, who had promised to send legates to it. In 787 the seventh Ecumenical Council met at Nicaea and restored the worship of images, without Charlemagne and the Frankish bishops having been invited to take part in the session. Thus not only was the Empress Regent making every effort to regain possession of Italy, she was also reviving her predecessors' prerogative of control over the Church. Her course of action totally disregarded the western Church, and appears in the last analysis to have been an unambiguous return to the universalist policies of the eastern Roman emperors.

This dual Byzantine offensive had considerable repercussions. Its immediate consequence was that the betrothal between Rotrud and Constantine VI was broken off, though it is not possible to be certain whether it was Charlemagne or Irene that took the initiative in making the breach. A further consequence was a vigorous military reaction in Italy, starting in the south. Grimoald, the new duke of Benevento, was not permitted to return to his capital until he had promised to have the name of the Frankish king inscribed on his diplomas and stamped on his ducal coinage. A Byzantine fleet landed troops in the southern part of the peninsula, but they were completely crushed in a battle that took place in November 788, probably on the borders of Calabria and the duchy of Benevento. Yet Charlemagne went still further: he put into action a plan that was clearly in embryo from the very beginning of his Lombard conquests, and occupied Istria, where a new duke was installed in place of Byzantine officials. From this centre, Frankish influence began to reach out to some of the Slav peoples such as the Croats, who had up till then been in Constantinople's sphere of influence. The tension between the two States persisted till 797. In that year a revolution fomented by Irene, who passionately wanted power for herself, led to the deposition of the young Emperor Constantine VI, who was blinded.

Irene mounted the throne and assumed the title of *basileus*.[1] She immediately sought to re-establish peaceful relations with Charlemagne, and sent an embassy to him. The following year, negotiations produced a settlement, under which Benevento and Istria remained with the Franks and Croatia was left with Constantinople. This was something of a military triumph for Charlemagne; and the same may be said of his political and intellectual victory. For along with his action in Italy he had also carried out a sharp doctrinal offensive against Byzantium, in the form of a legal action directed against the Council of Nicaea, which we must now proceed to study.

There can be no doubt that this action originated in Charlemagne's deep resentment at being ignored by the pope together with the whole western Church, both in the preparatory discussions and in the Council itself. He seems to have been informed of the event only through a Latin translation of the conciliar decrees sent to him by Hadrian. Now this was a very inadequate translation, full of mistakes, the work of a clerk who knew neither Greek nor Latin. A single example will be enough to convince us of this. In abrogating the decrees of the iconoclastic council held in 754 and restoring the cult of sacred images, the Nicene Fathers had established a clear distinction between adoration proper, which was reserved for God alone, and the veneration which might be paid to icons. Now the Latin translation explicitly spoke of the 'adoration' of images. The Frankish court was outraged, and Charlemagne, already infuriated by his exclusion from the debate, decided to have the Council of Nicaea's decrees refuted by his theologians. This was the purpose of the famous capitulary on icons (or 'Caroline Books', a translation of *Libri Carolini*), composed in 791–2, and intended to inform the whole Church, and first and foremost the pope, about the Frankish position in this matter. Moreover, it was intended in the king's mind to constitute a sovereign juridical act, in precisely the same way that the Byzantine government had given the canons of Nicaea the force of law. The capitulary was perhaps drawn up by Theodulf;[2] the style is vehement and incisive, and the thought is based on

[1] She figured as *basileus*, and not as *basilissa*, in all official docum ents.

[2] L. Wallach contests this hypothesis and thinks that the final compilation of the *Libri* was Alcuin's work ('The unknown author of the *Libri Carolini*', *Didascaliae*, New York, 1961).

scriptural, patristic and canonical foundations, from which there emerges a powerful line of argument reflecting a strong personality. There can be no doubt that this was the mind of Charlemagne himself, though it is impossible to be certain that the shorthand notes in the margin of the oldest manuscript of the *Libri* give us the king's reactions when it was read out to him in person. It is important for us to pick out from this document the ideas that are particularly relevant to our present purposes.

1 First, the titles assumed by Charles: 'Most illustrious and excellent (or greatly honoured), by the grace of God, king of the Franks, with the help of God, ruling over the Gauls, Germania, Italy and the adjacent provinces.' It will be observed that the geographical expressions included in the royal titles correspond to the provinces of the former Roman empire of the west. It is thus possible that Charlemagne considered himself to be occupying the position of the old emperors in this part of the Roman world. But that is not to say that he thought himself their successor, or that he had considered the consequences of such a claim; at the very most, it may be said that Charlemagne and his entourage considered the division of the empire into two parts as part of a plan being worked out by divine Providence.

2 We can now see clearly enough the view of the empire current at the Frankish court. The Caroline Books set out the theory of the four universal monarchies (the empires of the Babylonians, the Medes and Persians, the Greeks and Macedonians, and the Romans), and draw a parallel between Babylon and Rome, though they stress only the more sombre features, the impiety, the idolatry and the cruelty. It is as though the capitulary were rediscovering the terms of Christian polemics directed against the pagan Roman empire in the period before Constantine. That empire is well and truly dead: since the time of the Incarnation, there has been only one empire upon earth, the Empire of Christ, with its emblem the cross, 'which our cohorts follow into battle'. Such premisses, however, do not imply the denial or condemnation of the Byzantine empire. The point of view of the *Libri Carolini* is one of much more subtle distinctions. The Byzantine empire exists as a solid fact: yet it cannot lay claim to universality. The text often calls it 'the empire of the Greeks', and its sovereign is designated sometimes as king, sometimes as emperor, which perhaps shows that the ideas of *imperium* and *regnum* had lost some of their

original vigour since the period of antiquity, unless we suppose that the Frankish chancery had discovered the precise meaning of the title *basileus* (literally king), borne by the eastern emperors. The most serious charge made against them by the *Libri* is their failure to recognise that Christ was the sole emperor of the world, the *verus imperator,* since they continued to let themselves be worshipped as in pagan times. Everything connected with the imperial cult comes in for violent diatribes, because in the author's eyes it smacks of pure idolatry and thus appears to continue habits for ever condemned by the triumph of Christianity. But this is as far as the Caroline Books go. What they condemn is not the empire in principle, but its abuses, and particularly the arrogance of its princes, who give themselves out to be the equals of Christ and the Apostles, speak of their co-royalty with God, and deck themselves with the title of *divus* (divine).'There is as great a gulf between the Apostles and the emperors as between saints and sinners.' On that level, it was very easy to contrast the insensate pride of the *basileis* with the piety and humility of the Frankish royal line; and our document does not fail to do so. As the *Libri* observe, the honours due to a king are not paid him as such, but as the holder of an office that has been entrusted to him by God. He does not share either in God's divinity or in His holiness; he is merely the minister of the Most High, who alone reigns, in the full sense of that word, over all the earth.

3 As for the emperors' claim to govern the ecumenical Church as a whole, it is denounced as sheer error, for they have as little claim to universality as the Church of their empire. Confronted by the presumption of Irene and her son, by the so-called General Council summoned by them, which was really no more than a Greek synod, and by the part of doctor assumed in it by the empress, an assumption completely contrary both to divine and to natural law, the king of the Franks sets forth at length his own conception of catholicism. All that does not differ from the teaching of the Fathers and has been accepted after consultation by all the Churches—that is Catholic. On the basis of this principle Charlemagne recognises the dogmas proclaimed by the first six Ecumenical Councils, and pronounces the Roman Church to be the guarantor and interpreter of the tradition by virtue of its primacy in being established by the Lord himself. The universality of the Church thus rests upon the authority of the Roman

Church and on its acceptance by other Churches, both those of the Frankish realm, representing the majority of Christians, and the rest. Let us take particular note of this position. Far from opposing to the Byzantine Church (that of the emperor) a Frankish Church (that of the king), the *Libri Carolini* insist on the contrary upon the close links between the latter and Rome. If, as the prologue to the capitulary maintains, the king has assumed the government *in sinu regni*, in the interior of the kingdom, he is very careful not to break his communion with Rome, for which he holds himself personally responsible. It is noticeable, from this same standpoint, that there is not the slightest criticism of Pope Hadrian throughout the text, for he is deemed to have had no part in the Council of Nicaea. And this point of view enables Charlemagne to proclaim that everything decided at that assembly is innovation and schism.

4   Finally, conscious of his duties towards the Catholic Church, the king of the Franks puts himself forward as an arbitrator between the two Councils, the Council of Hieria, which had forbidden images, and the Council of Nicaea, 'which had commanded their worship'. The decrees of the latter are subjected to the most searching and virulent criticism, after which the king proposes a return to traditional doctrine, and refers his views equally to the teaching of the Church Fathers, especially Gregory the Great, and to the tradition of the Gallic Church. It is a question neither of worshipping images, nor of destroying them: to God alone worship is due, to the saints veneration, and to images neither of these; they should simply be used for the decoration of churches and should in no case be the object of worship.

The *Libri Carolini* do not confine themselves, however, to denouncing the errors of the Greeks concerning images; they are equally severe upon Tarasius, the patriarch of Constantinople, for having proclaimed that the Holy Spirit proceeds from the Father *through* the Son. This officially raised the question of the *Filioque* clause, on which the western tradition tended to differ from that of the east. While the creed of the Council of Constantinople (381) had declared that the Spirit proceeded from the Father, there had gradually crept into the western text of the creed the addition of 'and the Son' (*qui ex Patre Filioque procedit*). It seems to have been customary enough in Spain for the Council of Toledo (589) to accept it as canonical; and the same assembly contributed considerably to the popularisation of the creed with this addition, since it prescribed its recitation at Mass. From Spain the custom rapidly spread to Gaul. What are we to think of this development? Doctrinally, it does not seem that the *Filioque* clause can be considered a true innovation. In the east, as in the west, theological speculation had reached the concept of the double procession of the Holy Spirit, but their respective expressions of the mystery were different. In the east, the Spirit was said to proceed from the Father *through* the Son, in the west from the Father *and* the Son. Basically, as Mgr E. Amann observes, 'both Churches could recognise themselves in this addition to the creed'.[1] From the disciplinary point of view, the question looked rather different. The Byzantine creed was an official document, to which an addition had been made that was not recognised by part of the Latin west, and notably by Rome, where the creed was not recited at Mass, but during the baptismal liturgy—of course without the *Filioque* clause. In Francia, where there had been an increasingly clear recognition of what separated the Latins and the Greeks, the latter were reproached for not having sided with the western practice, which alone was considered orthodox. Hence the Caroline Books' attack on the patriarch Tarasius, which Pope Hadrian answered with a formal rejection.

Such are some of the salient ideas in the famous capitulary, which is not altogether easy to judge as a whole. It is rightly considered a kind of doctrinal manifesto on the part of the Latin Church, and an assertion of its right to make its voice heard. It is equally true that the spokesman for this Church was the Frankish king; and holding the faith to be a trust committed to him, he showed himself to be its watchful and jealous guardian. True, he intervenes in the religious sphere in a very different spirit from that of the *basileus*, and the nature of his authority is very different from that of the imperial power. Nevertheless, he considers himself to be invested with the same rights in matters ecclesiastical as those enjoyed by the sovereign of New Rome. He promptly gave an additional proof of this by using the traditional institution of a council to promulgate his decisions on the problem of images. Thus the Frankish Council convoked in 794 at Frankfurt to condemn Adoptionism—a heresy arising in Spain which held Christ to be no more than the adopted Son of God—likewise saw

[1] *L'Époque carolingienne* (vol. 6 of *L'Histoire de l'Église*, ed. Fliche and Martin), p. 175.

itself postponing the icon question. So this assembly appeared initially to be a reply to the *ineptissima synodus* of Nicaea. It was a very large gathering, including not only the papal legates, who presided over the debates, but bishops and abbots from all regions of the Frankish kingdom, and even from Galicia, though not, despite frequent statements to the contrary, from England. The only Anglo-Saxon at the Council was Alcuin, though not as a representative of the Church of his homeland, but as spokesman for Charlemagne.

At this gathering of the western Church Charlemagne took the leading part, opened and closed the debates, and in the final session was acclaimed *rector populi christiani*. The Spanish heresy was condemned; the Greek errors were denounced; but only one of the decrees of the Council of Nicaea was declared null and void, which is ample proof that in Charlemagne's mind the Council of Frankfurt was meant to be primarily a counter-demonstration to the Council held in the east. Two years later, in 796, a synod of Italian bishops held at Cividale in Friuli took up the question of the *Filioque* clause; and Paulinus, the patriarch of Aquileia, pronounced judgment against the Greeks and vehemently and capably defended the principle of the Spirit's double procession, which he showed to be a safeguard of the unity of the divine substance.

Finally, let us note that all this action—whose repercussions died down temporarily when peace was restored between Charlemagne and Irene—took place solely on the initiative of the Frankish court, which paid no heed to Pope Hadrian's efforts to salvage the decrees of the Council of Nicaea and the orthodoxy of the Greek Church. The pontiff, who had tried in vain to defend the conciliar canons approved by his authority, thus found himself thrown back into an extremely difficult position, from which he tried to extricate himself by manœuvre. While maintaining the validity of the seventh Ecumenical Council, he nevertheless let it be understood that he had not entirely approved of its decisions. In any case, towards the close of the eighth century, it was not under Hadrian's leadership, but under Charlemagne's, that the west was discovering its spiritual unity, and asserting it unceasingly against the Byzantine empire and its Church.

This growing awareness went hand in hand with the growing prestige of the figure who represented the unity of the west and who tended, in his own sphere, to place himself on the same level as the emperor. Nothing is more significant than the visible signs of this rise to power, which, though very diverse, are all none the less an expression of the *Imitatio Imperii* embarked upon by the king of the Franks. Some of these signs may be observed in the practices of the chancery. Such for instance was the monogram affixed to the diplomas, precisely as was the custom in Constantinople. This same custom likewise explains the use of the term *sacer* (holy) as applied to the king's diplomas, his palace and his court. Or again, there was the bull serving to authenticate the prince's acts: first it was in lead, then in gold, thus constituting a singular novelty for the west, which was accustomed to the use of wax seals. The obverse carries the bust of a crowned sovereign, and round it runs the inscription: 'Jesus, Son of God, powerfully defend Charles.' On the reverse is the formula: 'Glory to Christ and victory to King Charles', a legend apparently representing an abbreviation from the *Laudes*. It should be observed, moreover, that the model imitated is not a contemporary Byzantine bull, but a coin or medal of the fourth century, perhaps even of the time of Constantine, the first indication we have of a return to the traditions of the late empire, of which we shall discover still further signs.

Another indication—this time a literary one—of the *Imitatio Imperii* is the frequency with which Charlemagne is called David after the Council of Frankfurt. This seems to have been a genuinely political manifestation. When the emperor was acclaimed as David in Constantinople, he appeared as the head of a new chosen people who had taken up the inheritance of Israel. Pope Leo II had likewise recently saluted Constantine IV, the promoter of the sixth Ecumenical Council, as the New David: 'Let all the Churches sing with a loud voice and say: the new David, the staunchest of all the emperors, has overcome the devil.'

This was therefore an imperial title, reserved for the *basileus*. But, as we have already seen, at the height of the iconoclastic controversy Pope Stephen II and his successors transferred this glorious title to Pepin. There is an echo of this in a single letter written by Hadrian to Charlemagne; but after this, as I have mentioned, there is a break in communications from the papal side. To the reasons given above for this silence, we should now add that during the negotiations with Irene preceding the Council of Nicaea, Pope Hadrian no doubt wanted to abstain from any action that might wound imperial susceptibilities. On the Frankish side, 'David' was to start with no more than a term of comparison—as for instance in a letter addressed to the king by the Anglo-Saxon poet Cathwulf about the year 775. The atmosphere changed about 787, when the Franco-Byzantine conflict began. In that year a poem by Paul the Deacon applied this title to the king. In the Caroline Books, David is frequently quoted, but without being associated with Charlemagne. The examples of the Jewish king and his son Solomon, both famous as patterns of royalty, are invoked as a contrast to the attitude of the Byzantine emperors. David planned to build the temple, and Solomon carried out the plan, while the 'kings of the Greeks' have profaned the sanctuary. After the Council of Frankfurt, the court writers shed all reserve and often gave Charlemagne the name of David, as though to express the divine repudiation of the new Saul and the promotion of David as ruler over the chosen people.

Alcuin put himself at the head of this movement, and the letter he wrote to his master shortly after the Council of Frankfurt may be found at the end of this book.[1] Up to his death in 804, that is, even after the imperial coronation, he continued to call Charlemagne David in the body of the letters he sent him no less than in the address written after the Council of Frankfurt, where the predicate was accompanied by a whole series of epithets expressing their author's sincere admiration for the person of the 'most excellent' king, such as 'most gentle', 'most longed for', 'most worthy of all honour'. The example set by Alcuin led other writers, such as Angilbert, Theodulf and Modoin, to do likewise. One could quote from them almost indefinitely. What lessons are to be drawn from this practice? In the first place, what is being given to Charlemagne is a *nomen*—'David, thy other name', as Alcuin puts it; what is being recognised in him is no less than the sacred office and functions and qualities of the Hebrew king. Among these qualities the Abbot of Saint-Martin de Tours mentions especially mercy, good will, a steady piety and godliness, and above all wisdom—spiritual wisdom, as he goes on to explain—associated with a great clarity of mind. Moreover, David directly inspired by God also illustrates the theme embodied in

[1] See p. 233 below.

Charlemagne as *rex et sacerdos,* though we must once again emphasise that this should be interpreted with a certain shade of meaning. As regards sacerdotal power, only the teaching aspect is recognised in Charlemagne; so that it is in this respect alone that Alcuin attributes to him the possession of the two swords, as both sovereign and preacher of the word of God at one and the same time. Like David, Charlemagne has been invested by the Deity with a mission to turn his people towards the spiritual life. Like David too, he is directly inspired by God, whom he represents upon this earth, as Cathwulf wrote as early as 775. And like David, Charlemagne is the best ruler of the people of God, and will bear the responsibility for them at the Last Judgment. This is another thought of Cathwulf, which finally crystallises in the union of the notions of the *Regnum* and the Church in one and the same mystical body. In this present world, the exaltation of the New David will assure to Christian peoples peace and prosperity. Modoin had celebrated David as the prince of peace; Alcuin addresses Charlemagne as 'David, the peaceful king', and praises his might, in the shadow of which peoples and Churches can live in peace.

We can perhaps connect with this theme the adjective *serenissimus,* which figures in the headings of some of the royal diplomas between 790 and 800, and which certainly seems to designate the king of peace. But, strikingly enough, it also forms part of the imperial description used in Byzantium, and its adoption by the Frankish chancery would thus be a further indication of the *Imitatio Imperii* we have been seeking to portray. But what is only probable in this title becomes absolutely certain in that of *orthodoxus,* the holder and defender of the true faith—another epithet traditionally ascribed to the *basileus,* and in the last decade of the century frequently given to the king of the Franks by Popes Hadrian I and Leo III. Here too there are eloquent allusions to this royal quality in Alcuin's letters, which constantly find new terms in which to celebrate a sovereign 'whose right hand wields the sword of triumph, and whose mouth trumpets forth the sounds of Catholic piety', a sovereign who is 'ruler and teacher' of his people.

There is thus a great similarity in the titles, and they all have much the same tone as in the Byzantine empire. None the less, the interpretation of them by the Frankish intellectuals gives them a new meaning, emphasising the duties and moral concerns rather than the privileges of sovereignty. The western David is not altogether the David of the east, just as western Christianity differs in appearance from the traditional faith of the empire.

VII

Aachen and Rome

The open rivalry between the Frankish realm and the Byzantine empire during the crucial years outlined above is equally evident in Charlemagne's decision to give himself a fixed place of residence, a palace worthy of being the visible sign of his power. Such was the palace at Aachen from the year 794 onwards, which soon seemed to contemporaries the equal of those at Constantinople, since the term 'New Rome', reserved hitherto for the city on the Bosphorus, was now applied by a court poet to the Carolingian foundation. Now 'New Rome' at once suggests 'empire'. This then was the final approach to this idea. But it must at once be added that though the idea of empire began timidly to peep through, it could not detach itself from the ancient and true Rome, and the approach was thus made difficult. For the moment, it will be enough to indicate the problem. The first task will be to search out the meaning of Aachen, before going on to examine the situation at Rome and the tendencies prevailing there about the year 800.

Up to the end of the eighth century, Charlemagne's court, like his predecessors', had been itinerant, going round from one palace to another. Slowly, however, it tended to move from the valleys of the Seine, the Oise and the Aisne, formerly the centres of Frankish power, towards the north-eastern territories recently incorporated in the monarchy, which it was important to keep under scrutiny. And so the palaces of Thionville, Herstal, Düren,

Nijmegen, Ingelheim and Worms gradually supplanted Compiègne, Attigny, Quierzy and Verbérie. At the end of this tran-
sitional stage, Charlemagne took up residence between the Meuse
and the Rhine, in a gently undulating plain, watered by the Wurm,
a tributary of the Roer, where there were abundant hot springs
from which the place took its name (Aachen = *Aquae*, waters).
This former Roman military outpost with its hot springs, important remains of which have been discovered, had since the
Frankish conquest formed part of the royal domain; and it was
no doubt the Merovingians who, after their conversion, had
founded a church there for the inhabitants of their estates. The
centre of the 'villa' was a house arranged to accommodate the
king. Pepin spent the winter of 765–6 there—the year in which the
name of Aachen first figures in history. He built a round chapel
to hold an important treasury of relics; and excavations have discovered it beneath the altar dedicated to the Virgin in the church
built by Charlemagne, who stayed several times at Aachen, in 768,
777, 786, 788 and 789; and this was perhaps about the time he
decided to take up his abode there permanently, and turn his
palace into a residence. A fire in the palace at Worms in 790–1
hastened the execution of this plan.

It is difficult for us to picture this building as a whole, for
apart from the chapel (incorporated in the present cathedral of
Aachen), all its buildings have been destroyed, and since the
second half of the fourteenth century the Town Hall has stood on
their site. And so they can only be pictured with the help of
Carolingian documents and the excavations that have been carried
out. Situated on the slope of the hill running down from the
present-day market square to the cathedral, it consisted essentially of a large one-storeyed building, the *aula regalis,* the principal
room being a rectangular reception hall, 46 metres long and 20
wide, perhaps opening on to three apses or conchs; in the largest
of these, on the western side, there were steps leading up to the
royal throne. In front of the palace stretched a courtyard with
porticos and houses occupied by the king's attendants. After the
year 800 there was placed in its centre an equestrian statue of
Theodoric, king of the Ostrogoths, brought from Ravenna;
while to the west a wooden gallery, about a hundred metres long,
directly linked the *aula regalis* to the chapel.

Regarding the chapel, there is evidence giving at least an

approximate date of construction: a letter from Alcuin to Charlemagne in 798, telling him that he had been discussing with a lady of the court the columns that had just been built in the church. So the main work was complete by that date, and fairly certainly by the year 796, when an Avar chieftain came and was baptised there with great ceremony. Be that as it may, the chapel certainly dates from the years immediately preceding the imperial coronation. It was a building on a central plan, in the form of an octagon inscribed in a sixteen-sided polygon. The octagon, 31 metres in height, constituted the main nave; and round it was a cloister forming side-aisles, with galleries above it. The aisles and galleries opened through big arcades and bays with round arches onto the central space, which was covered in by an eight-faced cupola over a 'tambour' pierced with windows. On the eastern side, before the time of the present choir, there was only a rectangular choir of modest dimensions, also two-storeyed, with two altars placed well forward, the lower one dedicated to the Virgin, the upper to the Saviour. Opposite the latter, in the upper church, was the royal throne (still there today), from which the altar dedicated to the Virgin could also be seen. Facing the choir, the entrance to the chapel was perhaps by way of a small western block framed by two turrets with staircases giving access to the galleries. The chapel was very sober and even austere-looking from the outside, with its bare walls broken only by the fluted pilasters framing the bays of the tambour; but the interior was finely decorated. There were bronze doors, the balustrades of the upper galleries were finely wrought in the same metal, there was coloured paving, antique columns imported from elsewhere, particularly from Ravenna, with shafts of marble and variegated porphyry, and Corinthian capitals. The plane surfaces were covered in paintings, and the cupola with mosaics representing the Saviour in triumph[1] surrounded by the four and twenty elders of the Apocalypse. Such were the principal features of the decor, whose sumptuousness was decreed by Charlemagne and dazzled his contemporaries. The few elements that have been preserved enable us to get at least some idea of what it must have been like.

As I have described it, the palatine chapel presents a major problem in origins and meaning, about which the specialists are still arguing today. All are agreed that the building belongs to the

[1] Or the Lamb of God.

family of polygonal or circular churches, whether of the baptistery type or the *martyria* raised over the martyr's tombs, or simply containing relics, thus constituting 'monumental reliquaries'. Both of these have links with classical types, either with the hero's tomb (*heroon*) or the architecture of thermal baths. There were polygonal or circular churches in southern and central Gaul as well as in northern Italy, and it may be conjectured that in Charlemagne's time there were architects acquainted with the technique of this kind of construction. The architect of the chapel at Aachen, Eudes, must have been such a man, though all we know about him is that he was buried at Metz. Who was he? A Frank, or a foreigner? We simply do not know.

Having thus fixed the traditional type of structure, at least in its general lines, we may go on to ask what particular model or original inspired its architect. Here too we can only formulate hypotheses. A dozen or so years ago, one such hypothesis considered the chapel to be an adaptation of the chrysotriclinos at Constantinople, a building probably constructed by the Emperor Justin II (567–78), which served both as a church and as a throne-room. The monument was octagonal in form, and covered in by a central dome; and there opened off the ground floor eight vaulted niches, the most easterly of which contained the imperial throne. Above these niches ran a gallery surmounted by the sixteen windows of the cupola. There would thus seem to be striking similarities between the chrysotriclinos and the chapel at Aachen. Yet there is one considerable difference between the two structures. At Constantinople the most important element was the imperial throne in its eastward-facing niche. At Aachen, it is the altar, or more accurately the two altars, one in the lower and one in the upper church, faced by Charlemagne's throne in the west of the upper gallery. According to this interpretation, the chapel would on the one hand be another sign of the *Imitatio Imperii*, but also a correction on the part of the Most Christian and orthodox king of the traditional idea, showing that he considered himself as nothing but the servant of Christ, who alone is the King of this world. If this view is adopted it would be an illustration of the Caroline Books' devastating criticism of the 'kings of the Greeks', and their claim to be 'co-rulers with God'. This is an attractive hypothesis, but our ignorance of the conditions in which Charlemagne could have had such accurate information about the chrysotriclinos makes it preferable to seek for models of the chapel in the west.

For a good many years, the church of San Vitale at Ravenna has been advanced as a possible model, and with good reason, it seems. The influence of this church is undeniable, particularly as regards the arrangement of the octagon, and the part played by the columns in its decoration. We know that Charlemagne resided at Ravenna in 786 and 787, although our knowledge comes only from a later source; and he may, with Hadrian's permission, have brought the Ravenna marbles and mosaics north of the Alps and used them at Aachen. Recent research has shown that there is a second Italian monument to be added as a further source of inspiration, the mausoleum of the dynasty of Theodosius on the southern side of the basilica of St Peter's at Rome, consisting of two rotundas with eight niches, one of which, the eastern, was the actual mausoleum, the other having been transformed into a chapel dedicated to St Petronella, St Peter's supposed daughter, whose cult had been widespread among the Franks since the days of Pepin. This hypothesis might perhaps claim acceptance if we could know all the purposes for which Charlemagne intended his chapel to be used at the time of its foundation. The superscription on the altar in the upper church leaves us in no doubt that it was primarily a sanctuary raised to the glory of 'Him who loves the Franks', the supreme protector of the realm and the dynasty. But the very name specifically attached to the building, *Capella* or chapel, also suggests that it was meant to house the most splendid relic in the kingdom, the cope of St Martin, a symbol of the triumph of Christianity among the Gauls, and the *palladium* of the French monarchy. To this relic must be added all those already in Pepin's possession, which increased in number under Charlemagne, especially relics of the Virgin enclosed in a reliquary, which is thought to have been placed on a column behind the altar to the Virgin in the lower church. If the latter was thus a kind of 'monumental reliquary', the upper church could be considered a sort of parish church for the people of the palace, and before long for those of the locality who grew up on the fringes of the royal residence, the *vicus aquensis*. From that point of view, it is quite clear why the royal throne was placed as it was—to enable Charlemagne, when installed in it, to take part conveniently in the liturgical ceremonies going on in both the churches, one above the other. Finally, it is probable (though not certain) that the chapel was also intended as a mausoleum, to receive the last remains of the king who, as a Christian hero, woud find his last resting-place near the tutelary relics laid up in his *heroon*.

In short, the palatine chapel, though related to many preceding monuments, was nevertheless original both in its arrangement and in the multiplicity of its functions. Its sober grandeur expresses both a political and a religious idea, and also symbolises the power and prestige attained by Charlemagne's royal state, which by the end of the eighth century had reached a level not far below the emperor's. He had become *imperatori similis*. The atmosphere of the sanctuary is primarily biblical. The famous throne on its six stone steps, with its rounded back and arm-rests, copies Solomon's. 'May I soon be allowed,' Alcuin wrote to Charlemagne, 'to come with palms, accompanied by children singing psalms, to meet your triumphant glory, and to see once more your beloved face in the Jerusalem of our most dear fatherland, wherein is the temple set up to God by this most wise Solomon.' Thus Aachen seemed to be the New Jerusalem, prefiguring and announcing the eternal by its octagonal plan and the throne of the New David. Let us, however, beware of being too systematic in stressing this impression, which was by no means exclusive, for with the image of Jerusalem there was also mingled the great recollection of Rome.

I mentioned a little while ago the mausoleum of the Theodosian dynasty. Perhaps this reference should be taken further, for before the year 800 Charlemagne had made three stays in Rome, in 774, 781 and 788, and had come to know the monuments embodying the traditions of the Emperor Constantine. He must have been present on Holy Saturday 774 at the baptisms by Pope Hadrian in the Lateran baptistery, in the very place where, according to legend, Pope Silvester had assisted at Constantine's new birth into the Christian faith. One can scarcely fail to allow that some of these buildings may also have inspired the architects of Aachen. This baptistery was octagonal in shape; and we know that alongside the Palatine chapel there was a structure rather strangely known by the name of Lateran. Was it perhaps intended as the Pope's residence when he visited the court? In any case, we know that the Frankish councils met there under Louis the Pious. All these points would seem to indicate that recollections of the buildings associated with Constantine made a deep impression on Charlemagne. We may even conjecture that he saw his new residence as a kind of replica of Constantine's founding of the city on the Bosphorus. The phrases used by a court poet to describe Aachen, the New Rome, the Rome of the Future (*Nova Roma, Ventura Roma*), are certainly no empty hyperbole, but speak the same language as the pattern of bull, modelled on Constantine's, that was used by the Frankish chancery before the end of the eighth century for sealing the royal acts.

The fact remains, however, that this return by Charlemagne to the tradition of Constantine can have been no more than partial and external. Its deeper meaning was unknown to him. To understand it, we must trace out its genesis from the second half of the fourth century onwards.

The tradition of Constantine is primarily a reflection of the Christianised empire. It did not take shape immediately after his death, for his leniency towards the Arians was not quickly forgotten. But Constantine's conversion—the prelude to the triumph of Christianity—and the first Council of Nicaea, with which his name seemed to be indissolubly linked, were considered facts of another order of importance than the prince's defects, the memories of which grew dim with the passing years. In the church of the Holy Apostles at Constantinople, or New Rome, where his sarcophagus had taken its place alongside the cenotaphs dedicated to the memory of the twelve apostles, he was compared with St Paul, since his famous vision at the Milvian Bridge testified that he had been directly called by God, like St Paul on the road to Damascus. From the fifth century onwards at the latest, he enjoyed the right to liturgical honours in the east; furthermore, the Byzantine Church made him the eponymous hero of the Romano-Christian empire, who was reborn in each of his successors, especially in those who had rendered to the Christian faith services comparable to his. 'The New Constantine' thus became the imperial title *par excellence*. It occurs in the ritual acclamations, including those which concluded the councils. They all expressed the orthodox character and the divine vocation of the empire and its head. Even the popes freely used this epithet when seeking to express their gratitude to the emperors. Thus Hadrian I, hoping to see a rapid end to the iconoclastic crisis, had as early as 785 accorded Constantine VI the title of New Constantine, and hailed his mother Irene as the New Helen, recalling the mother of Constantine the Great, who was believed to have discovered the wood of the Holy Cross, and was almost as widely revered as her son.

In Rome, however, there was developing a picture of quite a different kind. The name of Constantine was attached to some of the most notable Christian monuments in the city given by him to the Church, such as the Lateran Palace and the papal residence, or built by him or his successors, such as the Lateran basilica (then called St Saviour's), St Peter's in the Vatican, Santa Croce, St Paul-outside-the-Walls, and others. Moreover the emperor would seem to have been closely associated with Bishop Silvester, whose pontificate had begun in 314, but was put back by St Jerome to 310, thus enabling him to point to the bishop of Rome as the person who had baptised Constantine. As in the east, it was considered advisable to forget the real baptism received by the prince, just before his death, at the hands of an Arian bishop; and it was also necessary to attribute this baptism to the pope in order to conceal the eclipse of the Roman Church after the decisive events of 313. In the second half of the fifth century there was composed in Rome a legendary story, perhaps of Syrian inspiration, known by the name of the *Actus Sylvestri*, which told of Constantine's leprosy, the barbarous advice of pagan priests who bade him, by way of cure, immerse himself in a bath of the blood of newly-slaughtered infants, and finally his healing and conversion through the grace of baptism administered by Bishop Silvester. We ought not to be surprised at the absence from this pious romance of any allusion to the vision of the Milvian Bridge. By silently passing over this miraculous episode, the narrator was disposing of the theme, prevalent in the east, of a Constantine who had received the charisma of apostolic mission direct from God. His story successfully produces quite the opposite impression: it gives the picture of a Constantine who, after baptism, guaranteed all the pre-existing rights of the Church, since it represents him as decreeing that throughout the Roman empire priests were to consider the pope as their head, just as the Roman officials obeyed the emperor.

The western Constantine's authority thus sanctioned the principle of the separation of powers, the doctrine formulated at the end of the century by Pope Gelasius, as well as the spiritual primacy of the Roman see. This story enjoyed great success not only in

Rome, but also in the east (from Justinian's time onwards) and the west (where it spread more slowly). It must not however be forgotten that in the Germanic kingdoms the double theme of Constantine—his conversion to Christianity and his protection of the true faith—was set before all the kings at the moment of their conversion. Let us remember at this point the famous account given by Gregory of Tours of the baptism of Clovis, the 'New Constantine'; and evidence of the same kind will be found among the Spanish Visigoths and the Anglo-Saxons. The emperor's memory was likewise preserved by the cult of the Holy Cross, whose principal centre in France had been at Poitiers since the days of St Radegonde and Venantius Fortunatus.

But we have now reached the point at which the image of the first Christian emperor was to assume the form that proved definitive in Rome and the west. This new version was preceded by the Roman revival of the cult of St Silvester, beginning at the close of the seventh century and reaching its climax during the pontificates of Stephen II and Paul I (752–7 and 757–67). It is imbued with the atmosphere accompanying the foundation of the 'Papal State', and it comes into the open in the most celebrated forgery of the Middle Ages—the Donation of Constantine (*Constitutum Constantini*).

Although its date is extremely uncertain, and although different scholars advance the date to 804 or even to the beginning of the reign of Louis the Pious, it still seems most probable, unless we take up the recent suggestion that the document evolved progressively, that it first saw the light in Rome in the period following Pepin's intervention in Italy. Not only has an examination of the style revealed many points of contact with the expressions occurring in the acts of Paul I, but the clauses of the *Constitutum* suggest with some likelihood that the forger wished to base the great political changes that had recently taken place in Rome on an imperial constitution. For—as E. Ewig, one of the most recent interpreters of the Donation suggests[1]—we must understand that though from the Frankish point of view it was perfectly lawful for Pepin to present the pope with the region he had just wrested from the Lombards (the Exarchate of Ravenna), in the eyes of its recipient the grant did not constitute a sufficient title. The emperor was still the temporal head of Christendom. In order to eliminate

[1] 'Das Bild Constantins des Grossen', *Historisches Jahrbuch*, 75 (1956), 31.

him from Rome, Italy and the west for good and all, it was necessary to create an exceptional status for the pope, like that of the
emperor himself in the east. This is why the forger of the Donation, having incorporated in his text the *Actus Silvestri* and established Constantine's sanction for the primacy of the Roman see,
shows the emperor as leaving Rome and founding a new capital
in Constantinople, because he could not conceive that 'where the
sacerdotal empire (*principatus sacerdotum*) and the capital of the
Christian religion have been founded by the Heavenly Sovereign,
the earthly emperor could possibly exercise his powers'. Moreover,
he represents Constantine as granting to Silvester and his successors a quasi-imperial rank in the west, and as part of this arrangement shows the emperor handing over Rome to the pope, along
with 'all the provinces, places and cities of Italy, and the western
regions'. Though the essential part of the Donation, as far as
later generations were concerned, consisted of this unprecedented
cession, the forger seems to have considered it as of only minor
importance, for he expresses himself in the vaguest possible terms
about the territories made over to the pope. The essential thing
for him, which he constantly stresses, is the attribution to the
bishop of Rome of prerogatives making him a person on the
same level as the emperor. The term *Imitatio Imperii*, which we
have constantly been using, figures in full in the Donation.
Splendid vestments, the insignia of power, the right to official
processions and to the use of ensigns—all these visible signs of
imperial authority are henceforth to adorn 'the successor of the
blessed Apostle Peter'. It is clear that such a prerogative could
not have been limited either to Rome or to Italy—it would have
then authorised the idea of an exceptional regime set up for
a territory that was no part of the empire—but was meant to
apply to the west as a whole, in order to provide a parallel to the
power wielded by the emperor in the zone set aside for his
rule.

I am well aware that this interpretation is no more than one of
those put forward to make some sense of this strange document.
If it is thought in some degree probable, we may go on to suggest
that the *Constitutum* was forged to detach the Roman Church from
all temporal power (and particularly from the imperial power
'relegated' to the east). In this way the text filled in the void that
had existed in Rome since 754; it finally created the type of 'the

good emperor', faithful and generous towards the papacy, and thus providing an example for imitation by his successors.

Let us dwell a little longer on this double donation, and try in the first place to form some conception of the peculiar position of Rome since the middle of the eighth century. The city and the duchy were under the governance of the pope. This was a *de facto* power, for no juridical act or decree had ended the dominion of the Byzantine emperor over the city and its territory. The only bond still existing between Rome and Constantinople—since Hadrian I, as we have seen, had ceased to date his acts by the years of the emperor's reign—was a spiritual bond, the bond of public prayers for the Roman empire, which were still said in Rome. On the other hand the imperial dominion had been succeeded by the Frankish 'protection'. Its basis was the renewal by Charlemagne in 774, when he visited Rome, of the pact of Ponthion, which replaced in written form the terms *adiutor* (helper) and *defensor* (defender), which defined Pepin's functions, by the formula *me protectorem et defensorem esse*, that is to say: 'I promise under oath to be the protector and defender of the pope and the city.' Now protection, according to the Frankish mind, as well as in the Germanic outlook generally, was not to be understood in the sense of the protector putting himself at his protégé's disposal in order to carry out his requests, but in a more strictly active sense. The protection was to be authoritarian, conferring on the protector the right to intervene in his protégé's affairs. It is highly significant that, from 774, the decrees issued from Charlemagne's chancery always gave him the title of Patrician of the Romans conferred on him when he was quite young, as well as on his father, by Pope Stephen II, which was not a political reality until he became master of Italy by right of conquest. We have only to follow the frequent interventions of the Frankish king and his officials (the counts and the *missi*) in the affairs of the 'Papal State' to become fully convinced of this fact. Moreover, these interventions were always tempered by the respect and affection existing between the king and the pope, and especially by the spiritual bond that united them. The royal unction conferred upon Pepin and Louis by Hadrian after baptising them made him Charlemagne's 'compeer'. It is difficult to know exactly what this *'compaternitas'* implied. Probably we should think of it as a pact—*pactum compaternitatis,* as Charlemagne called it—involving reciprocal undertakings, and creating between these two men, and more particularly between the offices they represented, a very strong bond, promising Charlemagne especially the help of the pope's prayers. The *ordo Romanus I* thus informs us that 'in Hadrian's time at the Station Mass on the Saturdays in Lent there should be a genuflexion for King Charles, which had not hitherto been customary'. One could quote further evidence of this public prayer which set the king of the Franks side by side with the emperor in the Roman liturgy. It should be noted, besides, that this *compaternitas* did not in any way abrogate the king-patrician's character as the pope's spiritual son. A letter of 791 from Charles to Hadrian bears the characteristic superscription of *compater idemque in Christo filius,* that is, 'compeer as well as Son in Christ'. In short, Rome really had no emperor: its government depended on the personal relationships between the pope and the patrician.

Did Hadrian instruct his spiritual son in the pattern of the good emperor? Once at least—in a famous letter of 778, which incidentally assumes the existence of the Donation, and reads as follows:

> Just as in the time of St Silvester the Holy Church of God,
> Catholic, Apostolic and Roman, was raised up and exalted
> by the most pious Emperor Constantine of blessed memory,
> who was pleased to grant him the power [*potestatem*] in these
> regions of Hesperia [that is to say, Italy], so likewise may
> she, in these present happy times in which we dwell, be
> increased yet more, so that all nations who have heard of her
> may say: Lord, save the king and hear us when we call upon
> Thee, for behold a new and most Christian Emperor
> Constantine has arisen in these days, through whom God has
> vouchsafed to give all gifts to the Holy Church of St Peter,
> prince of his Apostles.

The allusion is unmistakable: if only Charlemagne will support and assist the territorial claims being raised at that moment by Hadrian in Italy, he will in future deserve to be called the New Constantine. If we remember that this title traditionally belonged to the emperor, we shall realise that its attribution to Charlemagne was a further step towards placing him on the same level. It is however remarkable that this precise allusion occurs only in the pontifical correspondence of that one year. Less than ten years later Hadrian applied the title to Constantine VI; but that, it is true, was after the king of the Franks had refused his support for the pope's territorial claims. Moreover, the pope took good care not to reinforce the power that Charlemagne was already exercising in Rome. His pontificate is clearly marked by his anxiety to maintain as far as possible the independence of the papacy between the ancient empire and the new monarchy. The Constantine to whom he referred was not only the generous emperor, he was equally much the prince who had given Rome to the pope. Faced as he was with an all-powerful protector, Hadrian succeeded on the whole, by a combination of flexibility and firmness, in preserving a certain freedom of action for himself.

This was not true of his successor, Leo III, who hastened to revive the tradition of Constantine and project it upon Charlemagne; but this was to be a Constantine who would return to Rome whenever the pope called upon him to do so.

Elected in 795, the new pope possessed neither the prestige nor the broad outlook of his predecessor. He was of humble birth, and his career had been exclusively confined to his offices of the pontifical palace. His election seems to have been a matter of chance, and earned him the immediate hostility of a whole faction of the nobility, for the internal life of the Papal State was in fact governed by the antagonism between the military and landed aristocracy and the clerical bureaucracy. And so, from the moment of his election, Leo III drew as close as possible to Charlemagne and strove to ensure that his protection would be effective, for it was something of which he stood in urgent need. This explains a whole series of very significant steps. The first was to send the Frankish king a full report of his election, accompanied by a letter in which the pope begged Charlemagne to send him one of his notables to receive the oath of fealty and the submission of the Romans. At the same time Leo sent Charles the keys of the Confession of St Peter and the standard of the city of Rome. There are a number of strands interwoven here, as Schramm has shown;[1] and they need to be separated if we are to understand them. The dispatch of the account of the election, the *Decretum pontificis*,

[1] 'Die Anerkennung Karls des Grossen als Kaiser', *Historische Zeitschrift*, 172, 1951.

in a form dating from Hadrian's time, and now part of the official register of documents in the Roman chancery, the *Liber Diurnus*, was in accordance with fairly recently established custom. The transmission of the keys of the Confession of St Peter, or, more accurately, the keys placed on the Apostle's tomb, mingled with a few iron filings from St Peter's chains, did not have any political significance, but may rather be viewed as something to be valued as a relic, a mark of honour as well as a sign of the help expected from a prince devoted to St Peter, and nothing more. This tradition had begun with Gregory the Great, and Charles Martel had benefited by it before Charlemagne. But the same is not true of the other two gifts. The standard of Rome calls to mind in the first place the flying of flags which had greeted Charlemagne in 774, as had previously been done for the Byzantine Exarch. But on this occasion only one emblem was used; and in sending it to Charlemagne, Leo III was perhaps using it as an investiture standard, meant to symbolise the government to be exercised by the Frankish king over the city in the pope's name. There remains the receiving of the Roman oath of fealty by a *missus*: was this an oath to the pope or the king-patrician? Though we cannot be sure of the answer, it is clear that the participation of Charlemagne's representative in such an important act was a further sign of the increased protection from the king which it was Leo's intention to build up in Rome.

Charlemagne's reply to these papal initiatives was extremely subtle. As though with a presentiment that the newly elected pope would not be equal to the demands of his high office, he sent him his friend Angilbert, abbot of Saint-Riquier, to bring gifts, and also carrying written instructions and a personal letter to the pope. Angilbert was instructed to draw Leo's attention to the importance of an honourable way of life, the keeping of the sacred canons, the pious government of the Church and opposition to simony; he was also to remind the pope that 'the honour lately bestowed upon him is transitory, whereas the reward of good works is eternal'. Stranger still was the letter, drawn up no doubt by Alcuin, which Angilbert was to hand to the pope. First there were congratulations on his election, thanks for his prayers and his promise of fealty, and an invitation to discuss with Angilbert ways of strengthening the patriciate. Then come some weighty words upon the delimitation of the two powers. 'I desire'—so run the king's words—'to establish with Your Holiness an inviolable pact of faith and charity.' This makes it clear that Charlemagne wished to confirm, in fact to transform, the *pactum compaternitatis* which had hitherto governed his relations with the papacy. Then comes a closer definition of the substance of this *inviolabile foedus*:

> It will be my duty, with the help of divine goodness, to defend the Holy Church of Christ against the outside world by force of arms against all incursions of pagans or ravages of the infidel; and within, to protect it by assisting in the spread of the Catholic faith. Your part, Holy Father, will be to lift up your hands to God along with Moses, and thus by your prayers assist the triumph of our arms.

In short, the pope's role was the ministry of prayer; the king's was the defence of the Church, extended so as to cover its spiritual direction. Without in any way entering into the mind of Leo III, whose aim was to bind him to the cause of the papacy, Charlemagne sketched out for him a programme of Church government under the dual control of pope and king which was bound to work to the Church's advantage. We do not know whether Angilbert received the Romans' oath of allegiance. But there is no doubt at all that the pope, whose personal position became most precarious in the following years, was reduced to 'the role of Moses', and compelled to place all his hopes upon what help the patrician might think fit to give him.

In the course of the years 796-8, Leo III gave new expression to this hope in the famous mosaic with which he decorated the reception hall of the Lateran. It is no longer in existence today, but some idea of it can be got from an eighteenth-century reconstruction in the Piazza San Giovanni. At the back of the main apse was a representation of Christ sending the apostles out to convert the world. On either side of the principal scene were two detached groups: on the left, Christ is handing, to Pope Silvester and to the Emperor Constantine kneeling at his feet, repectively the keys and the standard, symbolising the spiritual and the temporal power. On the right St Peter, the Vicar of Christ, is handing Leo III the *pallium*, the symbol of supreme jurisdiction in the Church, and to the king of the Franks a blue standard powdered with red roses. Below the group runs an inscription, obviously inspired by the *Laudes*: 'Blessed Peter, give long life to Pope Leo and victory to King Charles.' The whole is crowned by a triumphal arch; and the first two verses of the angels' song inscribed upon it seem to suggest that the peace promised to men of good will can only be realised by understanding between the two powers. The essential message of the mosaic, however, is that Leo III was returning to the theme of Constantine and applying it to Charlemagne, while still delicately preserving a difference of degree between the two princes. Constantine is invested by Christ, but the king of the Franks by St Peter. The standard depicted in the mosaic perhaps embodies the memory of the one sent to Charlemagne by the pope in 796, and there can be no doubt about its meaning; it symbolises the dominion derived from St Peter, that is, in the Roman Church.

Can we go further still, and hold the picture of Charlemagne in the Lateran to be the equivalent of the portraits which the Byzantine emperors had by now ceased to send, or to have painted in Rome, as material evidence of their presence and their authority? This is an attractive hypothesis, and if pushed to the extreme would make us agree with Schramm[1] that even before his coronation Charlemagne had possessed the imperial prerogative in the Eternal City. The reality is perhaps rather less simple, if we remember that the Constantine facing Charlemagne is undoubtedly the emperor of the Donation, to which the pope owed his rank and imperial privileges. The most that may be conjectured is that in decreeing exceptional privileges to his protector, Leo III was acting in the name of this authority. This supposition is confirmed by a second Roman mosaic, destroyed in 1595 but still known from a sixteenth-century drawing, representing Charles in the apse of the church of St Susanna though, as it bears no inscription, we do not know whether it dates from before or after 800. It cannot therefore rank as more than a testimony to the exceptional honours accorded to Charlemagne by Leo III.

The strongest indication, however, of the position occupied by the Frankish king in Rome seems to lie in Leo's dating of his acts after the year 798, both according to the years of his pontificate and those of 'the Lord Charles, most excellent King of the Franks and patrician of the Romans, *a quo cepit Italiam anno XXV*', the twenty-fifth year after his gaining possession of Italy. The

1 See p. 113 above.

11 *Two miniatures of the so-called coronation Gospel, now in the Imperial Treasury at Vienna* (see also overleaf)
(From W. Koehler, *Die karolingischen Miniaturen*, I, Berlin, 1960.) Carried out between 795 and 810, probably in the Aachen studios directed by Einhard, in which there were foreign craftsmen, and particularly Italians, who had preserved the ancient traditions. This manuscript, unique of its kind, is the richest evidence we have of the imperial renaissance and the culture that flourished at the end of the eighth century.

Above: St Matthew, seated on a stool, is writing his Gospel in a book resting on a desk.

St Mark, with a scroll of papyrus (*volumen*) on his knees. A landscape of hills and trees in the background.

12   *A bull in use after the proclamation of the empire* (above)
(From J. Mabillon, *De re diplomatica*, Paris, 1704, suppl., p. 48.) There is
only one surviving specimen, in a very worn state (Bibl. nat., Cabinet des
Médailles, no. 995). The reproduction is from engravings and drawings of
the seventeenth and eighteenth centuries, and from bulls of the same type
from the later Carolingians, in a better state of preservation.

13   *Carolingian coins* (Bibl. nat.) (below)
(From E. Gariel, *Les Monnaies royales de France*, II, Strasbourg, 1883.)
N. 57, a denier. On the face, the legend: Charles emperor Augustus. On
the reverse, a tetrastyle temple, with a cross inside, and the legend:
RELIGIO CHRISTIANA (the Christian Religion).
N. 172, a third of a sou (in gold). On the face: the king, full-face and
half-length, with the legend: Our Lord King Charles.
On the reverse: A rosette, and round it the name of the mint, Flavia Luca
(Lucca, in Tuscany).

14 *Charlemagne the lawgiver*

A pen-drawing in a manuscript from the collection of capitularies of
Ansegis (Bibl. nat., Lat. 9654, tenth century, perhaps copied from a ninth-
century manuscript).

Under a portico of columns over which are draped the folds of a curtain
the emperor sits on a raised throne, his cloak fastened at the shoulder,
wearing a crown and holding a long sceptre (festuca).

pope was thus removing the difference between Charles's royal status in Italy and his patriciate in the Papal State, and consequently recognising without qualification that the king of the Franks was the master of Rome— but, we must add, no more than a *de facto* master, whose authority was derived from the pope's own.

It is on this note that we must bring this chapter to an end. Charlemagne was at the height of his power, a power attested by his new residence, a mark of the exceptional prestige he enjoyed in the west; and in Rome too his authority was unrivalled. But Rome, the former capital of the empire, had become St Peter's city, and although the Frankish king was its apparent master, the pope still sought to treat his mastery as delegated. The picture in the great hall of the Lateran could not be more eloquent; in Leo III's eyes, Charlemagne was to be the new Constantine, and hold himself at the Church's disposition. Was the pope already thinking of conferring on him the title and outward signs of the imperial authority which Charlemagne had created and of which he was to be the first beneficiary? We have no means of knowing. On the other hand, the king of the Franks assuredly had no intention of complying with Leo III's schemes and owing the additional prestige simply to the will of the Curia. Besides, what did Charlemagne know about Constantine? That he was a great builder; he was following the example. That he had given Rome, Italy and the west to the Papacy; we do not even know for certain that the Frankish king had ever heard of the Donation, except through more or less vague allusions, before his imperial coronation. His refusal to acquiesce in Hadrian's territorial claims shows him to have been far from ready to embark upon new concessions of that kind; and there is a genuine continuity between this refusal and his exchange of letters with Leo in 796. But Charlemagne certainly did not altogether believe Constantine to have been the model Christian emperor, since he had received from the archbishop of Toledo, in the midst of the Adoptionist controversy (792), a letter warning him not to follow in the footsteps of Constantine, who had lapsed into Arianism. In the last analysis, at the point we have reached in our study, it is clear once again that the path leading on to the imperial coronation does not follow a straight and simple line.

VIII

The birth of the imperial idea
in Charlemagne's circle

The successive lines of approach we have followed have brought before us three impressive facts: a royalty of great renown; Charlemagne's quasi-imperial rank; and the Constantinian tradition that Leo III was endeavouring to impose on the king of the Franks. Seen from these three standpoints, the rank of emperor may well appear to be no more than the strengthening and legalisation of a position already won, the crowning touch to a state of affairs that had been steadily developing throughout the reign. Once again, we must test this hypothesis against the notions of empire current at the Frankish court about the year 800. We must ask ourselves, moreover, whether these contained anything that could have made possible an imperial revival in the west. To these two problems we must therefore now turn our attention.

What idea could have been evoked by the term 'empire' in Charlemagne's circle during the last years of the eighth century? As far as we can see, it would not have been any original idea: the word 'empire' did not exist in any Germanic language, where *rîchi* (Reich) covered both the concepts of *regnum* (realm) and *imperium* (empire), and where the equivalent of 'emperor', *casere*, was an importation of Greco-Roman origin (*Kaisar*, *Caesar*). 'Empire' and 'emperor' corresponded to Roman ideas. But by the end of the eighth century these were remarkably diffuse in character. Thus it was possible to conceive of the Christian Roman empire as something universal, a great community of Christian civilisation, the body politic of an ecumenical Church. This was a religious and intellectual concept surviving in the liturgy. But this notion had developed by evolution, and one can trace at least three derivative forms of it, corresponding to three stages of its development. In one of these stages the notion had become fixed, regardless of reality, in the Byzantine imperial idea, Roman and universal in tendency, and strongly marked by the sacred character of the institution. Then there was a stage of dilution: the Christian empire, a conception which covered all Christian peoples and states. And, last, a spiritualised stage: the religious empire, clothed with the insignia of temporal power, corresponding to the papacy's claim to be entrusted with a mission of governance over kings and peoples. In the first of these stages, the centre of the empire was in Constantinople, the New Rome, considered as the authentic and sole heir of the old city; in the second and third stages, the centre was in Rome itself. Alongside these conceptions, which were all linked with Rome, there was another, not focused on any precise centre, but none the less Roman in origin, hardly distinguishable from the supremacy which a particular king might exercise over other princes. We have already come across the famous definition: 'the emperor is the man who is supreme [*praecellit*] in the world, and kings are under his orders.' A variant of this idea is to be found, for instance, in the title of emperor given by certain authors steeped in classical antiquity to kings who had become masters of several kingdoms, or where it was a question of underlining their pre-eminent authority over various peoples. This might perhaps be called a hegemonial conception of empire.

Such being the possible interpretations of the word empire, it will be readily admitted that Charlemagne could come round to the idea only slowly and with some difficulty. The picture most calculated to impress him was that of the Byzantine Roman empire. The Caroline Books have shown us what he thought of it. And the complete sincerity of his outlook is proved by his refusal to have anything to do with a Byzantine party hostile to Irene, whose emissaries came and offered him the empire in 798.

Was it not however possible to conceive of an empire of a different type from that of Constantinople? To find the answer, we must turn to the court intellectuals. We are now at the end of the eighth century, in the middle of the Carolingian Renaissance.

Its promoters, with their eyes on the ancient world, could not fail to be vividly reminded of the empire. To them the past was never completely dead: it lived on, and might be renewed. It is difficult not to believe that they projected the imperial concept onto the Carolingian monarchy as they knew it, and so set up a movement of thought favouring a restored empire. This hypothesis may be sound enough; yet it must be admitted that it rests upon slender support, seeing how few documents there are to supply any evidence.

The testimony of Alcuin, the most famous of these intellectuals, is of particular value, though its extent is small. Let us recall the contexts in which he conjures up the thought of empire. First there is the biography of St Willibrord, the apostle of Frisia, written before 797, where he surrounds Pepin of Herstal and Charles Martel with an imperial glow: 'Pepin who ruled gloriously over the empire of the Franks . . . Charles Martel who added many nations to the Frankish sceptres . . . among which he gloriously and triumphantly added Frisia to his father's empire'. Anglo-Saxon as Alcuin was, and familiar with the hegemonial theory of empire (which appears for instance in Bede's historical works), he must have found the word 'empire' a suitable one to define the power of the two Mayors over a multiplicity of peoples. Similarly, in a letter to the king of Kent (797), Alcuin speaks of the 'imperial royalty' of the king, no doubt because he enjoyed supremacy over kingdoms adjacent to his own. Did the same line of thought lead him to exalt Charlemagne's 'honneur du règne impérial'? It may well be so, but it should at once be observed that this expression, as applied to the Carolingian monarchy, is altogether exceptional. Alcuin sees only too clearly that Charles's royalty is not to be compared to these petty 'empires' founded only upon their holders' hegemony: it is something infinitely greater, and so he will set it in a quite different perspective.

It was from 798 onwards that the term 'empire' began to figure in some of his letters to Charlemagne. Alcuin expresses his good wishes for the king's health, 'so necessary for the whole empire of Christians'; may God grant him the power to exalt the Holy Church and preserve good government in the most sacred empire. Another appeal to Charlemagne in the Adoptionist question said:

Before this heresy spreads even further through the world of the Christian empire which has been entrusted to you and

your sons for rule and governance, arise, O man chosen of
God; arise, son of God and soldier of Christ, and defend the
spouse of the Lord your God, that you have received from
Him to govern and preserve.

How are we to interpret this 'Christian empire', which reappears
with new insistence in 799 and 800? It can certainly not refer to
anything but a spiritual reality, the community of believers. But,
as we have already noted, this idea was indissolubly linked with
that of the Romano-Christian empire, considered as the body
politic of Christendom, whose essential task it was to defend the
Church. The titular empire was making a poor showing in this
mission of defence; the Byzantine successors of Constantine and
Theodosius had put themselves out of court by their arrogance
and their religious tyranny. Something much nearer to the imperial Christian tradition was the whole group of territories
governed by Charlemagne, those western regions united beneath
his rule, with its spiritual metropolis at Rome, and a common soul
for all its inhabitants forged by the bonds of Christianity. In so far
as the 'empire of Christian people' could be defined geographically, its limits were those of the Carolingian kingdom's boundaries at the end of the eighth century. Alcuin himself said as
much in 799 when he wrote of the death of the two dukes,
Gerold of Bavaria and Eric of Friuli, 'those most valiant men who
preserved and extended the frontiers of the Christian empire'.[1]
The Christian empire is thus fairly clearly distinguished from the
titular empire, whose Christianity was by no means impeccable;
and this gives us some inkling of the extent to which iconoclasm
and the Caroline Books must have contributed to this awareness.
There is new evidence of this in the remarkable assimilation of
the terms Roman empire, Christian empire and kingdom (or
even empire) of the Franks—already taking place before the year
800—in certain sacramentaries, especially in the appendix bearing
the marks of revision by Alcuin. The text of the ancient prayers
shows that the name 'Roman' has sometimes been replaced by
'Christian' or 'Frankish', and even by the specific 'Roman empire
or empire of the Franks'. But we must not read into this more than
an attempt to express the Carolingian reality, which seemed to
be a revival of the ancient empire.

[1] This is F. L. Ganshof's conclusion in *La Révision de la Bible par Alcuin*,
Bibliothèque d'Humanisme et Renaissance, vol. 9, 1947.

If Alcuin's correspondence truly mirrors the problems discussed in Charlemagne's circle, it may fairly be taken as evidence of a trend of opinion in the Frankish court holding that 'the Christian empire' was already in existence. But this hypothesis cannot be taken any further. On the contrary, one must realise that there was really no need for an emperor at the head of this 'Christian empire': the Davidic king, the king inspired by God, was all-sufficient for its governance. Moreover, if we are to suppose that there was really an intention to transform the king of the Franks into an emperor, we have nothing to show us how this transformation was conceived. One single, very obscure allusion may be gleaned from a letter by Alcuin to his friend Arno, archbishop of Salzburg, who had gone to Rome to receive the *pallium* in 798. Arno is asked to let him know 'whether, thanks to God, the project that he [Alcuin] so ardently desired to see fulfilled had any chance of success'. Was this to do with re-establishing the empire? And if so, can we put forward the hypothesis that Alcuin was counting on the pope to play an important part in promoting Charlemagne to an imperial status? We must be very cautious here, for it is not easy to admit that the same person who, two years earlier, had written the letter in which Charles had given a fairly categorical answer to Leo III's proposals, could have invited the pope in 798 to take the initiative in reviving the empire. Certainly it may be said in reply that Alcuin was not politically minded, and that the men of the year 800 could not foresee the consequences that would later be deduced from the way in which the empire was re-established. I prefer, however, not to build too much upon the part Alcuin may have assigned to Leo III, for there is another and connected difficulty arising from the Roman character of the empire. To become emperor meant to become emperor of the Romans. How could it then be possible to adapt the Roman empire to the kingdom of the Franks without profoundly modifying its structure? The sequel was to show that these two difficulties, the conditions of imperial accession and the Roman character of the empire, both arose after the great event of the year 800. How can one then suppose that a clear and precise plan had existed long before that time at the Frankish court for re-establishing the empire? Aspirations there may well have been, and an awareness of the fact of a Christian empire with Charles at its head; that much is certain, but nothing more.

Finally, there is no evidence enabling us to prejudge the thought of Charlemagne himself. It will be readily seen that he must have had some hesitations. But to go on from there and claim that he did not want the empire, and that when the moment came he let his hand be forced, is to take a very big step indeed. It would involve forgetting that he had long been pursuing a course dictated by his people's interests and his own personal prestige. Our conclusion must be that he made no specific declaration for the time being, but was wise enough to wait for an opportunity to take the decisive step.

Was this opportunity given to him by the events that took place in Rome during 799? This is the question which we must now try to answer.

As far as it is possible to know the cause of these disturbances, they would seem to have been fomented by a party among the Roman aristocracy. Disquieting charges of immorality had been made against Pope Leo III in 798. Informed of these by Arno, Alcuin was much alarmed; so was Charlemagne, who sent Count Germaire to Rome to enquire into the matter. But before he arrived, a revolt had broken out in the city. One can hardly believe that its sole cause can have been the possibly dubious morality of Leo III: there must have been more solid motives playing a decisive part in it. Was there a pro-Byzantine party among the Roman nobility, intent on turning Leo aside from his alliance with the Franks? This seems unlikely, if we remember that the insurrection's leaders, the *primicerius* Paul and the *sacellarius* Campulus, were both nephews of Hadrian. It seems more likely that the aristocracy wanted to make a forcible change in the internal administration of Rome and the Papal State in order to recover the influence of which the pope had deprived them for the benefit of the clerical bureaucracy in the Lateran, to which he had formerly belonged.

The incidents of 25 April 799 remain extremely obscure when we compare the papal sources—in this case the biography of Leo III in the *Liber Pontificalis*, drawn up some years after the events—and the sources on the Frankish side. The general picture emerging is something like the following. On 25 April, the Feast of St Mark, the pope had left his palace on horseback to go to the church of San Lorenzo in Lucina, where he was to head the procession of the Greater Litany, when he was attacked in front of the church of St Stephen and St Silvester by a group of men who threw him from his horse, assailed him with blows, and tried to put out his eyes and tear out his tongue, while the people fled in terror. According to the *Liber Pontificalis*, the pope was left for a while on the public highway, and then taken inside the church by the conspirators, who set upon him once more and finally threw him into a cell in the monastery adjoining the church. From there he was taken that evening to the Convent of St Erasmus on the Caelian Hill and entrusted to the abbot's care. His faithful attendants, led by the chamberlain Albinus, managed to rescue him from this prison and take him back to the Vatican. Meanwhile, a miracle is supposed to have happened: Leo III, who had been unable to see or to speak, recovered the use of both faculties. The count of Spoleto, hastening to Rome at the head of a small army, merely took the pope to the city that he governed, while everyone was expecting him to re-establish law and order in the capital. At Spoleto Leo III was met by Count Germaire, who may have persuaded him to join Charlemagne in Saxony— unless it was the pope himself who took the initiative.

This story, in the summary we have given from the *Liber Pontificalis,* where it seems to be made up of several successive traditions, is admittedly not very comprehensible. It would seem that Leo III, after the first rough handling on the public highway by men posted near the church of St Stephen and St Silvester, was then pushed by them into the sanctuary, where the leaders of the conspiracy were assembled. What took place next may be conjectured by analogy with the facts which marked the proceedings instituted on 7 August 768 against Pope Constantine II, and by interpreting the data of the Royal Annals, which stress the conspirators' intention to depose Leo III. He was no doubt deprived of the pontificate, degraded and stripped of his priestly vestments. The putting out of the eyes and cutting out of the tongue (though in this case only attempted) were quite usual in an affair of this kind, and these mutilations were familiar enough in Constantinople from the seventh century onwards. It was also customary to shut the fallen pope in a monastery. This would explain the pope's incarceration first at St Silvester's, then at St Erasmus's. In the eyes of the conspirators, this abbey, which belonged to the Greek rite, situated in the southern part of the city, seemed a more appropriate place of detention for the pope than the other, where communication with Spoleto might have been possible. This manœuvre was in the end foiled by the speed with which Leo III's retainers came to his rescue; but it is hard to see why the conspirators did not at once provide a successor to Leo III.

The news of the Roman insurrection spread north of the Alps in the course of May, as can be gathered from some allusions by Alcuin in a letter to Arno. Having received official information from Charlemagne, the abbot of Tours wrote to him in the course of the summer a number of letters. The most characteristic of them is the one where he analyses with firm strokes the current situation in the Christian world. One passage is worth quoting in its entirety:

> Up till now, three persons have been at the head of the world's hierarchy. The representative of apostolic sublimity, Vicar of the Blessed Peter, prince of the apostles, whose seat he occupies; and the fate that has overtaken the present holder of this office Your Grace has been good enough to communicate to me. Next comes the titular holder of the imperial dignity, who exercises temporal power in the Second Rome: and the impious fashion in which the head of this empire was deposed,[1] not by foreigners, but by his own people and fellow-citizens, has been noised abroad throughout the world. Then, third, there is the royal dignity which Our Saviour Jesus Christ has reserved for you, so that you may govern the Christian nation. It is to be ranked above the other two dignities, for it eclipses them and surpasses them in wisdom. Now it is upon you alone that the Churches of Christ rely, to you alone that they look for salvation, you who are the avenger of crimes, the guide of the erring, the consoler of the afflicted and the support of the godly.

In other words, the order of the world had been overthrown by the events in Rome and Constantinople; and it could be restored only by the man who, next to the pope and the emperor whose authority had failed, was the *persona in mundo altissima*. We can hardly fail to set this invitation to act alongside the thoughts

[1] An allusion to the dethronement of the Emperor Constantine VI in 797; see above, p. 90.

that were running in the minds of Pepin's contemporaries half a century earlier. In 751 the idea of the world's order had served to advance the Carolingians to their royal position; and now it reappeared as a pressing call to the Frankish king to restore the Holy See. God had dispensed to him a full measure of wisdom so that the Church might thereby be raised up and recover her security. The king must act on his own; it was for him, as *rector populi christiani*, to solve the Roman crisis. Alcuin thus confronted Charlemagne with his moral responsibility. He could not speak of the juridical situation, since he was well aware that any judicial action against the Roman conspirators lay outside the competence of the patrician, and belonged to the imperial jurisdiction.[1] Others too were aware of this, not least Charlemagne himself. It must then be recognised that any plan to re-establish order in the world by a papal restoration involved, at least implicitly, the question of the empire. At all events, as another of Alcuin's letters informs us, the king himself seemed at that moment to have made up his mind to intervene personally in Rome for the restoration of peace.

When this letter reached Charlemagne, he was at Paderborn in Saxony, where he had been joined by Leo III at the end of July. The pope was received with all the honours due to his rank. The king sent his son Charles to meet him, and received him in the company of an imposing assembly of lay and ecclesiastical notables, 'grouped around him like a crown, in imitation of the world', if we are to believe the testimony of a witness who was present at that first meeting. Nothing could have been more significant than the adoption of this order, in which the intermingling of state and Church dignitaries was a telling illustration of the interpenetration of the spiritual and the temporal in Charlemagne's circle.

About what passed between the king and the pope we know extremely little. Leo III had undertaken the long journey in order to plead his cause. Unfortunately for him, there arrived almost simultaneously letters from Rome accusing him of 'wicked and criminal acts', of immorality, perjury and adultery, and declaring him unworthy of his office. These documents created a very bad impression, which comes out especially in the laconic tone of the

[1] The link between the exercise of supreme justice in Rome and the imperial power is one of the essential insights of K. Heldmann's book, *Das Kaisertum Karls des Grossen*, 1928.

Frankish sources. They give no account of the conversations, but merely note that 'the pope was received with great honours, and after a certain time[1] was sent back to Rome again in the same manner.'

A little more information is contained in Alcuin's correspondence. He was absent from Paderborn, whither he had not been summoned, perhaps because the policy he supported was thought too absolute, and because his outspokenness was feared. None the less he carried on from a distance a vigorous campaign on behalf of Leo III. Faithful to western Christian tradition, he saw him as 'the pontiff chosen by God, the Vicar of the apostles, the heir of the Fathers, prince of the Churches, whom all should venerate and accept as the Confessor of Christ'. His letters to Charlemagne were at pains to show him that the pope's innocence was beyond question. By allowing him to escape from his enemies, God had shown how the dispute must be settled; moreover, He had vouchsafed to work a notable miracle for him in restoring both his sight and his speech. It may therefore be supposed that this rumour, spread by Leo and repeated later by his biographer, was already coming to be widely believed. The Romans alone were guilty: they must be severely chastised, and steps taken to ensure that the pope could once more serve Christ in all peace and security. The way in which this restoration is to be realised Alcuin leaves entirely to the king's wisdom, for he will know how 'to correct what is in need of redress and maintain what should be preserved'. In his letters to other correspondents, however, Alcuin confessed his anxieties about the attacks of Leo III's enemies. Thus in a letter written to Arno we are told that they had succeeded in sowing doubt at the Frankish court, where some were of the opinion that the pope should be required to purge himself by an oath,[2] while others whispered that he should be deposed from the papacy and made to retire to a monastery. Alcuin deplores the fact that Leo III should have let himself be drawn into discussion of the accusations against him, and would rather have him treat them with haughty indifference. There is only one solution—to reinstate him in Rome without his being judged or obliged to justify himself. Has he, the abbot of Tours

[1] At the beginning of October.

[2] It may be noted that this was the first reference to the method which was in fact used (after a certain lapse of time) as a way out of the crisis.

not read that a pope cannot be accused except on the deposition of seventy-two witnesses of irreproachable reputation? Alcuin also quotes the famous axiom dating from the time of Pope Symmachus, according to which the Holy See judges all men, but can be judged of none. Accordingly Arno is invited to press his advocacy of all these ideas with Charlemagne for 'the well-being of the head of the Church, the authority of the Holy See, and the integrity of the Catholic faith'. But what was decided at Paderborn? For a long time Alcuin had no information, and he expressed his anxiety to his friend Adalard of Corbie: what would he not give to know what words had passed between the eagle (the pope) and the lion (the king)! Was Leo III to be fully reinstated? Would the rebels submit, or raise their heads again? Would Charlemagne go to Rome? These were all questions the abbot of Tours kept asking himself with anxious impatience.

The decision finally taken by Charlemagne reflects the advice given him by his master. Leo was to be taken back to Rome as pope, under escort and accompanied by royal commissioners, who would open an enquiry on the spot into the grievances against the pope, pending the king's arrival in Rome to examine the case in person. This decision is clear enough, and needs no comment, which might perhaps distort it. In particular, there is no suggestion that Charlemagne was thinking of sitting in judgment upon Leo III; we rather get the impression that he was reserving his own initiative as the holder of a royal status directly inspired by God.

Were other matters discussed at Paderborn, apart from the fate of Leo III? We would put forward a cautious suggestion that the question of empire must at least have been raised. It may well be imagined that Alcuin's letter about the three supreme dignities may have aroused in certain minds the feeling that the hour had struck for taking up the imperial title on behalf of the Frankish king, who was assuming functions traditionally reserved for the Christian emperor. We may also mention here in passing, the news, reported after the event in the chronicle of the bishops of Naples, that the pope had promised Charlemagne the imperial dignity as a reward for his good offices. There is, however, another piece of evidence admitting us to what may be called the 'imperial atmosphere' at Paderborn.

This is the poem, *Charlemagne and Pope Leo*, written by an anonymous poet familiar with events in the Frankish court. The work celebrates in the epic and panegyrical style the meeting in Saxony between the king, the 'father of Europe', and the 'supreme pastor of the world'. It consists of two parts. The first begins with a rhapsodic eulogy of Charlemagne and his family, which is followed by the description of a hunting scene, and of the building of Aachen. The poet's imitation of the ancient model, the founding of Carthage described in the *Aeneid*, is so close that we are even presented with the building of a port in the vicinity of Aachen. The reader of these lines is finally left with the impression that the poet wishes to win the king's favour for a request he is about to make of him. This comes out in the second part of the poem, which is centred on Leo III's tribulations. The anonymous author relates the Roman insurrection, underlining the rebels' blinding of the pope and the tearing out of his tongue, and then his miraculous recovery of sight and speech. God thus made an open proclamation of his innocence: let Charlemagne be his just judge. Leo is represented as asking the king 'to examine our acts in just judgment'. Unfortunately, we do not know how the poem ends. Yet even in the form that has survived, it is fairly clearly a plea on behalf of the pope. It is almost certain that it was composed while the latter was staying at the Frankish court. What is the main impression that it makes on us?

There is no denying that the poet is very much on the side of the pope. On the level of the affections, there is no difference between him and Alcuin. At the most, he slightly strengthens the view of the abbot of Tours by putting into the pope's mouth a request for just judgment. He thus recognises Charlemagne's right to judge Leo III, which makes him seem at this point to be speaking on behalf of a whole group of the royal counsellors urging him to undertake judicial proceedings. Yet we must observe the improbability of the words our author ascribes to the pope. Their force is admittedly much weakened by the supernatural intervention in his favour, which is set forth here as a judgment of God.

But if the anonymous poet seems to be basically in agreement with Alcuin on this problem, the imperial idea showing through his work is of firmer mould than the scattered allusions in some of the letters from the abbot of Tours. Having reached the highest point of his power, Charlemagne was already an imperial figure; he was 'the beacon and the summit of Europe', the greatest of kings (*summus rex*), the head of the world (*caput orbis*). The geographical area over which his authority extends is called empire (*imperium*). 'As, by virtue of the high position of the empire, Charles is above all other kings, so he is superior to them all through his activity.' The poet is obviously recalling the definition of empire in terms of the supremacy exercised by its holder over kings. As for Charlemagne's activity (*ars*), he sums it up in the end by its principal characteristics of justice, power and generosity. Repeatedly the *summus rex* is called *Augustus*, the imperial description *par excellence*, in particular when the poet is describing the construction of Aachen, the New Rome, the Rome of the future. A commentator on this poem, H. Beumann, pertinently notes that the anonymous author must have known Alcuin's letter on the three powers, in which Constantinople figures as the second Rome; and he in his turn projects this title onto the capital of the Frankish state. The poem thus gives the impression of standing on the threshold of great events. However, although the Frankish state is already called an *imperium*, its holder does not cease to be the new David; and among the profusion of epithets adorning Charlemagne, we look in vain for the title *imperator*.

It cannot be doubted that the anonymous poet is voicing an opinion very widespread in court circles. The essential feature of his poem is that it transfers the empire's centre of gravity from Rome to Aachen. Whereas Alcuin's thought, as far as it concerns our theme, is directed towards the traditional Romano-Christian empire, our author's is undoubtedly marked by a certain originality. The Byzantine empire was not exactly the Roman empire; the empire whose future capital, Aachen, is here celebrated, will not be Roman either. We may venture to say that it will be an empire at most very superficially united with Rome, but with its heart beating at the very centre of Frankish power, between the Meuse and the Rhine. Already the poet had caught a glimpse of this idea; and, as we shall see later, the idea was never entirely lost.

In summing up, it may be surmised that the Frankish court had become in a certain measure aware of the traditional imperial mission incumbent upon Charlemagne in going to help the head of the Church. We may go even further and grant that the notion of a Christian-Roman, or Christian-Frankish, empire had become familiar to a small intellectual and religious elite, and that they considered it to be already in existence. However, we shall never know how they conceived of Charlemagne's transition from king to emperor, or whom they intended to be the agents of the transformation. The empire could be reborn only in Rome; and, this being granted, a role of the first importance belonged to the Romans and to the pope, their temporal and spiritual chief. But, as things stood, the pope's authority was gravely compromised. One can well understand that in these conditions Charlemagne felt the need to let the situation become clearer. That is no doubt why he was in no hurry to go to Rome. In fact he let a whole year go by after the meeting at Paderborn before he set out for Italy.

✧ IX ✧

The revival of the empire in
Rome on 25 December 800

We have only very incomplete information about the long period of time that elapsed between the meeting at Paderborn and the imperial coronation. If the *Liber Pontificalis* is to be believed, everything was already decided by the end of the conversations between Leo III and Charlemagne. 'On the advice of numerous archbishops, bishops and other churchmen, it was decided, with the consent of the most religious king, and the agreement of all the notables among the Franks, that the pontiff should be conducted back to Rome with honour.' The account given by the same source of the pope's solemn re-entry into his city certainly suggests that the question was closed, and that Leo III was completely restored to his functions, leaving no doubt at all about the authority with which he was invested. The Frankish delegation accompanying him consisted of persons of considerable importance: two archbishops, Arno of Salzburg and Hildebald of Cologne; five bishops, including Atto of Freising and Jesse of Amiens; and three counts, among them Germaire. They proceeded to hold an enquiry lasting more than a week, in the course of which (we are still following the *Liber*'s version) Leo's enemies had nothing to say. The *missi* finally arrested them and sent them to Francia. At first sight, it is surprising that the Royal Annals (an official source) say absolutely nothing about the activities of the royal commissioners. Is this perhaps an indication that their position was considered of minor importance? The *missi* had certainly been commissioned solely to concern themselves with the conspirators and to determine how far they were guilty; in no case were they required to take action against Leo III. Their essential role was to re-establish peace between the pope and the Romans. 'Most holy father,' wrote Alcuin to Arno, 'see that you bear the olive-branch into the Ark of the Lord.'

All the same, it seems that things were in fact a good deal less simple than the *Liber Pontificalis* would have us believe. It is by no means certain that all the Romans were enthusiastic in greeting the pope's return, and less certain still, perhaps, that the Frankish commissioners were entirely at one on all points. They were not all friends of Alcuin, and, according to him, some of them were not altogether beyond the temptations of bribery. Arno, on the other hand, would appear to have met with some insults in Rome. More seriously still, there were still rumours going round concerning Leo III's misdeeds, including perjury and adultery. On this subject Arno wrote so specific a letter to Alcuin that the latter thought it advisable to destroy it, so that it might not fall into unauthorised hands. But the more anxious the abbot of Tours became in face of these facts, the more unshakeably he was convinced that the unity and peace of the Church depended on Leo III's full restoration, whether he was innocent or guilty; besides, as he wrote to Arno, 'let him who is without sin cast the first stone!' Even more insistently than in the previous year he turned to Charlemagne. Let us look at one of his letters dated early in 800, already addressed in imperial terms to 'the great and invincible victor, as well as the most merciful ruler of kingdoms'. Its object was a double one:

May you exert your will, and the power ordained by God
that is given you, to defend the Catholic and apostolic faith
in all places [an allusion to the struggle against
Adoptionism]; and as you strive valiantly to extend the
Christian empire by force of arms, so may you do your
utmost to defend, teach and propagate the true apostolic faith
[note that there is still the same correlation between empire
and the triumph of the faith]. . . . May Almighty God
preserve and increase the power of your royal glory for the
exaltation and defence of the Holy Church, for the peace of
the Christian empire and for your own well-being, O most
cherished and well-beloved Lord.

In spite of the somewhat veiled terms in which he develops his thought, Alcuin considers empire as an increase in prestige for the royalty of the Franks. Its essential function will be to defend the Church—and once again we must underline the very general terms in which this message is couched. About the same time, no doubt, Theodulf was addressing to the king a poem which, although not referring to empire, was likewise an invitation to intervene in the pope's favour. St Peter, we read in the poem, desired to rescue the pope from every danger, and he has presently charged the king of France to accomplish this mission in his name. The Apostle has already restored his Vicar's health; he will now, through Charlemagne, restore him to his functions. To the pope belong the keys of heaven, to the king those which control the governance of clergy and people; for 'it is by thee', as he very significantly says, 'that the pontiffs hold and possess their sacred functions.'

It is to this kind of evidence that we must turn in order to surmise that north of the Alps the Roman question was still present in at least some men's minds. For official sources rather give the impression that it was overlaid by more pressing problems. After spending the winter of 799–800 at Aachen, Charlemagne paid a visit to the defences installed along the Channel coasts, where the Normans had just carried out their first raids. Then, travelling by way of Saint-Riquier and Rouen, he reached Tours, where he had long discussions with Alcuin. These were continued at Aachen, where the abbot of Saint-Martin took an active part in the council called together to condemn Adoptionism, and won a victory over its principal exponent, Felix of Urgel. It is hard to avoid the conjecture that the discussions between Charles and Alcuin must often have turned to the Roman question. What is certain at all events is that at short notice the king convened the general assembly of the realm at Mainz, where he is said to have declared that, now that there was peace in his dominions, he remembered the attack which had been made upon the pope, and that the moment had come for him to go to Italy in person. Charlemagne explained the object of his intervention in Rome some weeks later. Among other things that had led him to the Eternal City, he said, the most difficult and important—a matter that had already engaged his attention—was to discuss (literally, to dissipate by destroying) the accusations levelled against the pope. The essential meaning of these words is clear enough; but there remain the 'other considerations'. Should we see this as an allusion to his imperial promotion, on which he must no doubt have decided by then? Or an intention to achieve a final settlement of his relations with the pope by a new organisation of power in the Church? These two questions can only be put, but not answered.

And so, for the fifth time, Charlemagne crossed the Alps, accompanied by his eldest son, Charles, and a splendid escort of prelates, counts and warriors. He spent a week at Ravenna, where he was joined by Pepin, king of Italy, who accompanied him as far as Ancona, and then went on to conduct operations against the principality of Benevento. On 23 November Charlemagne arrived at the town of Nomentum (Mentana), twelve miles from Rome; here Leo III was waiting to receive him 'with the greatest humility and the greatest honours', as the Frankish Annals tell us. Under this concise description, M Déer has discovered the great changes introduced that year into the reception ceremony for the king of the Franks. Traditionally, the Byzantine Exarch had been received at the first milestone outside Rome, and the emperor at the sixth. The pope came out of Rome only when the emperor was visiting him. Now in 774 we are assured by the 'Life of Hadrian' in the *Liber Pontificalis* that Charlemagne was greeted by the pope and the Roman clergy 'in the same way as it was customary to receive the Exarch or the patrician'. We do not know what course the ceremonial followed during the Frankish king's two stays in Rome during 781 and 788. But in 800 Charles was greeted by the pope in person, not six but twelve miles from the city. In 774 the king may have walked from the first milestone to St Peter's; now it was on horseback, in the midst of a distinguished procession, with waving banners and accompanied by the acclamations of the crowd lining his route, that he proceeded all the way from Nomentum to the square in front of St Peter's. Leo III, who had parted from him the previous evening, was waiting for him at the top of the steps and led him into the basilica to the accompaniment of psalms. This particularly solemn entry into Rome was nothing else but the *adventus Caesaris*, the arrival of the emperor: there could be no doubt about it. The atmosphere was charged with expectation: could this be yet one more sign of the imperial rank of

Charlemagne now being recognised in Rome even before the moment of his official accession?

The subsequent facts are so divergently related by our sources that it is far from easy to make out what actually happened. It will therefore be as well to begin by comparing the various accounts. According to the Royal Annals, the king held an assembly eight days after his arrival in Rome to discuss the accusations against the pope. Now as no one came forward to support them, the pope took an oath of compurgation; but the annalist does not say whether it was imposed on him or whether he took it of his own accord. Next we have the *Annales Laureshamenses*, a very important source, to which we shall return:

> In Rome, the king gathered a great assembly of bishops and abbots with the priests, deacons, counts and the rest of the Christian people;[1] and there appeared before them those who wanted to condemn the apostolic lord. When the king realised that they were moved not by reasons relevant to justice but by envy, it seemed good to him and to the bishops and holy fathers present at the council that, if this were the pope's wish, and if he himself expressed this wish, he should purge himself by an oath, not because they judged this best, but of his own free will. And this was duly put into effect.

This source authorises us, it seems, to allow that there was a form of judicial proceedings against the pope, though they did not lead to any clear result concerning his innocence or guilt. In this situation, Charlemagne proposed a compromise, namely an oath of compurgation. The laboured insistence of the *Annales Laureshamenses* that Leo III took this oath of his own free will should not put us under any illusions: the oath was no doubt imposed upon him. The silence of the Royal Annals is much more eloquent than the efforts of the other sources to maintain the pope's freedom. Finally, there is yet another version of the facts in the *Liber Pontificalis*. After reminding us that Charlemagne had called together in St Peter's an assembly of Churchmen and Roman and Frankish laity, Leo III's biographer continues:

[1] That is to say, the Romans and the Franks in Charlemagne's entourage, who were considered to represent, along with the others, the Christian people.

The great king and the most blessed pontiff took their places, and invited the archbishops, bishops and abbots to be seated, while the priests and Roman and Frankish *optimates* [notables] remained standing. The business before them was to expunge [literally, to file off] the crimes of which the august pontiff had been accused. When they heard this, they all declared with one voice: 'We dare not judge the apostolic see, which is the head of all the Churches of God; we are all judged by Him and His Vicar, who is judged by none; this has been the custom since the earliest ages. As the supreme pontiff decides, so we shall obey according to the canons.'

As for the venerable bishop, he answered as follows: 'I wish to follow in the footsteps of my venerable predecessors, and I am willing to purge myself of the calumnies that have been shamefully levelled against me.' This oath was to be taken by Leo *alia vero die*, on another day. Altogether, then, there are three accounts, basically very different: in the first, there was no discussion of the crimes imputed to the pope; in the second, accusations were formulated against him in the presence of the king, who took up a definite position; if the third is to be believed, no accuser came forward, and the assembly refused to judge the pope. But each of these accounts ends with a common element, the oath of compurgation. What are we to make of it all?

First, we can conclude that, contrary to Alcuin's recommendations, Charlemagne did not act on his own. No doubt because of the persistent rumours going round about the pope's unworthiness, he convened an assembly, a synod composed of both Romans and Franks. The deliberations were begun a week after the king's arrival, and went on during the following days, ending with a plenary session on 23 December. First there was an examination of the complaints against Leo III; as at Paderborn, and as in the enquiry held by the *missi*, it transpired—the *Annales Laureshamenses* explicitly say so—that the pope had been condemned out of hatred, and no witness came forward to confirm the accusations that had been levelled against him. Furthermore, there were mutual accusations among the conspirators as to their responsibility for the injustice committed against Leo III. In these circumstances, the examination of the case for which

Charlemagne had come to Rome rapidly changed into a trial of the instigators of the revolt. It seems also that this turn of events was helped by the scruples of at any rate the majority of the council's members, who refused to judge the pope. On this point the evidence of the *Liber Pontificalis* is authentic, and fits in with Alcuin's advice to Charlemagne; this would explain the king's lack of surprise at the declaration that the Holy See could not be judged by any man. But if this was the majority opinion, there must have been some Romans who thought otherwise, as well as some Franks who must have been impressed since the meeting at Paderborn by the accusations levelled against Leo III.

Thus Charlemagne imposed a compromise calculated to satisfy the majority as well as the minority. This was the oath of compurgation, which was taken by the accused in Germanic law when the accusation could not be supported by any proof. Leo III submitted to this requirement, and the oath was taken on 23 December, in the presence of the council assembled in St Peter's. Charlemagne presided over it, with Leo III seated beside him. The archbishops, bishops and abbots were seated, the other clerics and laymen, Romans and Franks, representing the whole body of Christians, stood round them in accordance with the order adopted by councils in the Frankish kingdom. Leo mounted the pulpit, holding the Gospel above his head, and pronounced the solemn oath. L. Wallach has shown that the formula, as it has come down to us, is apocryphal, and we are reduced to the very brief wording of the *Liber Pontificalis*: 'Of these false crimes heaped upon me by the Romans who unjustly persecuted me' (the pope is represented as saying) 'I know nothing, nor do I acknowledge having committed any of them.' It has been observed that this formula—if it really was pronounced—was equivalent to a 'public declaration of good conscience'; but it is certain—as our texts imply—that contemporaries considered it a *iusiurandum* or *sacramentum*, in other words a solemn oath. In submitting to this procedure, Leo III was imitating one of his predecessors, Pelagius I, who had used this form of public disclaimer, but without in any way binding his successors. The joy and relief of all those present expressed itself in the Te Deum which followed Leo's declaration. As regards the chief conspirators, they were judged some days later, not for their accusations against the pope, but for having disturbed public order by their attempt to depose him. They thus came under the law of *maiestas* which was to be applied by the new emperor.

The assembly of 23 December did not, however, confine itself to receiving the pope's solemn oath. Once Leo III's case had been settled, the prelates, clerics and laymen discussed the re-establishment of the empire. There is a source which many historians have long rejected because its interpretation of events seems of a *post hoc* and tendentious kind, but which modern criticism has shown to be entirely authentic: the *Annales Laureshamenses,* or Annals of Lorsch, already quoted above. These leave us in no doubt about this central fact. They cover the period 785–803; and in all probability their compiler was Ricbod, abbot of the famous monastery since 784, and then, while still retaining his abbacy, archbishop of Trier from 791 to 804. He too was a pupil and friend of Alcuin, and bore the name of Macharius in the Academy circle. The abbot of Tours speaks glowingly of his taste for Virgil and his profound knowledge of the Bible. These Annals generally provide a very useful supplement to what we know from the official sources. Whether they are dealing with Tassilo of Bavaria's deposition, or the Council of Frankfurt, or the Saxon campaigns at the end of the eighth century, or the expeditions against the Avars, all the comments bear the mark of an author remarkably well informed about what he was reporting. Fichtenau has succeeded in showing the existence of a whole private information service at his disposal, and even in naming some of the archbishop's probable informants—Bernard, archbishop of Sens and abbot of Echternach for Saxon affairs, Arno for the war against the Avars. This being so, why should we reject *a priori* Ricbod's account of the events in Rome? True, he did not accompany Charlemagne to Rome, but he was able to receive an account of what took place during those memorable days through his friend, Archbishop Riculf of Mainz, an eye-witness of the facts, whom he had an opportunity to see on his return. We should therefore pay due attention to the very precise tones of the *Annales Laureshamenses*, though of course without overlooking the personal element in the author's presentation of the story.

This source gives us the substance of the arguments put before Charlemagne by the assembly on the 23 December. The *nomen imperatoris* (that is, the title of emperor and the imperial dignity combined) was held to be vacant in Constantinople, where the empire had fallen into a woman's hands. The king of the Franks was in possession not only of Rome, where the emperors were formerly wont to reside, but also of the other imperial residences in Italy, in Gaul and in Germania. By the will of God, all these 'seats' had fallen into his power. Thus he was marked out by God to be chosen by the bishops and the Christian community. Therefore all the members of the assembly, the pope, the bishops and the laymen representing Christians as a whole, deemed it fit and proper that the imperial title should be conferred upon Charlemagne.

The terms in which this line of thought was expressed will require to be carefully assessed. The assembly's starting-point was two solid facts: first, the usurpation of Irene, which had been judged illegal in Constantinople itself by a whole party, which had offered the empire to Charlemagne in 798. In these circumstances there was nothing at all abnormal in talking about the vacancy of the imperial title. Second, in contrast with the crisis raging in the traditional empire, there was the picture of the Roman west unified under the rule of the Frankish king. We rediscover in the Annals the idea inscribed at the head of the Caroline Books: Italy, Gaul and Germania all ruled by Charlemagne. There are, however, two slight differences. Rome is explicitly mentioned—a reflection of the development that had taken place between 795 and 800, from Hadrian's time to that of Leo III. Second, it was now not so much a question of naming the sum total of Charlemagne's territories as the imperial residences in which he had become the successor of the Caesars of old: Rome of course, but also Ravenna and Milan in Italy, Arles, Lyon, Paris and Trier in Gaul. What *sedes* could Ricbod have had in mind in Germania? Perhaps former Roman towns that had become Carolingian residences, such as Worms and Aachen. This allusion to the western 'capitals' admittedly suggests the author's own thinking; nevertheless, there must have risen before the members of the Roman assembly the vision of a *pars occidentis*, comprising the former imperial provinces, under Charlemagne's rule. This double awareness led on to a logical conclusion: the king of the Franks, already wielding the effective power (*potestas*) in one zone of the empire, ought to receive the name of emperor (*nomen imperatoris*), valid not only for the west, but for the whole empire, of which Rome was the true metropolis. *Potestas* and *nomen*: this combination, in the background of Pepin's accession to the throne half a century before, now reappears in the full light of day. The *nomen imperatoris* has lost its real content; and Charlemagne's *de facto* power, acquired by his own efforts, needs only to be clothed with the impressive title to re-establish the world order which has been distorted by the disparity between theory and reality. Thus the proclamation of the empire, as set forth by the *Annales Laureshamenses*, would fit into the line of political thought emerging in 751, in the Caroline Books, and later in Alcuin's letter on the subject of the three powers.

Whatever may be our general interpretation, it cannot be denied that the initiative for these overtures to Charlemagne belonged to the council as a whole and not to the pope alone, and that the council included, along with the Romans—who, by tradition, bestowed the rank of emperor—Franks who represented the *universus christianus populus*. This combination of Romans and Franks together proposing to re-establish the imperial title for Charlemagne surely corresponds to the picture of the Romano-Christian empire glimpsed by Alcuin. We can hardly avoid conjecturing that an important share in the assembly's discussions, and perhaps even more of the preliminary conversations, must have been taken by the friends of the abbot of Tours, men who knew his thoughts and hopes, such as Arno, Hildebald, Riculf and others, including Wizzo, a Monk of Saint-Martin, sent to Italy by his abbot to keep him in touch with developments.

As for Charlemagne, the Annals tell us that he 'was unwilling to reject the petition of the bishops and people'; he accepted the proffered title—*imperii nomen suscepit*. Faced with the unanimous desire, he decided to accede to it. We have not up to this point seen any declaration of imperial ambitions on his part. But it is certain that he must have been gradually impelled towards empire by a variety of circumstances, and basically by a current of opinion ultimately originating in the Carolingian Renaissance. On 23 December the situation seemed to him sufficiently developed to warrant the decisive step.

We must, then, be grateful to Ricbod for having preserved for us such a faithful echo of the discussions of 23 December, and for expressing himself with such clarity. Fichtenau has subjected his style to the minutest scrutiny, and revealed certain borrowings from the language of some of Charlemagne's diplomas, in particular those that embody judgments pronounced by the king. This observation is of some importance, for it suggests that the compiler intended to create the atmosphere of a judicial proceeding. It is striking, too, that, in the later traditions referring to Charlemagne, this debate sometimes figures as an imperial election in the full sense of the term. As always, legend has hardened the outlines and simplified the tradition. On 23 December 800 Charlemagne was not elected emperor. But a wish was expressed by the Romans and the Franks, which encouraged him to take the imperial title. He assumed the *nomen imperatoris,* and therefore became emperor. Without the help of the *Annales Laureshamenses* we should be sadly astray in our interpretation of the events of Christmas Day 800.

But before reaching that point we must take note of a further act of homage offered to Charlemagne on 23 December from a distant quarter of the Christian world. It came from the Holy Land, whose defence had been assumed by the king of the Franks since 787, replacing the Byzantine empire in this function while it was preoccupied with wars against the Caliphate of Bagdad. Charlemagne thus resumed with Harun al Rashid the relations his father had had with the Abbasid state in the last part of his life. An embassy was despatched to Bagdad to beg the Caliph to put an end to the vexations—not habitual, it should be stressed—from which the Christian communities of Palestine were suffering at the hands of his subjects. This embassy also passed through the Holy Land, distributing alms from the Frankish king among the local churches. In this way contact was made with the patriarch of Jerusalem, leading to an exchange of honours and presents. Thus Charles's messenger to the Holy Places arrived back in Rome on 23 December, accompanied by two Palestinian monks bringing to the king from the patriarch the keys of the Holy Sepulchre and Calvary, together with those of the Holy City and Mount Sion, as well as a standard. This gesture reminds us of the similar action by Leo III some years earlier, and has very much the same significance. The keys in question were a religious symbol, a pledge of blessing from the head of the Christian Church in Palestine. The despatch of a standard had a further significance: it could be interpreted, if not as a sign of investiture properly speaking—for the patriarch, unlike the pope, could not dispose of the city—at least as a symbol of the protection for which the city of Jerusalem looked to Charlemagne. Coming from the head of Palestinian Christianity, this homage did not fail to produce a tremendous impression in Rome, and must have provided a further argument, if any was needed, for those who had offered Charlemagne the *nomen imperatoris*.

It remained only to express Charlemagne's promotion to the empire in an official ceremony. This took place two days later, on Christmas Day. Before analysing the acts and gestures constituting the rite, we shall make a few remarks that will pave the way for their easier understanding. One has only to glance at the sources which relate the event to see that their accounts differ considerably from each other. The *Annales Laureshamenses* are content to note, with their usual conciseness, that Charlemagne was consecrated emperor by Pope Leo III. The Royal Annals, however, allow us to catch a glimpse of what took place in St Peter's; and their account is reproduced, though with some modifications, by the narrative in the *Liber Pontificalis*. From these three major sources come all the echoes handed on by the others. On the other hand the remark by Charles's biographer Einhard, that his master felt dissatisfied after the imperial coronation, would appear to stand in complete isolation. Now criticism has sifted these data as thoroughly as possible, and efforts have been made to introduce a distinction between the so-called official sources and the unofficial ones, between contemporary sources and those written after a certain lapse of time, and between Roman and Frankish sources. The result has been to make the picture of Charlemagne's coronation entirely dependent on the degree of credibility accorded to one document rather than another. But today this matter is looked at rather differently. A contemporary historian, P. E. Schramm, thinks that for our purposes the traditional criteria of criticism should be set aside:[1]

> An event as unusual as that of 25 December [he writes] may well have been understood and related in several ways by different spectators; and the picture of it may well have been influenced by later controversy, and so been modified. So the historian must not confine himself to revealing the con-

[1] In the article cited above p. 113.

traditions between one text and another; he must explain why and how these contradictions arose.

This is therefore the point of view that I myself adopt, and I shall therefore do my best to take all the documents into account and to understand their influence and underlying significance.

The proclamation of the empire certainly was an unusual event for the west. According to what rites would it be performed? The Roman Church did not possess any of its own; it was therefore compelled to look to Constantinople, which had a fully developed liturgy for the imperial accession. It comprised in particular the principal rite, the acclamation, recognising the emperor as the elect of God; the coronation of the emperor by the patriarch of Constantinople, which had only gradually become a religious rite, and was never regarded as more than a 'corroboration' or confirmation of the election to the empire; and finally the adoration (proscynesis) of the emperor by the patriarch and the other high dignitaries of court and state, who thus acknowledged that they were the subjects of a prince clothed with a sacred dignity. Now examination of the documents bearing on Charlemagne's coronation shows that the Byzantine rites were in fact followed, but only up to a certain point. The differences we shall note can hardly be ascribed to improvisation. On the contrary, they reveal some very exact thinking on the part of Leo III, who indisputably played the leading role in the ceremony. It must be strongly stressed that there was a profound difference between the pope who on 23 December had exonerated himself by solemn oath and was then among those who offered Charlemagne the Empire, and the pope on 25 December who crowned the Frankish king. Leo III had regained the initiative, and proceeded to organise Charles's accession to the empire in such a way as to make certain that he himself would play the main part in it.

Let us now imagine ourselves in St Peter's on the morning of 25 December, when the Christmas Day Mass was about to be celebrated by Leo III. The basilica was filled with a great company of people, Romans mingling with Franks, just as their representatives had done two days before. It is generally forgotten that the choice of the Vatican basilica was not in accordance with the usual procedure, under which the ceremony normally took place at the church of Santa Maria Maggiore. This detail alone would be enough to suggest that the whole setting had been most carefully arranged. Fixing the Vatican basilica as the place where the rites should be performed provided a grander setting, which was calculated to impress not only the Romans, but also the Franks, among whom the cult of St Peter had long been very popular. Incidentally, this precedent established a custom: henceforward— with very rare exceptions, usually brought about by outside circumstances—emperors were crowned at St Peter's up to the end of the Middle Ages.

We shall now follow as closely as possible the way the ritual was actually performed.

Before the beginning of Mass, Charlemagne, accompanied by his son, who was to receive royal unction that day, had prostrated himself before the Confession of St Peter. When the king rose to his feet, the pope placed a crown on his head. This was the first act of the ceremony. It would certainly be pointless to consider what crown was used by Leo III, but for a suggestion—very tempting at first sight—advanced in recent years, namely that the crown was the one worn by the king of the Franks when he entered the church and removed from his head when he went to meditate before the apostle's tomb. By taking this suggestion to its limits, historians have pictured the coronation of Charles by the pope as basically no more than 'a festal coronation', a solemn placing of the diadem upon the sovereign's head, a kind of restitution to him by a high dignitary of the Church of what he had himself taken off out of humility. I cannot subscribe to this view, for though such *Festkrönungen* do certainly appear in our records from the tenth and eleventh century onwards, there is nothing to show that they already existed in the Frankish period. Furthermore, there is no certain documentary evidence that the crown was part of the Frankish royal insignia before the year 800. In the second form of the *Laudes*, the expression *a Deo coronatus* is a translation of a Byzantine formula, but does not necessarily imply any material object. It may therefore be said that the first coronation of a Frankish king was in fact the coronation of Charlemagne as emperor. Let us agree that this diadem came from the treasury of St Peter's, which must have possessed a number of them; and let us further note—as Leo III's biographer tells us— that it was 'most precious'. But what is much more important is that the handing over of the crown was accompanied by a prayer said by the pope. The very precise term 'consecration' used in the *Annales Laureshamenses* leaves no doubt on this point. The word *consecratio* in an episcopal ordination meant the form of blessing which admitted the candidate into the order of bishops; and since 751 Frankish sources had also spoken of the 'consecration' of the king. So it is clear that Leo III pronounced aloud a form of blessing; and whether it was short, like the one used by the patriarch of Constantinople when handing the diadem to the *basileus*—'in the name of the Father, the Son and the Holy Spirit'—or something longer, we do not know. The essential point is that contemporaries interpreted this 'benediction' or 'consecration' as a sign of Charlemagne's accession to a sacred function or 'order'; it was thus a sign of his ordination, in the strict sense of that term. Finally, let us dispose of a constantly repeated error. Consecration did not as yet necessarily mean anointing. At that time, Rome had not yet adopted the anointing of bishops, nor did it occur in the Byzantine ceremonial for the emperor. Charlemagne was not anointed emperor, but simply crowned, or—if the term is preferred —'ordained'. It was his son of the same name, Charles, who during this same Christmas Mass was anointed by the pope with holy oil, as his younger brothers Louis and Pepin had been in 781.

Here then was Charlemagne, with the crown on his head, kneeling before the Confession of St Peter. At that moment there burst forth from the crowded congregation the acclamation whose wording has been preserved for us both by the Royal Annals and the *Liber Pontificalis*: 'Long life and victory to Charles Augustus, crowned by God, great and peaceful Emperor of the Romans.'[1] There is no difficulty in recognising the formula contained in the *Laudes*, though with this difference, that the titles 'Augustus' and 'Emperor' have taken the place of the royal predicates. According to the *Liber Pontificalis*, the acclamation was repeated three times, and 'they called on the name of numerous saints', which would suggest that the initial acclamation was followed by the invocations contained in the *Laudes*. This moment is surrounded by a number of obscurities. In the imperial Roman accession rite, as it continued to exist in Constantinople, the acclamation possessed

[1] Both sources contain slight variants: in the *Liber Pontificalis*, the title Augustus is preceded by the epithet 'most pious'; on the other hand, 'Emperor *of the Romans*' does not occur in the Royal Annals, but the determinant 'Romans' comes a little later on in the *Liber Pontificalis*.

constituent force: when pronounced by the Senate and the army, it was considered tantamount to the prince's election; it created the emperor. This is the character obviously recalled by the compiler of the account in the *Liber Pontificalis*, when he concludes with the remark: 'And so by all present he was constituted emperor of the Romans.' But this first impression is diminished by the invocation of several saints, in which we have discovered an echo of the *Laudes*. Now these do not have, and never can, any constitutive force; they are simply a profound recognition that the wearer of the crown is the elect of God. This at once raises the question whether the acclamation of 25 December had constituent force, or was simply a recognition of the imperial quality just conferred on Charlemagne by the placing of the crown upon his head. There is no lack of documents alluding to the election of Pepin's son by the Roman people; and the time was soon to come when the Roman nobility saw the imperial acclamation of Christmas 800 as a revival of their own right to dispose of the empire. But things had not yet reached that stage; and on this Christmas Day the acclamation properly speaking and the *Laudes* were probably intermingled in one tumultuous chorus of voices in which, as E. H. Kantorowicz writes, 'it would be futile to try and distinguish what was constituent from what was not.' One fact alone remains certain and extremely important: it was Leo III's action that was the signal for the universal shout.

The full importance of this fact can be seen by looking at it in parallel with the order of the rites established in the Byzantine imperial liturgy. In Constantinople, the emperor's coronation by the patriarch followed upon 'election' by the army, the Senate and the people. In St Peter's, however, Charlemagne's coronation took place before the acclamation. If Leo III had crowned Charles after the acclamation, he would have been acting as the people's mandatory, or rather, as that of the ecclesiastical and lay assembly which had promoted the Frankish king to the imperial status. He would have been imitating the patriarch, who conferred on the emperor elect the outward and visible sign of his office. But he made a point of preceding the acclamation by crowning Charles 'with his own hands', as the *Liber Pontificalis* most significantly observes. He acted in his capacity of head of the Roman Church; and as such he was the first and most important of the actors, the others not doing more than ratifying his gesture and recognising

that he had acted—and here again we quote the *Liber Pontificalis*—
'according to the will of God and the blessed Peter, who holds the
keys to the kingdom of Heaven', and that the act confirmed 'the
exceeding great defence and love of the Frankish king testified by
him to the Church of Rome and its Vicar'. In other words, the
inversion of the rites—which was undoubtedly the result of
careful forethought—set forth Charlemagne as the emperor
crowned by the pope, as the emperor whom Leo III was thus
aiming to bind to his own person, to the see of St Peter and to the
'holy Roman republic', whose head—it must not be forgotten—
possessed imperial attributes and status. Hence the acclamation
was reduced to a quite secondary role, and the highly important
act of 23 December was overshadowed by Leo III's initiative,
which had made him assume the part of a creator of an emperor.
In this way, from the moment of its revival, the western empire
was encumbered with a burden of debt which it never managed
to throw off.

Finally, it is equally remarkable that the *Liber Pontificalis* should
avoid mentioning the third and last of the rites constituting
Charlemagne's accession to the imperial dignity. The Royal
Annals alone inform us that after the ending of the *Laudes* the
new emperor was, like his predecessors, 'adored' by the pope.
This adoration corresponded to the Byzantine rite of proscynesis.
Leo III was acting like the patriarch, and so paying to Charlemagne the supreme homage reserved for the emperor alone. Who
can ever say what impression was produced by this rite upon the
man who, in the Caroline Books, had been so harsh in denunciation of the 'idolatry' which was displayed at Constantinople.
Leo III must certainly have regretted his action—hence the silence
of the *Liber Pontificalis*; and never again did proscynesis form
part of the imperial ceremonial in the west.

Such were the rites that made Charlemagne an emperor. 'Having
laid aside the title of patrician,' write the Royal Annals, 'he was
henceforth called emperor and Augustus.' The empire had come
into existence, but not—it must at once be added—in a form that
entirely satisfied its recipient. For we cannot ignore a remark
made by Einhard. When he recalls in his *Vita Karoli* Charlemagne's last sojourn in Rome, in the course of which he received
the *nomen* of emperor and Augustus, he remarks on this subject
that 'at first [*primo*] Charles was so averse to it that he said he

15 *Illustrations referring to Louis the Pious* (see also overleaf)
A seal (from E. C. F. Babelon, *Histoire de la gravure sur gemmes en France*,
Paris, 1902, pl. IV, 1): an antique gem of the same type as the seal of
Charlemagne.

 An imperial bull: see below, no. 19.

 A coin (from Maurice Prou, *Catalogue des monnaies françaises de la Bibl.
nat.*, Paris, no. 994): a denier, like no. 57 in fig. 13. Legends: Louis
Emperor Augustus; Christian Religion.

The Christian Sovereign wearing the cross and the shield of the faith
(from P. E. Schramm, *Die deutschen Kaiser und Könige*). MS. 652 in the
National Library of Vienna, the work of the Fulda school (836–40). The
emperor's portrait stands out against a background consisting of the first
fifty lines of the *Liber de Laudibus S. Crucis* by Walafrid Strabo, abbot of
Reichenau.

16 *The Emperor Lothair I*
Miniature from a gospel made at his request at the abbey of Saint-Martin
de Tours about 850 (Bibl. nat., Lat. 266).

The emperor in majesty, seated on a throne between two warriors; his
head is crowned, and he wears a flowing mantle, fastened on the right
shoulder by a buckle, and holds a long sceptre ending in a knob.

17 *Charles the Bald receiving the Bible from Vivian*
Middle of the ninth century, the work of the Tours school (Bibl. nat.,
Lat. 1).

Charles the Bald is seated on a high-backed throne under a portico
draped with hangings, wearing his crown and holding the long sceptre.
He is surrounded by dignitaries and warriors, and is bending towards
Vivian, abbot of Saint-Martin, who has come in procession to present the
Bible specially made for him. Above him, the hand of God sheds forth its
beams; and in the top corners there are two female figures (Virtues)
holding out crowns.

would never have set foot in the church that day if he had been able to foresee the pope's intention, in spite of its being such a solemn feast day.' These words are much more than a sudden outburst of ill-temper or a 'historic saying': they are irrefutable evidence which must certainly be taken into account. Not that it should be set alongside the *Annales Maximiani*, according to which Charlemagne was crowned emperor without knowing what the pope intended to do (*nesciente domino Karolo*). From this, certain historians had concluded that the king of the Franks did not desire the empire, and that Leo's gesture took him by surprise. This misinterpretation has however been cleared up by L. Levillain, who has recognised in these Annals a simple recasting of the Royal Annals, and has shown that Charles could not have been either surprised or displeased with the re-establishment of the empire as such, to which he had himself agreed, according to the testimony of the *Annales Laureshamenses*. For a correct interpretation of Einhard's words, we must in the first place remember that this writer was steeped in the Carolingian renaissance, and full of reminiscences of antiquity. The imperial Roman biographies which helped him to fill out his narrative are full of examples of emperors—good emperors—who at first refused the dignity to which they had been raised, for this note of humility was a requisite element in the portrait of an ideal prince. In the ecclesiastical world, too, it was considered correct for a newly elected bishop to refuse for a moment the honour conferred upon him. But we must pass beyond the dictates of convention, and not isolate Einhard's remark from its context. Following the same train of thought, Charlemagne's biographer is careful to show us at least one cause of the emperor's first aversion: he had a foreboding of the irritation his coronation would provoke in Constantinople. But Einhard at once adds that Charles's patience and magnanimity triumphed in the end over the ill-will of the Byzantine rulers. It must never be forgotten that the primary purpose of the *Vita Karoli* is to be a moral portrait of the emperor, and to show how his lofty qualities enabled him to get the better of his most dangerous rivals.

It seems, however, that Einhard's explanation needs to be completed. Charlemagne's discontent may also be explained by the way in which the ceremony of 25 December was performed. The coronation preceding the acclamation; the role adopted by

Leo III and the Romans, which made them appear as the joint dispensers of the imperial dignity; the very secondary place occupied by the Franks in this procedure; the utterly ill-defined scope of the imperial title: all these were points that must have been a considerable embarrassment to the new Caesar. And these are certainly no mere suppositions, as is proved by one fundamental fact: from 25 December 800 up to the year 813, Charlemagne never ceased to clarify—even to correct—the situation arising from the rebirth of the western empire. And so the imperial promotion of Christmas Day is only one striking link in a chain of facts beginning in the last decade of the eighth century and continuing to the eve of Charlemagne's death.

The empire in theory
and practice

The days immediately following the imperial coronation take on a very different look according to whether they are viewed from Rome itself, or from Charlemagne's entourage.

In Rome, the situation seemed to be suddenly clarified. 'History, tradition, and written law defined the *imperator*'s prerogatives beyond any shadow of doubt,' says L. Duchesne; 'the Emperor was sovereign in Rome: everyone, including the pope, was subject to him.' From now onwards, everything went on as though the slender link between Rome and Constantinople had been severed, and as though the imperial dignity gave Charles, in the city and in the Papal State, a more definite authority than he had possessed before. There were several signs, moreover, that the days when Rome had been without an emperor were at an end. From 801 onwards Leo III dated his acts by the imperial years, and even—no doubt in order to restore fully the ancient tradition—by the years of Charlemagne's consulate. The coins struck in Rome bore on one side the pope's monogram and the inscription *SC Petrus,* and on the other, Charles's name and the imperial title. Finally, the subsequent letters written to Charles by Leo III are drawn up in the official form of correspondence *ad principem* (to the emperor) and are addressed: 'to our most pious and serene son, victor triumphant, lover of Christ and God, Charles Augustus', and end with the wish that 'the grace of the Most High may preserve the Lord's most holy empire and subdue all the nations under its feet.' Thus the pope and the Romans had once more found a master to whom they could swear allegiance like all the other subjects of the empire. But this emperor was their own creation: in their eyes, this reborn empire was the empire of the Romans.

But this was not at all Charlemagne's view of things. His conception of the empire was infinitely more subtle and complex; it gradually comes out through precise pieces of evidence, the first of which appear in 801–2, and it continues to be elaborated during the years that followed. Let us look at the beginnings of this development.

To start with, we are somewhat in the dark, for we possess knowledge of only one sovereign act by Charlemagne as emperor soon after the Christmas festival: his judgment on the conspirators of the year 799. It will be remembered that they were condemned in the name of the Roman law of *maiestas*. This is all we have over a period of many weeks. Was this time taken up, as some historians have conjectured, by conversations with Leo III leading to an exact definition of the implications of the imperial coronation? This might well be suggested by the slowness with which Charlemagne's title was established. As it appears on the first diploma we have from the year 801 (given in March in respect of the bishopric of Arezzo), it is, strangely enough, still the royal title, incidentally in an irregular form, 'king of the Franks and the Romans, as well as the Lombards'. Some have deduced from this that Charles avoided calling himself emperor. In fact, the text has come down to us only in a copy from the end of the ninth century, and there is some likelihood that a copyist's error has crept in. It has also been suggested that the text of 801 may have been drawn up before the imperial coronation. I prefer to conjecture, along with others, that the chancery was reluctant to fix the imperial title before finding the formula corresponding most accurately to Charlemagne's own ideas. A second document gives evidence that a step in this direction had already been taken. In a capitulary for the kingdom of Italy the superscription is as follows: 'Charles, crowned by the will of God [*nutu Dei*], ruling [*regens*] the Roman Empire, Most Serene Augustus.' There are three elements here, the first coming from the title of the Caroline Books, like the word *regens* in the following element, where the Roman empire has replaced the enumeration of the three provinces; and the third element is composed of the imperial predicate *par excellence.* The clear impression given by the whole is that the writer of the capitulary is in the process of discovering the notion of a Roman empire governed by an emperor who does not reside in Rome.

It was on 29 May, in a diploma issued at Reno in the territory of Bologna, that the full imperial title made its appearance in the form it maintained almost to the end of the reign: 'Charles, Most Serene Augustus, crowned by God, great and peaceful Emperor, governing the Roman Empire, and by the mercy of God, king of the Lombards and the Franks.' In its unaccustomed length, the title is at first reminiscent of the royal *Laudes*, but with slight differences ('most excellent, crowned by God, great and peaceful king of the Lombards and Franks'). It was from this, as we have already mentioned, that the acclamations were derived which had re-echoed through St Peter's. But between the imperial predicates and the double expression of royalty there has been inserted the formula *Romanum gubernans Imperium.* Contrary to what was long supposed, this is no new formula, and it can in no way be adduced in support of the hypothesis that Charles had some reservations about accepting his new dignity. On similar grounds it was also thought that by adopting this element into his title Charles intended to spare the feelings of the Byzantines. Now recent research has shown that, far from being new, the expression *gubernans* etc. was traditional. It occurs in the *Corpus Juris* and in the forms of solemn oaths used in Italy up to the middle of the eighth century. Perhaps it was in the archives at Ravenna, where Charles stayed in May 801 on his way back to Aachen, that the Frankish chancery came into contact with this formula.[1] Having thus thrown light on the origin of this title, we must now attempt to get a good grasp of its significance. On what grounds could Charlemagne have been reluctant to take the title emperor of the Romans to replace that of patrician of the Romans, the title he had borne up to the year 800? The most probable answer to this question is the one proposed by H. Beumann: because in the eyes of the Franks and the Lombards, the title *Imperator Romanorum* would have made the Romans, that is to say the inhabitants of the Eternal City, the dominant people in the new empire. Now Charlemagne did not want to introduce any changes into the structure of his states: he intended to remain king of the Franks

[1] P. Classen, 'Romanum gubernans Imperium', *Deutsches Archiv*, 9, 1951.

and the Lombards. Hence the persistence of his old title, expressing the personal character of his rule over these two peoples. On the other hand the expression '*Romanum gubernans Imperium*', which derived from Justinian, would express the essence of the imperial magistracy, exalted above the level of personal royalty. It belonged to an institution separate from the prince's person, the Romano-Christian empire. Now since Christ is the true emperor of that Empire—'He whose banner [that is, the cross] is followed into battle by our cohorts', as the Caroline Books stated—it is by no means impossible that Charlemagne may have renounced the title of *Imperator Romani Imperii* out of humility. On that view, the title 'Governing the Roman Empire' could be understood in the sense of lieutenant of Christ the Emperor, and could even be taken as a form of devotion.

The essential fact, however, remains the new awareness of the Roman empire's resurgence and the imperial Roman dignity. This is proclaimed by a number of signs, both in the coins and in the chancery enactments from the second half of 801 onwards. The new coins struck in the numerous mints, much superior to those of the eighth century, are a revival of the imperial coinage types of the third and fourth centuries. The face is stamped with the head of the new sovereign in profile, wearing a laurel wreath, with the inscription: 'Charles emperor'; the reverse represents a tetrastyle temple surmounted by a cross—no doubt a stylised version of St Peter's at Rome—and round it runs the device *Christiana Religio*, proclaiming the mission of the new empire, namely the defence of religion, as defined by Alcuin and many others, through the spread of a Christian empire. The language of the second bull, used from 802 onwards to seal all diplomas and public acts, is perhaps even more instructive. The face bears a bust of the emperor, full face this time, wearing a crown *en fleuron*, and surrounded by the group of letters D.N. KAR. IMP. P.F.PP. AUG., reading as follows: Our Lord (*Dominus noster*) Charles (*Karolus*), emperor (*imperator*), pious (*pius*), happy (*felix*), perpetual (that is, guaranteeing the eternity of the Empire) (*perpetuus*), August (*Augustus*). Here we are confronted with the traditional imperial title, and resurrected in its complete form, for since the seventh century it had survived only at Constantinople in an abbreviated form. The reverse side represents the gate of a city flanked by two towers—the city of Rome, for it is expressly named (*Roma*); and round the picture runs the inscription *Renovatio Roman. Imp.*, the Renewal of the Roman Empire. This formula made its appearance at the end of antiquity; and the idea it expresses is, as it were, the corollary to the powerful belief in the empire's eternity, which would be assured by successive renewals reviving the institution's youth and vigour. And thus it would be with the renewal in the year 800. So the adoption of this device by the Frankish chancery shows that something of the Roman outlook had entered into Charlemagne's ideology and that of his entourage. But it should also not be forgotten that their biblical education made them ready to assimilate this concept; for had they not read in the Book of Ecclesiasticus (46:16) that 'Samuel renewed the kingdom and anointed the king of the Hebrews'?

In short, from the moment when Charlemagne left Italy—which he was never to see again—and withdrew to his palace at Aachen for a long period of meditation, one result at any rate was certain: the Empire to which he had just succeeded in Rome was not the empire of the Romans, but emphatically the Roman empire. What had been restored was the classical empire, but in a renewed form. Thus one of the problems presented by Charlemagne's coronation had been solved; but it was also necessary to give the idea a definite content.

In order to get a glimpse of how the Frankish elite interpreted the empire, and what functions they assigned to the emperor, we shall go back for the last time to Alcuin, whose letters between 801 and 804 are most instructive. The abbot of Tours had seen the realisation of his desires; and now, during the last years of his life, he continued to direct his disciple and help to make him conscious of his high calling. Let us first note how he addresses Charlemagne in these letters. 'David' always comes into them, showing that, as far as one of the intellectual currents in the imperial entourage was concerned, there was no lack of continuity between the period before and that following the coronation. But in the period after it, 'David' was the title most often associated with 'emperor' and accompanied by the traditional epithets—most serene, most great, most good, most victorious, most Christian (especially), August Emperor, and even Most August (*Augustissimus*). Along with these ancient expressions there were new titles, painting in lively colours the imperial dignity conferred upon Charlemagne: rector and emperor of the Christian people, protector of Holy Church, and even—an authentic Roman reminiscence—Father of the nation.[1] It will also be noted that all this profusion of titles and predicates still leaves out the Roman link of the imperial title. Yet there can be no doubt at all that for Alcuin, the empire to which Charles had just been exalted was the former Roman empire, for he quotes Constantine, Theodosius, Honorius and Valentinian III as models for the new emperor, in a letter reminding him that he is bound to his predecessors' constitutions, so that the prince is not *legibus solutus*. But above all, this reborn empire is Christian. And it is therefore by virtue of that character that Alcuin sketches out for Charles what his government ought to be.

He seems quite certain that the imperial dignity conferred on him is first and foremost a homage to his person. 'Blessed be God who has honoured you and exalted you to this point.' It is a homage too to his wisdom, like that of Solomon, thanks to which he always knows better than anyone else what is pleasing to God and beneficial to his Christian people. Now by conferring the empire upon him, God has raised even higher the *decus sapientiae* (honour of wisdom) and the *regni potentia* (royal power) of Charlemagne; and these are two gifts to be used for the Church and Christian people—two ideas that are always mentioned in very close connection. By his wisdom, the emperor will spread the Word of God, assure the defence of orthodoxy, and teach the

[1] Here, by way of comparison, are the addresses of some letters sent to Charles by other correspondents. From Paulinus of Aquileia about 800: 'To Lord Charles, decorated by the largesse of God with triumphal crowns, most earnest promoter of the orthodox faith, elevated to the summit of royal power.' The letter in question can easily be discovered to belong to the period before the imperial coronation. About 809–12, a letter from a bishop: 'Most glorious emperor and prince [*princeps* = emperor] of the Christian people'; from Maxentius of Aquileia about 811–12: 'To the most pious and most Christian, glorious prince, crowned and protected by God, peaceful conqueror and victor, most serene perpetual Augustus Lord Charles the Great, emperor and governor of the Roman Empire.' There are two letters of this same time from Leidrade of Lyon, the first addressed: 'To the most glorious and truly pious Lord, emperor and conqueror in Christ, undefeated victor and perpetual Augustus'; the second is a contrast to the first by reason of its sober tone: 'To the most happy [*felicissimus*] and august emperor.' These examples could easily be multiplied. The accumulation of words certainly seems to be a sure sign of the impossibility of expressing in a single word all that Charlemagne's new authority suggested to contemporaries.

faith to his subjects (*subiectos*)—a very strong term, no longer implying simply the king's faithful followers, but a new reminiscence of Roman absolutism—subjects of the emperor, whose faith he will shelter and protect. By his power, the invincible emperor (*invictus imperator*) will overcome the proud and defend the humble —a statement in which we recognise the mission assigned to Rome by Virgil (*parcere subiectis et debellare superbos*). So great would be the fear inspired by Charles that all the peoples he had been unable to subject 'by the works of war' would voluntarily accept his dominion. At this point an almost unlimited perspective opens up of this 'empire of wisdom and power'. But it must not be forgotten that this was also the prospect of the universal Church, since, in the words of Alcuin quoted a few lines above, these same peoples will abandon their idol-worship and so ceaselessly swell the ranks of 'the vast multitude of Christians'. Thus the empire that had just been reborn was universal by reason of the Church's universalism, which is tacitly taken for granted, and not by its own essential nature, as it was in the outlook of the ancient world. Ultimately, in the double role assigned to him by Alcuin, Charlemagne would be an incarnation of the *felix imperator* as glimpsed by St Augustine. And his own happiness would shower forth over all his people. 'Happy the nation,' exclaims Alcuin, 'which is ruled by a wise and pious emperor', rather as Plato had declared those kingdoms happy that were ruled by philosophers. Thus there would be realised the *Imperium terrenae felicitatis*, a prelude of the City of God upon earth. Let us emphasise once again that at the centre of this idea of a Christian empire, or empire of felicity, there is a very firm underlining by Alcuin of the notion of peace—in the first place between individuals, then between the peoples, a peace which included the concept of justice guaranteed by the 'peaceful' emperor, and securing tranquillity to all Christendom.

As far as we can outline it, such was Alcuin's vision of the empire; and it may be allowed that the upper ranks of the Carolingian Church shared in the essentials of this outlook. It was to be a 'renewed' Roman empire, but its substance was to be fundamentally Christian; a universal empire, an empire of wisdom in which spiritual and temporal were mingled under Charlemagne's authority, implying that he had the duty of directing his Christian people and above all of serving them (*praeesse, prodesse*).

Charlemagne was very far from insensitive to the advice showered upon him both by Alcuin and by the disciples of the abbot of Tours, Wizzo, Nathanael and the assiduous Arno, who were all at the palace in 802. On the contrary, it seems that as he spent that year at Aachen *sine hoste*—without any military expedition—meditating upon the exalted dignity with which he had been clothed, he realised his increased responsibilities, and thought of himself even more than in the past as responsible to God for what should be the manner of life among his Christian subjects. Nor can we doubt that he came under the influence of the memories of imperial Rome, which had given laws to the whole world. 'The imperialists in his entourage,' writes Ganshof, 'certainly contributed to a heightening of this awareness; and they perhaps attempted to convince the emperor that he was the source of all law and the lawgiver in the full sense of that term, as his predecessors had been.' Be that as it may, these various themes dictated to Charlemagne the intense legislative activity he showed in 802–3 in particular, as well as in the following years. Let us try to capture its essential moments and aspects.

In March 802 the emperor presided over an assembly at Aachen, after which he sent throughout the empire *missi* entrusted with a capitulary outlining the necessary measures to enable every man to live according to the law. First of all, the *missi* were to require from all free men an oath of fealty to Charlemagne as emperor. The instructions laid it down that clerics and laymen who had already sworn to be faithful to Charles as king were to renew their vows, and swear by the *nomen Caesaris*; those who had not yet done so were to be called upon from the age of twelve and upwards. This general requirement of an oath is interesting on two counts in particular. On the one hand, it appears to have been a kind of ratification by the Franks of the creation of the empire, thus both correcting and ratifying the act of 25 December; on the other, the form of the oath incorporated an element of the vassal's oath of fealty. 'I am faithful as a man [that is, as a vassal] must be by law to his lord for the good of the state and its law.' The intention here is clear enough: subjects are equated with vassals and, like the latter, must bind themselves to a faithfulness that is both more exacting and more extensive, since it covers a field far wider than that of the traditional fealty.

One has only to read this 'programmatic' capitulary of 802 to be convinced of this. The *missi* administering the oath would indeed have to explain the weighty and numerous duties to which subjects of the empire would be bound by their oath of fealty. Up till then, the text tells us, many had thought that their oath created only a personal bond between themselves and the prince, limited to defending him and promising not to treat with his enemies or with those who had broken faith. But from now on there were to be other obligations and other prohibitions as well. In the first place, the primary duty of all was to keep themselves in the holy service of God 'because the emperor cannot personally give the help necessary to each individually', which implies that Charlemagne expected each man to do his utmost in this respect. Then there is a prohibition of all actions harmful to churches, widows, orphans and strangers, whom the emperor—next after God and the saints—takes under his protection and defence. It will be noticed that the formula used by Charlemagne since 774 to define his duty to the Church is now broadened by the addition of three new categories. Once the oath has been taken, it is forbidden to oppose the emperor's orders, or hinder their execution, to avoid the obligations of military service and financial levies (*cens*), to usurp royal lands, to hinder the execution of justice, or to despoil a benefice held from the sovereign for the benefit of one's own possessions. Every man serving the emperor must do his utmost to assure that equity shall triumph.

It is impossible to overstress the nobility and originality of this language. The general impression is that Charlemagne was trying to substitute for duties owed to the person of the prince obligations owed to the cause that he himself was also serving. As L. Halphen has written, 'this cause was in keeping with the higher interests of the community, or—to use our political language— with the interests of the state.' This same historian also observes that the powerful idea of *respublica*, 'a living composite of all the citizens, who were represented by a higher power delegated to and incarnated in a person whose duty it was to watch over the collective interests', an idea that had disappeared after the collapse of the Roman empire, though not explicit in documents of this kind down to 814, is reflected in the idea that the emperor has duties towards all, and that his acts must be in consonance with the public interest. On the same principle, the content of the oath of fidelity can be extended indefinitely. Nothing could be more significant than to read in a capitulary that to give asylum to a robber is a breach of fealty, for 'all robbers are faithless both to ourselves and to the Franks, and all who harbour them are like them.' Thus anyone who betrays the emperor's interests and those of Frankish society in its solidarity is held to be unfaithful. In the final analysis, then, it would seem that the newly reborn *imperium* opened the way to a rediscovery of the idea of the state. This was a lengthy and sporadic rediscovery. The notion was dimly seen by Charlemagne, and matured during the first part of his son's reign, but once again disappeared in general until the renaissance of Roman law. But we must return to the year 802.

Having taken note that his capitularies were quickly forgotten, and that popular laws had many gaps and contradicted each other or Christian justice and the authority of the Church, Charlemagne called together in October 802 a great assembly. The *Annales Laureshamenses*, which alone describe it, call it a 'council'; in reality it was a mixed assembly, where churchmen and high officials of the laity sat in parallel, but separately. There were in fact three groups, since the monks sat separately from the secular clergy. The agenda put before the great laymen comprised nothing less than the restoration, amendent and completion of the civil legislation then in force. 'The emperor,' we read in the *Annales*, 'caused to be read aloud to the bishops, priests and deacons all the canons received by the holy council and the decrees of the pontiffs'—no doubt the collection *Dionysio-Hadriana*—'and ordered that they should be published in full before all.' To the assembled abbots, wise men (we should call them experts today) read the Rule of St Benedict. 'Then Charlemagne ordered all the clergy to live each in his own place according to the constitutions of the Holy Fathers of the Church, and commanded that anything done in these monasteries contrary to the rule of St Benedict should be amended in accordance with it.' During the sessions of the council, the emperor gathered round him the dukes, counts and 'all the rest of the Christian people', that is, representatives of them, such as great landed lords and royal vassals, with the 'legislators', that is to say lawyers belonging to the various national groups and knowing the local laws of the particular peoples living in the empire. 'To this assembly he caused to be read all the laws of the realm, and introduced corrections wherever they were necessary. Then he put this amended law in writing, in order that the judges might pronounce sentence according to all that was written.' The results of these deliberations are to be seen partly in several capitularies concerning the clergy, the monks, the laity, and the part played by institutions in the empire, and partly in a series of complementary additions to certain national laws. It is important to grasp the full significance of this fact, as Ganshof has shown. 'Up till then,' he writes, 'ancient law was something venerable, almost sacrosanct and untouchable, a heritage to be preserved intact.' Here, too, we see the initiative taken by Charlemagne under the influence of the imperial idea; for was he not the successor of Constantine and Theodosius, and so able to carry out reforms in his people's laws? Although Salic law, already revised under Pepin, received only superficial corrections, the Ripuarian law was drastically revised, at least in certain of its articles, and new articles were added to the law of the Bavarians. All the national laws received a common addition in the shape of a *Capitulare legibus additum* in 803. Finally, the laws of the Thuringians, the Chamavian Franks, the Frisians and the Saxons were put into writing.

Altogether it would seem that, on the information brought in by the *missi* sent throughout the states in the spring of 802, Charlemagne made a tremendous effort to fix the ecclesiastical and secular law of the empire. He was following the example of Justinian; yet this legislative work remained unfinished.

On the other hand it is certain that, under the influence of the imperial idea, Charlemagne was intent upon promoting the triumph of Christian principles in the working of institutions and in everyday life. The tone of the capitularies became more and more charged with emotion, so much so that one or two of them read more like sermons.[1] The emperor was unremitting in calling upon his representatives to administer sound justice to all, to the exclusion of all fraud, subterfuge or arbitrariness, reminding them of the Gospel precept: 'For as you judge others, so you yourselves will be judged' (Matthew 6:2). But the laws and customs found side by side within the empire had brought about such variety in judicial practice that it was necessary to find some more general principle capable of animating and fertilising social life as a whole. This was the principle of peace for which Charle-

[1] In particular the one quoted in the series of texts at the end of this book, p. 243.

magne, ever since the *Admonitio generalis* of 789, had been attempting to win acceptance as the most imperative of all requirements.

The capitularies towards the end of the reign repeated unceasingly what peace is, elaborating the theme of St Augustine: 'The peace of all created things is the tranquillity bestowed by order' (*City of God*, XIX, 13 and 14). It is first of all defined as perfect harmony between all the working parts of the social organism, assured by the perfect adjustment of all the different elements composing it: peace between the bishops and the counts, the bishops and the abbots, between great and small, 'for nothing is pleasing to God without peace.' This *concordia pacis* is also and above all the union of hearts (*unanimitas*); and as such, it is the force that enables the emperor not to be crushed by the load of responsibilities laid upon him by God. No government is possible unless all observe among themselves the relationships of justice and peace. This is an essentially religious conception, for interior use, and suitable for a Christian people, whose members are all made children of God, a fact which is symbolised by the kiss exchanged by the faithful at Mass. The peace the emperor is attempting to promote is also supported by the Church, the body of Christ, of which every Christian is a member bound to respect its unity. Thus the Church's unity is to sustain the unity of the empire, and the Church's peace to reinforce the imperial peace. It is of the utmost significance that one of the five great councils towards the end of the reign, the council of Chalon in 813, proclaimed peace to be based on the collective good will and no longer on the strength of the emperor, who cannot be held responsible for it by himself. All must work together for peace, and this order will be brought about more by the common will than by the sole authority of the emperor, who nevertheless reserves the right to judge all major infringements of the law of concord.

We can pick out certain practical applications of these principles, such as the defence of free men against oppression by the great and the exactions of officials; the reform of weights and measures and the coinage, with severe penalties against offenders; the obligation of every Christian to help support a poor man; or the law against hoarding victuals, and the measures taken against the illegal rise in prices in 806, a year of severe economic crisis. But the most original measure adopted by Charlemagne in the name of peace was the condemnation of the principle of exacting one's own vengeance (in 802 and 805), and the order to those who had suffered hurt to accept legal reparation from their adversaries. Very early on, Charlemagne had striven to suppress private warfare, as we learn from the capitulary of Herstal of 778. This intention was reaffirmed after the imperial coronation—witness the second capitulary of Thionville (805) prohibiting within 'la patrie' the carrying of certain arms (bucklers, lances and cuirasses). If a case of vendetta occurred (a dispute involving—according to ancient custom—recourse to arms),

> enquiry is to be made as to which of the two parties is opposed to a peaceful settlement; and the two parties are to be compelled to settle peacefully, even if they are unwilling [*distringantur ad pacem etiamsi noluerint*]; and if they will not be pacified in any way at all, let them be brought into our presence.

There is no need to press this point any further: basically, the emperor in the service of peace as far as the Franks were concerned was what the imperial idea amounted to at the end of Charlemagne's reign.

This ideal received so much emphasis that it brought about a gradual transformation in the conception of public service. Even more insistently than before the imperial coronation, the term *ministerium* (service) was extended to cover the functions of bishops, counts and in particular the *missi*, as well as the territorial districts in which their power was exercised. It was as if the emperor were intent upon associating the great laymen and ecclesiastics with the tasks belonging to a Christian empire, and primarily with those of his own ministry, even if the words 'imperial ministry' do not actually occur before the time of Louis the Pious. But this idea of Charlemagne's concerning ministry contributed in its turn to dilute the notion of the state, which seems to be absorbed into the high religious functions with which the supreme head of the City of God on earth was invested. It must never be forgotten that the empire's unity was founded upon a common faith, and that its universalism was in keeping with that of the Church and Christianity. There has been no better expression of this than the words uttered by the council of Mainz in 813: 'Let peace, concord and unanimity reign among Christians, for we all have one Father in Heaven, one Mother Church, one single faith and one baptism.' In the first decade of the ninth century the concept of the empire was really equivalent to the idea of imperial Christianity, blending the notions of empire and Church, in which both clerics and laymen were governed in things spiritual and temporal by the emperor. It is also to be noted that when interpreted along these lines, the empire has no special name, but is simply known in the capitularies as *Imperium*, *Imperium nostrum*. But there can be no doubt that this empire is that of the *populus Christianissimus*, which is often cited in conjunction with it.

This was a grandiose conception, worked out by a chosen band of clerics, before it was taken over by the higher ranks of the Church and used for their own advantage during the reign of Louis the Pious; but it was a conception that failed to make a permanent impression upon events. One has only to study the end of Charlemagne's reign in detail to see how disorder, corruption and violence, far from being eradicated, spread alarmingly in the huge body politic of the Frankish empire, despite all the preaching of the emperor. The ideals of Christian empire, and Charlemagne himself, were betrayed by men.

Whatever form the empire might assume within, it was urgent that Charlemagne should obtain Byzantine recognition for the promotion which had come to him. He applied himself to this task without delay, and we must now follow the efforts he made in this direction.

One can more or less imagine the impression produced in Constantinople by the news that an emperor had been instituted in the west by the pope and the Romans. Since getting rid of the unfortunate Constantine VI (797), Irene had assumed the title of *basileus* (emperor) and not *basilissa* (empress), and was exercising full imperial power. In face of this reality, the argument that the imperial power was vacant, used in Rome to justify Charlemagne's proclamation, could not but seem utterly without foundation in the eyes of the Byzantines, who continued to regard Rome as part of their empire. In these circumstances, Charlemagne's coronation was considered an act of rebellion against the legal authority, identical in character with the revolts of generals against the imperial power which had occurred several times in the empire, and notably in Italy from the seventh century onwards.

On the other hand, the eventual accession of many Roman and Byzantine emperors who had begun by opposing the reigning sovereigns shows that acclamations of the kind that greeted Charlemagne in Rome might well be the first steps towards the establishment of legitimate power; provided always that the person acclaimed in whatever region of the monarchy succeeded either in winning recognition from the titular *basileus* at Constantinople as an associate emperor, or in eliminating him and obtaining the constituent acclamation of the senate and the inhabitants of the capital. As long then as Charlemagne could not establish himself in one or other of these ways, he would remain a rebel. Now it is very interesting to note the manner in which the Byzantine historian Theophanes relates the events of 25 December. He is obviously intent first and foremost upon stressing the illegality of the act, saying not a word about the acclamations, and describing Charlemagne's imperial dignity as proceeding solely from his coronation by the pope. He shows a scarcely veiled contempt for the procedure, coupled with a certain sarcasm, when relating that the king of the Franks was anointed by Leo III from head to foot.

On the other hand, not even Constantinople could overlook the fact that Charlemagne had been acclaimed emperor of the Romans. Now the imperial Byzantine acclamation as fixed in the time of Heraclius generally included the double title of *basileus* and *autocrator*, without any particular geographical addition, even if 'of the Romans' was sometimes added. How could Constantinople then escape the conclusion that Leo III and the Romans wanted to adorn the new empire with Roman prestige, and perhaps also regain for ancient Rome the right henceforth to create the emperor? The imperial accession of Charlemagne must have seemed to Constantinople the act of a usurper, and a revolutionary act into the bargain.

Charlemagne's great merit was to have clearly sized up the situation and lost no time in seeking for ways of solving the problems presented by his coronation. There were two possible solutions. Either to make war on the Byzantines, capture Constantinople, and supplant the legal power there—a policy which carried many risks, and was rejected; or to negotiate, and try to obtain Byzantine recognition for what had taken place. Charlemagne adopted the latter solution, whilst recognising that it would mean making some sacrifices. We already know the first of these: Charles had not assumed the title of emperor of the Romans. By taking good care not to link his name with the city of Rome, he studiously avoided provoking Constantinople.

Now Irene was also inclined towards diplomatic rather than forcible measures. Unable to fight on account of Bulgarian and Arab pressure on the imperial frontiers, and likewise put on her guard by the rumours of an imminent Frankish expedition against Sicily, the empress sent an embassy to Aachen in the Autumn of 801 in order to find out Charles's intentions. The Byzantine envoys had no difficulty in establishing that there was no thought in Charlemagne's entourage of a campaign against Constantinople or Sicily, but at the most an expedition against the principality of Benevento, which was once again in revolt. They also took note that the Frankish Court appeared ready to negotiate. In the course of these conversations, did they take up the former project of a marriage alliance between the two dynasties? This seems to have been so, since Count Helgaud and Bishop Jesse of Amiens travelled to the shores of the Bosphorus in April 802 and proposed as a solution for all difficulties a marriage between Charlemagne and Irene. This is at first sight a surprising piece of information: there is not a word about it in the Frankish sources; Theophanes alone gives it. Although his evidence has been called in question, there seems no reason to reject it out of hand. The main point is to know how to interpret this plan, supposing that it was really proposed. Charlemagne certainly did not see it as a way to establish his dominion over the eastern empire. We can safely say as much from all that we know of his cautious temperament, and his reluctance to embark upon adventurous courses. But perhaps he glimpsed in this plan the possibility of legitimising his coronation by a match with the empress, which would temporarily at least have restored unity to the *orbis Romanus*, with perhaps one emperor residing in the west and another in the east. Be that as it may, the plan did not mature, for on their arrival in Constantinople the Frankish ambassadors witnessed a palace revolution, in which Irene was overthrown and Nicephorus I (802–11) came to power. He too opened early negotiations with Charlemagne, sending him his own messengers, who accompanied the two Franks on their return journey. The Byzantines met the emperor at Salz in Thuringia (803) and took home to their master proposals for a treaty. We do not know its clauses, for none of our sources mentions them. At the very most —to adopt Dölger's conjecture—it may be supposed that Charlemagne was to be recognised as associate emperor, but without any matrimonial alliance or transfer of residence for the Frankish sovereign to the east. But Nicephorus firmly rejected these proposals; diplomatic relationships were broken off, and war between the two empires began. As in the years before 800, it was conducted both on the religious and on the military level. But above all, this new tension with Constantinople led Charlemagne to clarify still further the idea of his own empire, and thus give the monarchy a solid intellectual armament. We must turn first to this attempt, before giving a brief account of some aspects of the Franco-Byzantine conflict.

Once again, it must be noted that the documents sometimes appear to speak with contradictory voices. Yet it would seem that a single tendency was gradually coming to the fore, a tendency not altogether unfamiliar to us, since it is connected with the ideas expressed some years earlier in the poem *Charlemagne and Pope Leo*.

First of all, let us take the so-called first Annals of Metz (*Annales mettenses priores*), dating from about 805, whose author was certainly in touch with the court, and thus obligingly gives us the view of things it wished to be taken, portraying each Carolingian prince's reign as a stage towards the events of the year 800. Thus the empire is seen as in preparation ever since Pepin of Herstal's Mayoralty; and the word *imperium* itself is used—*Imperium Francorum*, corresponding to the Christian empire.

Now we come to the most controversial document, which was long considered a sort of renunciation by Charlemagne of the dignity to which he had been raised, the famous *Divisio Regnorum* of 806. It is a complex document, the first five chapters of which put into writing the arrangements made by the emperor in the course of an assembly (*plaid*) held in February 806 at Aachen. The rest of it appears to be a capitulary of the usual type, whose prescriptions (chapters VI–XX) are chiefly concerned with the maintenance of peace. These two elements were fused into a single constitution during the summer assembly at Thionville. The particularly significant point for us here is first of all the way in which Charlemagne arranged for the succession. At first sight, it looks like a division of the kingdom between the emperor's three sons, Charles, Pepin and Louis, who had all three already received royal unction, the two latter being already subordinate kings in Italy and Aquitaine. But do not let us hasten to assume that Charlemagne returned purely and simply to the old Germanic custom of partitioning the monarchy. Although contemporaries called the act in question 'a division of the kingdoms', it is striking to note that the text calls it an *ordinatio regni*, a way of arranging the kingdom. And in fact, as H. Mitteis has clearly shown, the whole document reflects a scholarly dialectic between the ideas of partition and unity. Though the former is the more obvious, and is clearly expressed by the division of the empire into three *regna*, the other element recurs throughout the text in a certain number of characteristic expressions, such as *regnum* (the kingdom), *totum corpus regni* (the whole body of the kingdom), *imperium* (the empire). Critics have especially pointed out the frequency of the word *regnum*, in contrast to the relatively infrequent occurrence of *imperium*, and have been over hasty in concluding that Charlemagne was in some way indifferent to the latter idea. But apart from the fact that the two terms are often quoted together (*regnum et imperium*; *dominatus regalis atque imperialis*), we must not forget that *regnum* is the very substance of empire—a point to which we shall be returning. So there was to be a unity of the *regnum*: the three sons, even in their father's lifetime, became *consortes regni et imperii* (his associates in the kingdom and the empire), according to the term borrowed from the political language of the late Roman empire from the time of Diocletian onwards. And such they were to remain when they succeeded Charlemagne after his death. In order to avoid any altercation among them, the *totum corpus regni* was divided into three zones, and each of them handed over to one of the co-heirs' administration. Thus there were three kingdoms, but a single people, without any separation into sections through the boundaries of these *regna*—three kingdoms, but a single political entity. The three brothers were co-guarantors of the empire's unity, and were to give each other aid and assistance, and undertake in common the defence of the Church. The kingdom, then, was to be a single whole, yet there were three kingdoms within it: our contemporary political vocabulary simply does not possess any term that would adequately describe this structure. H. Mitteis has most aptly suggested a comparison between the arrangements of the *divisio-ordinatio* and the efforts of the Frankish court about the same time to work out a precise formula for the doctrine of the Trinity (Alcuin's treatise on this mystery in 802, and the *Filioque* controversy); and we may well wonder with Mitteis whether a mentality imbued with the notion that this present world ought to reflect the organisation of the other world did not project onto the political order the theme of unity in diversity characteristic of the doctrine of the Trinity.

The act of 806 is thus much more than a division of the empire, and it can therefore not be used in support of the thesis that at this particular moment Charlemagne abandoned the principle of unity for the monarchy. It has also been maintained that the imperial idea, as such, was by 806 growing dim in Charlemagne's mind. Here, too, the reality would appear to be somewhat different. The *divisio* has come down to us in six manuscripts; in only one of them—the London one, incidentally in a fragmentary state, perhaps representing the version meant for the interior of the empire —does Charlemagne take the imperial title that had been customary since 802: 'Governing the Roman Empire . . . king of the Franks and the Lombards', with the classical promulgation 'to all the faithful of Holy Church and all our subjects present and future'. The other five manuscripts carry a quite unusual title and promulgation, which suggests that the act underwent two redactions, each with a different protocol. Here is the version contained in the five manuscripts:

> The emperor Caesar Charles, most invincible king of the Franks, ruler of the Roman empire, pious, happy, triumphant victor, and always August, to all the faithful of Holy Church and to all Catholics present and future [belonging to] the peoples and nations in his empire and under his rule.

Taken as a whole, this would seem to be one of the most important testimonies to Charlemagne's conception of the empire. H. Beumann's remarkable analysis of it shows that the title properly speaking and the promulgation are very close to those of the famous Donation of Constantine. This discovery seems to be of cardinal interest, for it shows that Charlemagne deliberately followed in the footsteps of the first Christian emperor and applied to his own empire the image and type of a prince hitherto exclusively reserved to Constantinople. From this point onwards, there can be no doubt about it: the 'renewed' empire of 800 is the Romano-Christian empire, the empire of Constantine; and Charlemagne, for his part, is the new Constantine.[1] Then the problem immediately arises: when did the Frankish chancery come to know about the Donation? A probable supposition is that a copy of this document was brought along to the emperor by Leo III during his visit of 804-5, when he consecrated the chapel at Aachen. Without altogether taking over the Donation's arrangements, Charlemagne partly adopted the protocol and transferred it to the copy of the *Divisio* intended for the court of Rome. But was this adoption destined to turn the idea of empire into a different course from that which it had pursued since 801? With the help of Beumann, whose analysis I am following here, we must take a closer look at the title and the address. The terms *Imperator Caesar pius, felix, victor et triumphator atque semper Augustus* come directly from the Donation. 'Most invincible king of the Franks' is a customary title, whilst *Romani rector imperii* is a formula probably borrowed from the Gelasian Sacramentary. Let us take a further look at the place of the predicate 'king of the Franks', enclosed as it were between the two imperial titles. Whereas the 801 titulature contrasted the impersonal notion of Roman empire with the personal government that Charlemagne exercised as king over the Franks and the Lombards, here the two concepts are brought into the closest proximity. In other words, the Franks are the people of the empire *par excellence*, or—as I expressed it above—the Frankish kingdom constitutes the substance of the empire. Thus the imperial dominion extends beyond Italy and Rome: it is supported by the Franks and stretches out over other nations too, but only in so far as they are placed under the emperor's governance. This reservation makes a clear difference between the promulgation of the 806 act and that of the Donation. Constantine was considered to have addressed himself to the whole population and to all the nations constituting the total *orbis Romanus*, and this was bound to be so; but Charlemagne rejected these universalist pretensions. The addresses in the two versions are very similar in form: Charlemagne was legislating only 'for

[1] This is why I have thought it possible to use this document as one of those from 803 onwards with an anti-Byzantine tendency.

the faithful of the Holy Church' and for the populations of which
he was actually head. Although distinct, these two categories
formed one single entity, the Christian people. This stage therefore represents the full maturity of the theocratic conception
beginning to emerge in Pepin's time, which tended to fuse the
Frankish Church and the Frankish state into a single politico-
religious whole. But we shall also observe how careful was the
description of 'peoples really placed' under the government of
Charlemagne. It is as though the empire was brought in to crown
the fact of royalty, and the *nomen imperatoris* was superimposed
on a power that was already an accomplished fact.

Thus a new step had been taken towards the clarification of the
imperial idea. Face to face with the eastern empire, the empire of
Charlemagne affirmed its originality. Whilst claiming the Roman
succession, it based itself upon well-defined ethnic foundations
and abandoned the principle of universalism. Though also
'Constantinian', it was so in a more superficial sense than its
rival, and above all more indissolubly linked to the Christian
Church. And if there were any need to give it some supplementary
description, it could also be characterised as the champion of
orthodoxy. Let us add a further word or two in connection with
this anti-Byzantine action.

The problem of the *Filioque* clause, though widely debated during
the last decade of the eighth century, had been dormant since the
council of Cividale and Paulinus of Aquileia's striking manifesto,
which concluded that the affirmation of the Spirit's double procession was equivalent to confessing the unity of the Divine
Substance. The debate revived even more vigorously in the conflict between Charlemagne and Nicephorus, and denunciation of
the Greeks for their heterodoxy became part of the classical
method of making war on the Byzantine empire. The controversy
was re-opened in the Holy Land. Two Latin monks from the
convent of the Mount of Olives in Jerusalem had been sent on a
mission to the Frankish court in 806. They had occasion to be
present at the celebration of the liturgy in the chapel at Aachen,
and hastened to introduce its forms into their own church on their
return home, in particular the singing of the creed during Mass
with the *Filioque* clause. When denounced to the patriarch by the
Greek monks of the St Sabas convent, the Latins recognised that
the form used by them was different from that used by the eastern

Church, but they protested that their faith differed in no way from that of the Church of Rome, and appealed to Leo III to pronounce on the matter. The pope, who had also received information about this affair from the patriarch of Jerusalem, sent the two letters to Charlemagne.

The 'orthodox' emperor promptly seized this chance of coming down heavily on the Greeks on a question of religion. Three theologians were appointed by him to study the question. Theodulf of Orléans proceeded to conduct a patristic enquiry, and recorded its results in a highly learned treatise (*De Spiritu sancto*); Abbot Smaragd of Saint-Mihiel defended the *Filioque* clause from Holy Scripture, whilst an anonymous writer treated the subject along dialectical lines, by theses founded upon scriptural and patristic arguments. These works served as a basis for discussion at the council held in Aachen in November 809. Although this assembly is known to us only through a mention in the Annals, it is clear that the *Filioque* doctrine was recognised as an expression of the traditional faith.

As regards adding this clause to the creed, the council, ready enough to counter the Greeks, expressed the opinion that the pope should be asked to take this step. That was the purpose of the embassy which set out for Rome in the year 810. But Leo III, while agreeing in principle to the double procession, was anxious not to involve the Church in a new quarrel generated above all by political motives. He refused to commit himself on the second point, and confined himself to suggesting that they should stop singing the creed in the Mass at Aachen. Coming from on high, the example could not fail to be followed, and this in itself would lead to the contentious clause being dropped. We do not know what Frankish reaction was to this proposal. It is certain all the same that the chapel at Aachen went on singing the creed with the additional clause as before. The conflict died down, however, after the close of the year 810, when negotiations started between Aachen and Constantinople with a view to ending the military operations that had begun in 804.

These took place in the zone where the two empires met, Venetia and Dalmatia. Bordering on Frankish Istria, though theoretically Byzantine, both of these territories were in fact more or less independent, and were just then enjoying remarkable economic prosperity. But they were also gravely torn by party struggles between rival groups, which offered an easy excuse for outside intervention. Thus in 805, Charlemagne, profiting by one of these quarrels, succeeded in placing Venetia and Dalmatia under his own authority. Constantinople reacted vigorously, and in 806 the patrician Nicetas inflicted a heavy defeat on Pepin, king of Italy, and forced him to declare a one year's truce. He then put Venetia and Dalmatia again under the influence of the eastern empire and temporarily eliminated the pro-Frankish party. When hostilities broke out again in 808, a new Byzantine fleet cruised along the Venetian coast, whence it launched a raid on the town of Comacchio south of the Po estuary, while the Greeks from Sicily came and ravaged Populonia on the coast of Tuscany. The following year brought a new turn of events, for the Venetian doges turned against Constantinople, and this *volte-face* allowed Pepin to reduce Venetia to submission and ravage the Dalmatian coast (810).

These facts decided Nicephorus, who was incidentally waging a difficult war against the Bulgarians, to negotiate peace with the king of Italy through an embassy led by Arsaphus the *spatharius*. When it arrived in the peninsula it received the news of Pepin's death. But Charlemagne summoned the embassy to Aachen, where he received it in October. The conversations, which were supposed to relate solely to the Venetian question, were very probably extended to cover the question of the imperial title; and Arsaphus may well have taken back to his master the general lines of a projected treaty. In 811 a Frankish embassy consisting of two counts and Bishop Heitho of Basel was sent to Constantinople to ratify them. But they were not destined to be received by Nicephorus, for he had recently been defeated and killed by the Bulgarians; it was his successor, Michael I Rangabe, who received them. Grappling as he was with external and internal difficulties, he was compelled to make peace with Charlemagne as quickly as possible, all the more so since the latter was willing to give up Venetia and Dalmatia to him; in exchange for which Michael recognised his imperial title.

For the Byzantines, this was an unprecedented concession, for— as one of their chroniclers puts it—'barbarians and those who have arisen from among foreign peoples were not eligible for the imperial dignity.' It would be interesting to know what justification the Byzantine mentality was able to contrive for this extraordinary

novelty. A remark made a century and a half later by the Emperor
Constantine Porphyrogenitus in his book on the administration
of the empire may perhaps serve as an attempt at interpretation.
Charlemagne, he writes, was emperor because he had been sole
sovereign of several kingdoms in the zone over which he exercised dominion. From this point of view, the Byzantine politicians
considered Charlemagne's royalty as something more considerable
than others, a kind of reinforced royalty, so to speak, but nothing
more. Be that as it may, a Greek embassy arrived at Aachen in
812, bringing sumptuous presents for Charlemagne, and acclaim-
ing him *imperator* and *basileus*. It is also possible that the official
document handed to the emperor contained the word 'brother'
instead of the word 'son', which was customary in relationships
between the *basileus* and kings. All the same, it should be noted
that Charlemagne had already used it in the letter he wrote to
Nicephorus. The essential point, however, was that the imperial
title conceded to Charlemagne by Constantinople did not carry
any geographical label, and in particular was not linked in any way
with Rome. Only the *basileus* had the right to call himself emperor
of the Romans, and this usage became customary henceforward
in all the official acts of the chancery in Constantinople. Charlemagne had no difficulty in adjusting himself to these realities. We
have already seen that from the day of his coronation he had cut
free from the purely Roman conception; and after his recognition
by Michael I he abandoned, in correspondence with his 'brother',
the title of *Romanum gubernans Imperium*, though it was maintained
in the final diplomas of the reign, in favour of the simpler 'by the
bounty of the divine grace emperor and Augustus, as well as king
of the Franks and Lombards'. But it is just as significant that the
address of the letter to Michael, where this protocol appears for
the first time (early 813), likewise carries after the name of the
person addressed simply the titles emperor and Augustus, without
further definition. In Charlemagne's eyes, then, it was as if henceforward there were two emperors co-existing side by side, equal in
quality and in rights. As regards their respective zones of authority,
this same letter gives us very reliable information: they corresponded
to the west and the east (*Orientale et Occidentale Imperium*). So there
were now two empires side by side, as there had been between
395 and 476. The substance of the western empire was Christianity;
it is therefore not at all surprising that in liturgical manuscripts

the appellation *Imperium Christianum* often replaces *Imperium Romanum*. But by no means always.

Thus from the Byzantine side the problem created by Charlemagne's coronation seemed to have been solved, at least in appearance. Charlemagne's recognition as emperor had satisfied his self-esteem; but Constantinople had reserved to itself the rights that it judged to be imprescriptible. The Byzantine empire alone was the Roman empire. In fact, however, there were now two empires side by side, and their co-existence was often to prove difficult in the years to come.

After the peace with Constantinople the western empire took on for a certain period a complexion that was already in process of formation even before the year 800. Although it had been born in Rome, it abandoned the Roman title and setting, and fell back upon the Frankish reality. We have seen how this increased in importance in Charlemagne's titulature from 806 onwards: after 812 it alone remained, and the Constantinian tradition faded from the picture for the time being.

These new features were seen in their full light when in 813 Charlemagne for the second time arranged for the succession. The situation seemed considerably simplified, for only the youngest of the three co-heirs of 806 now remained alive, Louis king of Aquitaine. Charlemagne therefore summoned him to Aachen, where he convened a general assembly of 'the whole army, the bishops, the abbots, the dukes, the counts and their subordinates' from all the peoples of the empire. The only ones missing were the Lombards and the Romans, whose absence can no doubt be explained by the hastiness of the proceedings, in view of the very indifferent health of the emperor, whose days appeared to be numbered. Charlemagne then asked all those gathered together at Aachen, on a day in September which cannot be precisely fixed— 'all of them, the highest in rank down to the lower-placed in the hierarchy of duties'—if it was their pleasure that he should confer 'his name', that is, the *nomen imperatoris*, on his son Louis. Let us be quite sure what this really meant. Even if the person of his successor was not in doubt, it was still necessary to know if the imperial dignity could be made consonant with the customs of the Franks. In principle, at least, it was the Franks, the people who had since 802 sworn fealty to the *nomen Caesaris*, who were now called upon to pronounce on the continuance of the empire. The response of the assembly to this consultation was a general acclaim, and this was taken to confer imperial power upon Louis. It could also be interpreted as an election in which the emperor had played the part of first elector, the Franks taking the place of the Romans in the conferring of the empire. In a word, as one contemporary source most pertinently observes, 'Louis succeeded Charlemagne by general consent of all the Franks and by the gracious good will of his father.'

As for the succession rites proper, they ignored both the pope and the part he had played in 800 as creator of the empire. The ceremony that took place in the chapel at Aachen on the Sunday after the assembly was grandiose in its sheer simplicity. Charlemagne addressed his son, instructing him as to the duties he was assuming, and then asking him whether he was ready to fulfil them. Louis's affirmative reply took the place that later was filled by the oath at the anointing. This was followed by the coronation. Our sources give different accounts of the way it was performed. The Royal Annals state that Charlemagne placed the diadem on his son's head; according to Thegan, the biographer of Louis the Pious, Louis took the crown from the altar and put it on himself. The first account would seem to be preferable, since it is in keeping with Byzantine usage, according to which the reigning emperor crowned his successor. But whatever the actual manner of the second imperial coronation in the west, it is noteworthy that no Church dignitary took part in it. The general acclamation *'vivat Imperator Ludovicus'* was followed by the 'great litany', that is to say, by the *Laudes*, which denoted that all those present recognised that Louis had indeed been created emperor. As Charlemagne's appointed successor, Louis was henceforward *consors totius regni et imperialis nominis heres* (associated with the monarchy as a whole and heir to the imperial title), as Einhard appositely expresses it. The ceremony was completed by celebration of Mass; and it was the general opinion that what had been done was according to the will of God.

And so, thirteen years after the revival of the western empire, the imperial question was solved by the action of Charlemagne. Let us briefly recapitulate the long course that had been travelled by him. Almost at once, he had detached himself from Rome as centre of empire. His own empire was a reborn Roman empire (801); but in it, although he posed as the new Constantine (806), the Franks occupied the chief place. From 806 onwards, the empire could be historically and geographically defined; and when peace was signed with Constantinople, Charlemagne was led to abandon the title 'Roman', so that only the Frankish reality remained. In accordance with this it was possible to modify the imperial accession rites of the year 800. In the coronation of Louis of Aquitaine we have just seen how this modification was carried out. When this evolution came to an end, Rome and the Romans may be said to have been replaced by Aachen and the Franks.[1] The anonymous poet's vision of 799 had just been translated into reality. There was an empire whose roots were Frankish, yet which was bound to Rome by its rebirth; an empire that was the instrument of renewal for the kingdom of the Franks. It is most striking that this idea of renovation, officially Roman, should have been directed towards the Frankish monarchy, as is shown by the inscription on the new bull used by Louis the Pious from the time of his accession: *Renovatio regni Francorum*. But whether Roman in complexion or Frankish in hue, the Carolingian empire remained fundamentally what Alcuin had declared it to be—the Christian empire. And in the eyes of his faithful followers its chief remained the 'great and orthodox emperor who nobly increased the kingdom of the Franks', as he is proclaimed in the funerary inscription on the gilded vault placed over Charlemagne's tomb in his Church at Aachen.

[1] H. Beumann draws attention to a passage in Modoin's famous eclogue (about 804–14) where it is said in so many words that 'the place where the head of the world resides may indeed be called Rome'. One can clearly see the link between this idea and the one expressed in the poem *Charlemagne and Pope Leo*, where Aachen was called the New Rome ('Die Kaiserfrage bei den Paderborner Verhandlungen von 799' in *Das erste Jahrtausend*, vol. 1, Bonn, 1962).

Part Three

Charlemagne's successors

18 *Charles the Bald*
Miniature from a psalter, perhaps made in the court workshops (Bibl. nat., Lat. 1152).
A triangular pediment, supported by antique-style columns. The throne is studded with pearls and precious stones between the two raised folds of a drapery. Purple tunic and golden cloak; crown, short sceptre and orb; and above the sovereign, the hand of God.

The Latin inscription (in gold capitals on a purple background) proclaims Charles the Bald to be like Josiah and the equal of Theodosius.

19 *Seal and bulls of Charles the Bald*
(From P. E. Schramm, *Die deutschen
Kaiser und Könige*.) Inscription on the
seal: *Karolus gratia Di rex* (Charles,
king by the grace of God).
A royal bull: reproduced from a copy
in the Cabinet des Médailles at the
Bibl. nat. (no. 996a). The legends are
those of the bull used in Charlemagne's
reign (see above).
(Below) Sketches of various bulls
(from Mabillon, *De re diplomatica*,
suppl., p. 48). Top left, one of Louis
the Pious's reign; on the face, the
legend: Our Lord Louis, Emperor; on
the reverse (the symbol of Rome has
disappeared), the legend: *Renovatio regni
Francorum*. Centre left, one belonging
to Charles the Bald, with the legends:
Charles Emperor Augustus, and on the
reverse, *Renovatio regni FNCO* (cf. 3rd
row on the left).
   Of the imperial bull mentioned in
our account there exists only an old
description.

20 *Charles the Bald enthroned in majesty*
(From P. E. Schramm, *Die deutschen Kaiser und Könige*.) A miniature from
the famous *Codex aureus*, made about 870, which passed from France to the
Abbey of St Emmeran at Ratisbon and from there to the Munich Library
(c.l.m. 14000).

The sovereign faces the Lamb of God painted on the opposite page.
Canopy with four pillars, the hand of God, and two angels; round the
throne there are two warriors, one carrying a lance and the other
a sword, and two female figures holding cornucopias, the one on the left
representing *Francia*, and the right-hand one *Gotia* (Septimania).

21 *The nine worthies*
(From *Mémorial d'un voyage d'études de la Société des Antiquaires de France*,
1953.) An illumination from the *Livre au Chevalier errant* (Bibl. nat., MS.
franç., 12559). Charlemagne (last but one from left to right), in the company
of Hector, Caesar, Alexander, Joshua, David, Judas Maccabaeus, Arthur
and Godfrey de Bouillon. Typical illustration to a romance of chivalry
(1394).

✦ XI ✦

The fate of the
Carolingian empire (814–87)

When Charlemagne died, it looked for the moment as if the Empire would follow a path of steady consolidation.

Louis the Pious, born in 778, had now reached the prime of manhood. He had received a very careful education. In Aquitaine he had distinguished himself as much by warlike enterprise—the conquest of the Spanish March was largely accomplished under his direction—as by his zeal in promoting Church and monastic reform. This last received his attention under the inspiration of Benedict of Aniane, whom he brought with him to Aachen in 814, and who remained his most devoted and influential adviser up to his death in 821. The new emperor was deeply religious in temperament, and it was with high ideals that he approached his duties. He considered himself to be invested with supreme authority in order to protect the Church within and without. In his outlook, Church and empire were intimately linked and scarcely separable conceptions. The empire could be defined in terms of its people's religion; diverse as they were, they nevertheless formed as a whole the *populus Christianus*, held together within the framework of a Christian empire, the *respublica Christiana*. *Respublica*: this word, which was in only tentative use under Charlemagne, becomes from now onwards firmly established in the texts. It is as if the notion of the state were being reborn, the state as an institutional and secular clothing for the Church conceived as the mystical body of Christ. This was an abstract notion elaborated since Charlemagne's death by the clerical elite, but totally incomprehensible to the bulk of the laity. Moreover, it was a dangerous idea to handle for it contained the germs of future misunderstandings. It remained to be seen how far the emperor would be able to keep his independence in face of a Church tending to impose on him its own directives. This problem was all the more serious because Louis the Pious—also known in France as the Debonair—was a very weak character, alternating between obstinacy and submissiveness. All the same, before the outbreak of any dissension, it seems as though Charlemagne's successor did really set about giving more cohesion to the empire at every point, and providing the Church with the means of promoting the Christian life more effectively in the great complex of territories for which it was spiritually responsible.

The title he adopted after his accession, 'By divine Providence August Emperor', is in itself most revealing. Louis gave up the royal titles constantly used by his father, thus affirming that there was now only one reality that mattered: the empire as an idea and an institution. As has been very truly said, the supreme power accordingly found itself 'depersonalised'. The inscription on his coins, *Christiana Religio*, the iconographical representation of the emperor with the cross and the shield of faith, the quality which a writer recognises in Louis of being 'the emperor of the whole Church spread throughout Europe' (that is, in the west), are evidence of the supremely religious character of the imperial dignity.

During the four years 816–19 a series of councils, all held at Aachen, carried through the reform of the clergy, the monasteries and the episcopate; and the measures taken by them tended to limit the influence of the lay world upon the Church. Nor was the papacy forgotten, for in 817 it obtained a guarantee of its political independence and the freedom of papal elections. This was the end of the authority Charlemagne had wielded in Rome.

It was in this same year that there took place the act fraught with the greatest consequences in the whole reign, an act intended to guard against any possible disruptions in the empire, the mainstay of the Church. Since the Church was one, the empire must remain one, as it was at that moment in the emperor's hands. That is why Louis, 'moved [as he himself said] by divine inspiration', after due deliberation in an assembly of notables, promulgated the constitution known as the *Ordinatio Imperii*, by which his eldest son Lothair was proclaimed emperor, crowned with the imperial crown, associated with his father in the exercise of power, and proclaimed sole and only heir to the empire. As to his two brothers, Pepin remained king of Aquitaine—which he had been since 814—and the other, Louis, became king of Bavaria. Both of them ruled their respective kingdoms under the emperor's orders. The same was true of the kingdom of Italy, which Louis the Pious kept for his nephew Bernard, Pepin of Italy's son, to whom Charlemagne had given it in 813. Similarly it was laid down that when Lothair, after his father's death, became sole emperor, he should allow his brothers to control the internal administration of their kingdoms, but that they should be under the supreme authority of their elder brother. In the event of any of them dying, it would fall to the people of that kingdom to elect one of his sons as successor; and after Lothair's death, his followers should proceed to elect one of his brothers, who would then assume the imperial title.

The *Ordinatio Imperii* certainly seems to be a compromise between the unitary idea, first put forward by Louis the Pious, and the traditional custom of dividing up the Frankish state, though with a requirement that the brothers should govern in common as though forming a single whole. It will be remembered that this idea was strongly brought out in the constitution of 806. But between that decree and the one we have just analysed, there had been a complete change of outlook. It was no longer a question of kingdoms side by side, united by the mutual love of the brothers associated in the government of the *totum corpus regni*, but of kingdoms within the much larger and better defined framework of the empire, zones more or less reserved for younger sons strictly subordinate to the eldest, who bore the imperial title, and was responsible for the supreme direction of the whole. In this sense it may be said, with H. Mitteis, that the constitution of 817 tended to create not only a unitary empire, but 'a unitary state comprising autonomous districts'. It should be added that the *Ordinatio* was not intended to come into immediate force, but rather to make arrangements for the future, which were not necessarily any assurance for the present. The emperor reserved to himself the right to modify it as circumstances might require. Thus the value of the act lies much more in the idea inspiring it than in its immediate practical effects.

Nevertheless, it is certain that the *Ordinatio* immediately aroused a certain opposition, which crystallised round Bernard of Italy in 818. It was harshly repressed, and finally resulted in a strengthening of the principles set out the year before, since Italy was simply taken away from the rebel prince and joined to the territories reserved for Lothair. Moreover, at the Nijmegen and Thionville assemblies (May and October 821), the emperor required an oath from all present to respect the arrangements of the *Ordinatio*. Finally, throughout those years he strove to organise the imperial administration along more rational lines. The general assemblies (*plaids*) lost once and for all their former military character, and became much more frequent. Between 816 and 828 there were most often two, if not three, a year. The intention was clearly to encourage contact between the supreme power and the administrators, and to strengthen the bonds of unity between the various parts of the empire. At the same time, under the influence of the revival of learning then at its height, the capitularies began to be drawn up in a clearer and more orderly form, and to be more effectively circulated; and copies were carefully kept in the imperial palace archives. Putting all these signs together, we can say that the empire was gradually taking on a sounder appearance.

Nevertheless, from this time onwards, the emperor began to show signs of weakness. Distrustful of himself, and consumed with remorse since Bernard, of Italy's death, he granted an amnesty in 821 to the accomplices of his nephew who were still alive, and recalled certain old fellow-workers of his father's dismissed by him when he came to power, chief of whom was Adalard, formerly adviser to Pepin and Bernard, the kings of Italy, and his brother Wala, who had been governor-general of Saxony and was soon to become abbot of Corbie. Along with prelates like Agobard, archbishop of Lyon, Arch-chaplain Hilduin, abbot of Saint-Denis and Jesse, bishop of Amiens, they formed an active and energetic group intent upon preserving the unity of the empire and exercising strict control over the emperor in the name of religion. The first sign of this party's hold upon the emperor was the public penance they imposed on him at the time of the Attigny assembly (822). Furthermore, in their efforts to consolidate the *Ordinatio Imperii*, this same group persuaded Louis to have Lothair anointed and crowned emperor in Rome by Pope Pascal I in 823. A year later, Lothair, with Wala's help, and acting in his father's

name, succeeded in replacing a papacy under the empire's protection by the famous *Constitutio Romana*, which imposed imperial
control over the papal administration, and required in addition
that a newly elected pope could be consecrated only after he had
taken an oath of loyalty to the emperor or to his representative.
The Romans for their part were compelled to swear fealty 'to the
emperors Louis and Lothair'. Seven years after the weakness that
had characterised the early years of the reign, we are now confronted with a complete reversal of the situation, and Rome comes
once again into the imperial grip. This empire is now administered
by two emperors in effective association, whose names appear in
the protocols of all public acts after 825. Thus the principle of a
unified monarchy appeared to be triumphant.

But in the following years, for one reason and another this
development took an entirely different course. A conflict broke
out over the defence of the Spanish March, which was in a state
of insurrection against the Franks and was being invaded by the
Saracens (826). King Pepin of Aquitaine was in open disagreement
with his father, who handed over the command of the March to
Bernard of Septimania, son of the famous Guillaume de Toulouse.
The victory that he finally won was in marked contrast to the
inertia of the relieving army sent out under counts Hugh and
Matfrid, both of whom were severely punished and deprived of
their commands.

These events brought about a *rapprochement* between Pepin and
Lothair, who was a close relative of Hugh (brother-in-law) and of
Matfrid (his future son-in-law). We can surmise that there were
violent struggles for power going on around the emperor. The
tension was increased even further through the propaganda let
loose by Wala for a reform of the abuses then widespread in the
Church through the encroachments of great laymen. At his in-
stigation Louis the Pious consented to the setting up of four
councils to sit simultaneously in 829 and propose remedial measures for this state of affairs. Now the acts of one of these councils,
the council of Paris (the only ones that have come down to us)
proclaim the empire to be no more than a part of the Church.
The Church is a single body, whose head is Christ; and this body
is governed by two powers, the authority of the bishops and royal
power. But as already laid down in the Gelasian Decree quoted by
the council, the former is the more weighty, since the bishops are,

under God, responsible for the actions of kings. Whereas—especially in the closing years of his reign—Charlemagne 'had merged the empire and the Church in his own person', the episcopate was separating them once more, reserving to itself all religious authority, taking the place of a prince who was judged too timorous, literally taking charge of the empire, denouncing the rivalries of the men invested with Palatine powers profitable only to the enemies of Christ, and inviting the emperor to govern according to the law of God. For the immediate present, the bishops dictated certain measures to the emperor, such as freedom of elections, and the end of lay interference in the administration of Church property, the application of which would have completely upset the relationships between the Church and the secular power as established since the time of Charlemagne.

This is a striking manifesto, marking the 'first appearance of the Frankish episcopate' as an established body pronouncing on the great interests of Church and state. There is no doubt that it had deeper underlying causes not mentioned in the text, but discoverable if we take into account the moment when it was drawn up. In 819 Louis the Pious, who had lost his wife Ermengarde, had married Judith of the Bavarian house of Welf. Four years later a son was born to the emperor, who was given the name of Charles, the future Charles the Bald. This at once raised the problem of provision for this child: would the emperor have to reconsider the *Ordinatio Imperii*? Judith, who had great influence over her husband, was urging him to take this course. Now in the eyes of the 'party of unity', the 817 constitution possessed an absolute value. The empire, whose head was under the Church's orders, must necessarily, as the Church's upholder and sustainer, remain a unity. They were aware of the empress's manœuvres to win Lothair to her side, and of the hesitations of the latter, caught between Judith and those who were urging him to defend the sacrosanctity of the *Ordinatio*. In face of all these intrigues, Louis the Pious summoned up the strength to reply by a series of vigorous measures. In the course of the general assembly held at Worms in 829 he decreed certain measures of reform to satisfy the episcopate; but most important of all, he announced that he had created in favour of his last-born son, Charles, an appanage comprising Alemannia, Rhaetia, Alsace and part of Burgundy. There was no question of any alteration in the *Ordinatio*, which was neither modified nor abrogated. These provisions, however, were reinforced by two others of great significance: Lothair was sent to Italy, and his name struck off from the protocol of all official acts; and Bernard of Septimania became chamberlain, and so one of the principal personages at court. Thus there had come about a real palace revolution, foreshadowing even more important changes in the future.

This brings us to a turning-point in the reign of Louis the Pious. A major crisis began in 830; and after first noting the chief problems involved, we must go on to give a brief account of its essential features.

The palace revolution following upon the Diet of Worms sent the emperor's eldest son into opposition, making him the leader in a party including men of every shade of opinion. Alongside empire doctrinaires, intent upon an empire under the Church's control—men such as Wala, Agobard and Hilduin—were ambitious great lords like Hugh and Matfrid, greedy for offices and lands. In putting himself forward as the defender of imperial unity, which had been compromised in the opinion of himself and his supporters by the award to Charles, Lothair was nevertheless continually torn between two solutions. On the one hand, there was the possibility of negotiations with Louis the Pious with a view to recovering his place alongside his father; but in that case he would have to recognise the decisions taken by him, and the decisions still to come, in favour of Judith's son. On the other hand, there was the possibility of rebellion, aiming at the overthrow of Louis the Pious and his own promotion to be head of the empire. Whichever path he chose, Lothair would come up against his two brothers, Pepin and Louis the German, who had also entered the revolt with the avowed intention of seizing as large shares of the empire as they could for themselves. As a result, it seemed as though the forces making for partition of the empire were suddenly unleashed about the year 830. But Lothair's brothers had equally to choose between agreement with their elder brother and good relations with their father. The first course meant the elimination of Charles's rights in the succession of their father; the second meant their recognition. The complexity and the divergence of the interests involved explain the chaotic course of the last ten years of Louis the Pious's reign. Three moments need to be singled out for special examination.

In 831 the emperor came to an understanding with Pepin and Louis the German against Lothair. He granted them a considerable increase in their future kingdoms and divided the empire into three equal lots, with the exception of Italy, which remained implicitly reserved for Lothair. The king of Aquitaine accordingly had his share increased by the territories between the Seine and the Loire as well as by a large part of Neustria; and Louis the German was allotted all the territories east of the Rhine (except for Alemannia and Rhaetia), together with Austrasia, Brabant, Hainault, Flanders, and the extreme north of Neustria. As for Charles, his original domain was increased by the Moselle valley, the counties of Rheims and Laon, the whole former kingdom of Burgundy (except for certain districts reserved for Pepin since 817), Provence, Septimania and the March of Spain. This division was obviously inspired by the partition of the empire among his three sons effected by Charlemagne, though it was only to come into force after the emperor's death. It was also bound up with the principle of complete equality between the three brothers, who would have to take common measures in defence of the Roman Church. No question was raised of their relationship with Lothair: it seemed to have been completely forgotten, as was the empire. But we must repeat that all this was only a plan for the future; the *Ordinatio Imperii* was not annulled, any more than in 829.

Two years later there was a complete reversal of the situation: Pepin and Louis joined together with their elder brother against Louis the Pious. They let loose a powerfully concerted campaign against the latter, against his evil counsellors, and especially against Judith, who was held to be the cause of all the trouble. The central argument of the party of unity was the scandal provoked by the breach of the oath of fealty caused by the emperor's successive changes of plan, and this was made a major theme in the propaganda, which was handled in masterly fashion by Agobard. The new factor in the situation was the intervention, instigated by Lothair, of Pope Gregory IV, the rebels declaring him to be 'coming to the rescue of peace', Louis's partisans regarding him as 'a tool of the sons in the revolt against their father'. In reality, the pope was tempted to come to Francia by this exceptional opportunity of acting as arbiter in a quarrel between kings. Lothair appeared not to realise that he was making use against his father of an authority which he had handed over in 824 to the imperial power, and certain of his adherents, such as Agobard, justified Gregory IV's intervention in the name of papal supremacy, which called on the pope to re-establish the unity of the empire and of Christendom. On the other hand, some bishops who remained faithful to Louis the Pious, headed by his half-brother Drogo, archbishop of Metz, protested energetically against the papal intervention and even threatened the pope with deposition. The result is well known: on the field at Mensonge (south-west of Colmar), where the adversaries were encamped facing each other, Louis the Pious found himself completely abandoned after a few days; his sons had succeeded in corrupting all his vassals. His deposition was announced there and then, and Lothair was proclaimed sole emperor. But difficulties arose immediately. Lothair, unable to impose the constitution of 817 and compelled to satisfy his brothers, had to consent to a partitioning of the empire, and to recognise Pepin's and Louis's right to the greater part of the territories promised them by their father in 831. So the outcome of this tragedy was nothing more nor less than the overthrow of Louis the Pious, Judith and Charles. The empress was shut up in an Italian monastery and her son at Prüm, whilst the unfortunate emperor was made to go through the show of a voluntary abdication in the sinister comedy staged at Saint-Médard de Soissons by Archbishop Ebbo of Rheims in October 833.

But this situation was quickly reversed. Louis and Pepin were afraid of their elder brother, and not at all anxious to put themselves under his protection. They accordingly agreed to act together in order to set their father free. By March 834, Louis was restored to full power, whilst Lothair fled to Italy. The general confusion in men's minds was then at its height, and was only increased by the expiatory ceremonies and the reprisals that marked the following year. The emperor, for his part, thought only of assuring for his youngest son, at all costs, as large a share as possible in the empire. As the negotiations to this end with the conspirators of 833 had produced no result, he took independent action. In 837 Charles was given a kingdom comprising the whole region between the middle Meuse, the Seine and the sea. The next year, when he came of age, he was girt with a sword and crowned by his father at Quierzy. Since Pepin of Aquitaine had died at the end of 838, his kingdom was at once made over to Charles, in defiance of the rights of the dead king's son, Pepin II, whose supporters immediately took up arms. After an indecisive campaign south of the Loire in order to force his youngest son upon Aquitaine, Louis resumed negotiations with Lothair, setting him in opposition to Louis the German, on whom he had called as early as 838 to evacuate all the lands he had occupied since 833 on the right bank of the Rhine, and to withdraw to Bavaria. In 839 Lothair consented to appear at the Assembly of Worms, where he was pardoned by his father, who proceeded to divide the empire into two equal parts, except for Bavaria, which was left to Louis. As the eldest, Lothair was invited to choose his share, and he chose the east, that is, besides Italy, all the territories beyond the Meuse, the Saône and the Rhône, except for Toul, Lyon, Geneva and Provence, which went to Charles, who took all the west. This division was to come into force upon their father's death. The two heirs were placed on a completely equal footing. There was no longer any question of the empire: the imperial idea had perished in the midst of the great crisis, except perhaps in the minds of Lothair and a few clerics. Death came to deliver Louis the Pious from the appalling drama provoked by his vacillations while he was warring against his eldest son, Louis the German, in order to bring him to his senses (22 June 840).

The division of the empire into two in 839 became four years later a division into three by the Treaty of Verdun.

As soon as Louis the Pious was dead, Lothair, taking his stand upon the *Ordinatio* of 817, proclaimed his intention to have himself recognised emperor in all the former imperial territories, sending out messengers everywhere to receive the oath of allegiance to him from all the inhabitants. Strictly speaking, he was within his rights with regard to Louis the German, who claimed all the territories east of the Rhine assured to him by the agreements of 831 and 833. But as regards Charles the Bald, Lothair's actions were a violation of the treaty of 839, and a grave abuse of power. There gathered round him an 'imperialist' party, containing, along with his former faithful adherents, his two brothers' vassals, especially Charles's, whom he had succeeded in winning over; and among his protégés was Pepin II of Aquitaine.

This policy brought Charles and Louis together against the emperor, and they succeeded in defeating him at the bloody battle of Fontenoy-en-Puisaye on 25 June 841, which they considered to be a judgment of God. The following year they consolidated their alliance by taking, in the presence of their warriors, the famous oaths of Strasbourg by which they undertook to support one another and not treat separately with Lothair. Louis used the Romance language in order to be understood by Charles's warriors; and Charles spoke in Thiois (a germanic dialect) in order to be understood by Louis's men. After this, each of the warrior groups declared in their own language that they would refuse to follow their king if he attempted any unjustified military operations against his brother.

It is not to our purpose to enter here into the philological controversy about the text of the Strasbourg oaths, the first written document we possess in the vernacular spoken in Charles's kingdom at a time when the written Thiois tradition was clearly a good deal older. We will confine ourselves to stressing the extreme importance of the feudal order that shines through the oaths. They do not so much represent a contract between two sovereigns as a collective agreement based upon personal loyalties. No doubt Charles and Louis wanted to protect themselves against the deleterious effects of Lothair's propaganda by a solemn reinforcement of the feudal bonds. Very significant too is their insistence on consulting the Church upon the political measures they might be led to undertake. When they arrived at Aachen and found that Lothair had rejected all their proposals for negotiation, they assembled a council to discuss the fate of the Empire and the emperor. The bishops drew up a formal indictment against Lothair, who had 'heaped crime upon crime' and so incurred the punishment of God. Now that Lothair was a fugitive, the empire would pass to his two brothers, provided that they undertook to govern it justly. Charles and Louis at once declared their consent, after which the bishops handed over the empire to them 'in order that they might govern it according to God's will'. After the councils of 829, the council of Aachen, pronouncing Lothair's deposition and giving a free hand to his two brothers, marked a new stage in the part the Church intended to play in the destinies of the Christian state.

The two kings then agreed to share the empire between them. Thanks to the historian Nithard, we are in a position to follow the principles and methods of this operation. To begin with, it was only a question of dividing the northern territories between the two brothers. Nothing precise is known about this plan, except that it was inspired by the ideas of *affinitas* and *congruentia*: in other words, the countries to be shared out to each of them must have contact with the regions already actually held by them, and the personal convenience of the two kings was likewise to be taken into account. But this first partition was soon swept aside by a new turn of events.

Lothair had in fact not fled to Italy, as was believed, but to the valley of the Rhône, and was busy gathering another army. In April 842 he let his brothers know that he was ready to make peace, and demanded a share in the partition of the empire, leaving Pepin of Aquitaine to his fate. Charles and Louis agreed to parley, and laborious discussions went on up to the end of October. It was agreed that the division of the empire should not touch Italy, Bavaria or Aquitaine, the first being considered as reserved for Lothair, the second for Louis and the third for Charles; and the same applied to Provence and to the Burgundian part of the Rhône valley, both of which were held to belong to Lothair (no doubt because he had been in possession of them since the battle of Fontenoy). This, then, was the first solid fact— the omission of those southernmost parts of the empire; and this goes some way towards explaining the peculiar structure in which the three kingdoms, side by side along a north-south axis, were to be arranged a year later in the treaty of Verdun.

The only regions to be divided were the central and northern parts of the empire. To the principles of *affinitas* and *congruentia* Lothair added that of *aequissima portio*, or complete equality of the three shares, each of them to be contiguous with one of the three reserved regions. But it was still necessary to know the exact size of what was to be shared, so that the division could be carried out *pari sorte* (into equal lots). The three brothers each appointed forty commissioners for this purpose, to meet in October and proceed to draw up an inventory (*descriptio*) of the empire, and then to divide it. The commissioners duly assembled at Coblenz on 19 October; but it was very soon evident that they could not reach agreement in defining the territory of the empire. So the three brothers undertook the task themselves. After renewing their armistice at Thionville in November, they agreed in principle that the empire should be divided in July of the following year, and at once sent *missi* throughout all the regions to collect the necessary information for an inventory. During the winter and spring of 843 the commissioners worked on this inventory; and in August of that year the treaty was ready.

We must now go on to look at what was in fact divided. And here our best guide will be Ganshof, who helps us by analysing the tenor of the *descriptiones*, which were part of the current administrative technique. An inventory drawn up at the demand of the imperial government (and—be it emphasised—with the definite purpose of partition in view) involved an enumeration of the bishoprics, abbeys and collegiate institutions with their property titles, the counties—with information of the counts' endowments (*res de comitatu*)—and finally a list of the imperial domains (*fisci*) let out as fiefs or worked directly. Once this is understood, the question becomes relatively simple. We have only to understand the way in which the treaty of Verdun was prepared to grant that within a broadly agreed framework—the lands east of the Rhine bordering on Bavaria to go to Louis the German, those between the Meuse, Saône, Rhine and Alps adjacent to Italy and southern Burgundy to Lothair, and those west of the Meuse and the Saône and near Aquitaine to Charles— it was a matter of sharing out an aggregate of Churches, counties, rights and domains which constituted the means of governmental action and provided the subsistence of the sovereign. And the fact that this partitioning was done as fairly as possible is well shown by the case of Lothair's share, which was extended, between May 842 and the treaty of Verdun, in a north-westerly direction as far as the Sambre-Dyle line in the first place, and then as far as the Scheldt. The question of dividing the royal domains seems to have been foremost among the three kings' preoccupations. Lothair was given those in the Ardennes and those between the Meuse and the Rhine; Charles, those between the Somme, the Aisne and the Seine; and Louis the German, because there was relatively little of these lands in the east, was compensated by an additional sector that was peculiarly rich in them, on the left bank of the middle Rhine, round about Speyer, Worms and Mainz.

Private considerations undoubtedly played a part as well, such as the problem of the lands to be distributed by way of reward to each king's supporters, though no one was allowed to hold fiefs in more than one kingdom. Again, there was the desire to include in each of the three shares the *pagi* of the counts who had sided with each of the three kings during the civil war. The faithfulness of Count Guérin to Charles would thus seem to explain the allocation to Charles the Bald of the counties bordering on the Saône and even extending beyond it at one point (the county of Chalon). On the other hand it is quite certain that, apart from the

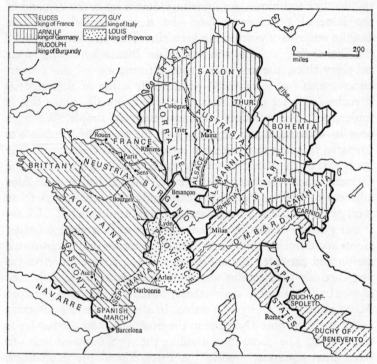

MAP 3 Territories of the Frankish empire in the late ninth century.

territory east of the Rhine, the languages and historical setting of the various peoples of the empire played no part at all in the division. Lothair's domain extended over two language zones; *Francia* and *Burgundia* were divided between Charles and Lothair, and Alemannia–Alsace between the latter and Louis.

The treaty of Verdun has not come down to us in any written document, so that the final division of the territories can be determined only by the evidence of historians, and in Lothair's case—quite exceptionally—by a precise inventory dating from 870. With this information, which is strikingly less precise than the records we have of the preliminaries to the treaty, we can reconstruct the partition of the Carolingian empire as follows. Charles was given the countries situated west of the Scheldt and of a line running from Cambrai through Sedan, the Argonne, the valley of the upper Marne and the Langres plateau towards the Saône, which it follows throughout its course (with the county of Chalon as an enclave on the left bank). Beyond Lyon, the boundaries of his kingdom did not include the Lyonnais, the Vivarais or the Uzège, but rejoined the lesser Rhône south of Nîmes and included the whole of Septimania and the Spanish March. Compared with what he had received in 839, Charles the Bald's new kingdom was greatly diminished, not only in the north, but also in the south, where he had lost an important section between the Cévennes and the Alps; and he never ceased to think of the boundaries of 839. Louis received all the Germanic lands east of the Rhine, less Frisia, but with the addition, on the other side of the river, of the enclave already mentioned. This was a considerable gain as compared with the situation in 839, when the whole of the German *bloc*, less Bavaria, had been given to Lothair. But it must be remembered that since 831 and 833 Louis had extended his dominion over these lands, and that Lothair had not been able to supplant him. As regards Lothair's share of the empire, it stretched between these two kingdoms from the North Sea to the Mediterranean. It was very extensive towards the north-west, where it included the present-day Low Countries from the Scheldt to Frisia, no doubt to compensate for the nominal losses east of the Rhine; and it also included Frankish Italy. 'The possession of the two capitals, Aachen and Rome,' says Louis Halphen, 'gave a certain sanction to the imperial title which Lothair continued to use.'

Thus the treaty of Verdun marks the end of Charlemagne's empire. Less than thirty years had been needed to bring about its downfall. Its vast size; the difficulties of administration; the absence of a regularly paid body of officials as a part of the economic structure; the strong sense of ethnic separatism in Aquitaine, in Burgundy, in Italy and in the land across the Rhine; the growth of the feudal system alongside the decay in the notion of fealty as a result of the multiplication of conflicting oaths; the rivalry between the lay aristocracy and the higher clergy; the emancipation of the Church from the imperial power: all these were factors contributing to the rapid collapse of the edifice constructed by Charlemagne, and the dynastic quarrels were played out against a gradually crumbling scene.

Thus Charlemagne's empire was replaced by three Francias, western, central and eastern, whose masters were on a completely equal footing. One of them, Lothair, continued to bear the imperial title, which contributed a certain prestige, it is true, but nothing more, though its holder tried during the years that followed the treaty of Verdun to give it some solid substance. He had little success, however; for north of the Alps the imperial idea was well and truly eclipsed after 843. On the other hand, it was never forgotten that the three Francias continued together to constitute one *Regnum Francorum*. In a letter from Lothair to Pope Leo IV, the kingdom was said to be not so much separated as 'in three distinctive parts', whose unity seemed secure in the notion of a single body constituted by the three brothers (*unum corpus fratrum*). This unity explains the maintenance of a common understanding between the three kings by means of a common government for the *regnum* as a whole. This was the regime of so-called 'brotherly concord', a substitute for the imperial idea, which functioned more or less adequately up to Lothair I's death in 855. The new divisions occasioned by this event then presented Charles and Louis with the temptation to increase their own states at the expense of their nephews; and Charles was even tempted to make a bid for the empire.

Charles the Bald's promotion to emperor is the last episode in the policy of regrouping a part of the territories of the ancient Frankish monarchy which had occupied the attention of the king of the western Franks since 860. But the empire during the last quarter of the ninth century was no longer the same in substance as it had been before the treaty of Verdun, for its centre had shifted south of the Alps, and it appeared a foreign institution to the Franks of Charles the Bald. These features require some further explanation before we go on to trace the story of the imperial adventure undertaken by the grandson of Charlemagne.

After the treaty of Verdun, the idea of the empire was gradually limited to Rome and Italy. As early as 844 Lothair had delegated his power in Italy to his eldest son Louis II, and had had him anointed king of the Lombards by Pope Sergius IV. Six years later Leo IV anointed him as emperor and invested him with the imperial crown. This fact should give us pause for thought, for it is of the greatest importance for the history of the accession to the empire. Charlemagne had been crowned emperor. As we have seen, there was no question of anointing, all the more so because Charlemagne had already received royal unction in 754; and he himself crowned Louis the Pious, who had been an anointed king since 781. It is commonly thought that, when Pope Stephen IV visited the new emperor in 816, he anointed him and crowned him afresh. But we are very far from being certain about this. Certainly, the pope placed a diadem on the head of Charlemagne's son; but did this act renew and repeat the first coronation, or was it simply a piece of display in honour of a prince on whom the pope had many demands to make? The sources which give an account of the scene would rather incline us towards the second hypothesis. As for the anointing Louis is supposed to have received on this same occasion, it seems doubtful also because only two sources mention it, and the normally precise Royal Annals make no reference to it. It seems then that we cannot rely with any absolute certainty on these data. The anointing and coronation linked together in a single ceremony are reliably attested only in the case of Lothair, in the year 823. He too had been proclaimed emperor and crowned with the diadem by his father in 817, but in that year he was not yet (unlike Louis the Pious in 813) an anointed king; and so it must have seemed necessary to the 'union' party, who were then in control of the empire, to have Lothair anointed and crowned, in order that he might be placed upon exactly the same footing as his father, with whom he was now associated in power. Since the years 754 and 800 the pope had been the dispenser *par excellence* of these two rites; he was the normal and natural person to turn to. But with Louis II, the situation was different in another way. He had received unction as king of Italy; nevertheless, the pope anointed him a second time as emperor, and then crowned him. If we also take into account that, contrary to the procedure in 813 and 817, Louis II was not proclaimed emperor in the midst of an assembly of notables at Aachen, it must be admitted that between 844 and 850 there were two radical innovations: not only the idea that one became emperor by virtue of an anointing and coronation of a special kind, both performed by the pope, but also that the two rites must be conferred in Rome, even if the king had already received royal unction previously. The triumph of these two ideas very quickly gave the papacy a considerable right to have a hand in conferring the supreme dignity. Thus the initial mortgage, of which Charlemagne had thought he could relieve the empire in 813, became a new burden upon it half a century after its rebirth.

The fixed form now given to the imperial accession was accompanied by other conditions which transformed the notion of empire as such. First there was the fact that, on the death of Lothair I, Louis II did not enter into possession of any of his father's transalpine possessions,[1] and so was reduced to Italy alone. From this point onwards, the empire seemed to become confused with the former kingdom of the Lombards. Thus after Lothair's death it is possible to talk of an Italo-Roman empire.

Moreover, it did not simply have this character on account of its territorial basis; it was also powerfully influenced by ideas that found their way to Rome. As far as these can be grasped and isolated from one another, there was first and foremost a strong consciousness of a renaissance, or—as it was then called—a renewal of the empire of ancient times, whose centre had been Rome itself, with all its prestige, which still made it the capital of the world (*caput mundi*). Men were conscious, too, that the empire belonged to the Romans, who had the right to dispose of it and to elect the emperor; it was they who had acclaimed Charlemagne on 25 December 800. The social milieu in which these ideas were most vitally alive was the landed and military aristocracy. But the horizons of those who considered themselves the heirs of the ancient Romans appeared to have shrunk, for they now hardly extended further than the city and the duchy of Rome. For them, the possession of an emperor meant the hope of using the cover of his pre-eminent power to lay their hands upon the states and the lands belonging to the Church.

Thus the papacy needed a protector against this turbulent and greedy aristocracy. This protector was the emperor, and the essential task committed to him by the papacy was to defend the Roman Church. This meant a considerable restriction of the imperial mission, which, in Charlemagne's time and even in the

[1] See p. 200.

early years of Louis the Pious, extended to the Church universal, and assigned to the emperor the governance of Christendom. But the Carolingian empire had crumbled into ruins; and the greatest pope of the ninth century, Nicholas I, whose pontificate (858–67) fell in the reign of Louis II, took the fullest advantage of this fact. It was the business of the universal Church, and specifically of the papacy, to assure the moral unity of Christendom, and to inspire and control the conduct of its kings. The emperor was one of these, a little higher in prestige than the others because he was Constantine's successor. Having been appointed by the pope, he must accomplish the tasks that the pope assigned to him. Thus the empire had a particular office to fulfil in the Church, 'the defence and exaltation of the mother of all the Churches', to quote the famous letter written by Louis II himself to Basil I, the Byzantine emperor, in 871; and again, 'the imperial dignity is no empty phrase: it resides in the summit of godliness.'

Such was the new interpretation that gradually took shape when the institution became confined to Italy and Emperor Louis II was playing a difficult role between the local aristocracies and the Church. This was also the time when he was waging energetic war against the Saracens, who periodically ravaged the coasts of the peninsula, and were making alarming progress, particularly in the south. His recapture of the town of Bari in 871 restored to the imperial idea something of its former glory, at any rate south of the Alps. But from that moment onwards Charles the Bald began to keep a very close eye upon the question of Louis's successor.

Since 843 he had been at the head of a kingdom in which the first requirement was to make his power decisively felt. Yet he was obliged at first to pursue a cautious and moderate policy, for he was confronted by a number of serious difficulties. There were the Bretons, intent upon securing expansion and independence; the Aquitanians, who had partly gone over to Pepin II; and the Normans, whose raids were throwing the whole western part of his states into terror and confusion. The essential thing for him was to keep a hold on the lay aristocracy; this he succeeded (to some extent) in doing by basing his royal power upon the idea of contract, identical with that which governed the relationship between a lord and his vassals, involving reciprocal duties, and subject to the judgment of the notables of the realm as regards any breaches of agreement. But at the same time he drew closer in his links with Church. Its most famous representative, Hincmar, archbishop of Rheims, was not only the king's most influential adviser up to about the year 870, but also contrived to invest the Frankish monarchy with an exceptional prestige, which helped greatly to strengthen it morally and spiritually. Charles's relations with his brothers were sometimes difficult, but open conflict was avoided thanks to the 'regime of brotherly concord' founded on mutual assistance and non-aggression pacts, which was repeatedly renewed in a series of meetings held from 843 onwards. This triple entente was however jeopardized by a tendency for two of the brothers to combine against the third. As far as it is possible to get any general idea of a constantly changing situation, it may be said that after 851 Charles the Bald was more often than not in league with Lothair against Louis the German.

The death of Lothair in 855 meant that the principles regulating the relationship of the Frankish kings since the treaty of Verdun were once again uncertain. The emperor divided his states into three portions. To Louis II he gave Italy and the imperial title; to Lothair II, the northern region of the former *Francia media*, from Frisia to the Langres plateau, with Aachen as its capital, the area then known as *Lotharii regnum* (Lothair's kingdom) and later as Lotharingia, from which comes the modern name Lorraine; to Charles, the youngest, the southern territories, from the Lake of Geneva to the Mediterranean. The former empire thus became a mosaic of five *regna* of unequal size and lacking in cohesion; and none of the new reigning sovereigns seemed capable of holding the balance, as Lothair—at any rate during the later years of his reign—had sometimes attempted to do. Charles the Bald and Louis the German still confronted one another distrustfully; and in 857 the latter did not hesitate to support certain lords in revolt against his brother, and to invade his kingdom in an attempt to get himself recognised as king. They were both ready to take advantage of their nephews' difficulties and extend their own power at their expense. Their mutual distrust was abated only when they combined to impose their will upon one or other of these princes, obviously considering themselves as representatives of the older generation and upholders of order, whereas Lothair's sons were mere upstarts. Of these three sons, Louis II seemed at first to be the least vulnerable. Charles of Provence, on the other hand, appeared an almost negligible quantity. He was incapable of governing, and had been confided to the care of a powerful feudal magnate, Count Girard of Vienne, whose task it was to defend the kingdom against the numerous competitors ready to pounce upon it, such as Louis of Italy, Charles the Bald and Lothair II. As king of a Lorraine which lay between the two Francias, and seemed to be a kind of buffer state but was really not firm enough in structure to play this part, Lothair II made simultaneous efforts to recover the regions of the Rhône, the Jura and the Alps, and to defend the independence of his own kingdom against his two uncles. All these fiercely opposed ambitions give the diplomacy of the period that opens in 855 a singularly tortuous and complicated character. It was important to bring out the chief facts in order to understand Charles the Bald's manœuvres, which we can now proceed to study in their principal phases.

It was towards the south-east that the king first tried to extend his power, invading the kingdom of Provence in 861 at the instance of a party of notables hostile to Girard. But his expedition was halted. Two years later, Charles of Provence died, and his two brothers made a friendly division of his inheritance, paying particular attention to the local vassals' interests. Lothair II took the centre (Lyonnais, Viennois, Vivarais and Uzège), where Girard was his representative, and Louis II the north (the bishoprics of Belley and Tarentaise) and Provence proper.

Being thus for the moment cut off from the south-east, Charles the Bald concentrated all his attention upon Lorraine. Indeed, the question which dominated Carolingian diplomacy from 860 onwards was Lothair II's divorce, which may be briefly summed up as follows. The king wanted to repudiate his lawful wife, Theutberga, who was barren, and marry his mistress, Waldrada, by whom he had had a son called Hugh. If he could be legitimised, he would one day be enabled to succeed to the throne, thus preserving the kingdom's independence and removing all fears of partition. It was to this end that Lothair applied all his efforts; he made numerous diplomatic approaches, and did not hesitate to use violence and forgery, or even to allow the dismemberment of his realm, ceding successively Geneva, Lausanne and Sion to his brother Louis II, and Alsace to Louis the German in order to gain their support.

The complications of the drama were many and various. Whilst

the Church of Lorraine was compliant enough to the king's desires and authorised him to break off his union with Theutberga
and marry Waldrada, Hincmar, having weighed up all the possi-
bilities in the situation, vigorously espoused the opposite cause.
He and Charles the Bald constituted themselves Theutberga's
protectors and she appealed to Rome. Pope Nicholas I, considering
himself invested with the supreme *auctoritas* empowering him to
rule the Church and direct the lives of kings, denounced the
scandal and declared the new marriage null and void. Furthermore, he deposed the archbishops of Cologne and Trier, the heads
of the Church in Lorraine, and threatened to excommunicate all
the bishops that had supported them. The firmness of his tone
provoked a violent protest from the two former, but brought the
others to submit. But the pope did not stop there. He called together an Ecumenical Council in Rome to settle all outstanding
matters at issue in Christendom. Alarmed by this turn of events,
Charles the Bald and Louis the German forbade their bishops to
attend the council, and met one another at Tusey-sur-Meuse in
order to invite their nephew to put an end to the scandal himself.
The latter then requested Nicholas I to settle the dispute. He was
compelled to separate from Waldrada and take back Theutberga,
who was brought back to him by a papal legate (865–6). But he
refused to admit defeat, and took up the matter again with
Nicholas's successor, Hadrian II. He replied with soothing pro-
mises and this was the state of affairs when Lothair II died in
August 869.

Legally, his kingdom ought to have reverted to his only surviving brother; but Louis II was occupied with war against the
Moslems in Italy, and could not intervene in time. Moreover, his
rights had been rejected by his two uncles when they conferred
together at Metz in 868, producing an arrangement which was undoubtedly the most cynical of all the pacts agreed between the
two of them. They agreed that when the right moment came,
Lorraine should be divided into two equal parts, and that Louis
II's states should suffer the same fate. The empire would thus be
extinguished on the death of its present holder. Some historians
have not unreasonably seen this as a kind of reply to the 'imperial' policy of Nicholas I.

In the normal course of events, then, Lorraine would have been
divided between Charles and Louis. However, taking advantage

of an illness that incapacitated his brother at Ratisbon, and without paying any attention to what had been decided, the king of the western Franks immediately fell upon his nephew's kingdom, in response to a call from a group of lay and ecclesiastical nobles from the west. On 5 September 869 he entered Metz, to be anointed king of Lorraine four days later by Hincmar and a number of the bishops of Lorraine. He pressed on northwards, reaching Aachen and then Cologne, where he asserted his sovereign rights. But Louis the German protested, alerted Louis II and Pope Hadrian, and threatened to resort to arms. In the end the two brothers agreed at Meersen-sur-Meuse, in 870, to divide Lorraine between them. The whole of the west as far as the Meuse, with a third of Frisia and the lands between the Rhône, the Alps, and the Durance, passed to Charles. On the other hand Louis the German entered into possession of everything between the Meuse and the Rhine. This was a far from perfect treaty, the frontiers often being drawn quite contrary to common sense; nevertheless, the agreement represented a great advance upon previous partitions. If it had been maintained, it might perhaps have prevented the later conflicts between the two Francias.

The territorial additions Charles the Bald had just obtained in the south-east turned his attention towards Italy. It may be that he was influenced by Bishop Ado of Vienne, who stood for a revival of the imperial idea; or he may himself have seen the possibility of taking possession of Italy and the empire in order to reconstitute the Frankish state as it had been about the year 774, before its great expansion towards the east. At all events, it is certain that after 870 he figured as a candidate for the succession to Louis II.

Louis II had no son. His wife, the Empress Engelberga, was carrying on a complicated diplomatic game, sometimes negotiating for the succession to Louis II with Louis the German, sometimes with Charles the Bald. The latter avoided committing himself, knowing that there was a strong party in Rome who were thinking of putting him forward for the empire. The spiritual father of this scheme was probably the librarian of the Lateran Palace, Anastasius, who judged Charles the Bald to be the most capable Carolingian successor to Louis II. Charles's culture, his devotion to the Church and his almost invariably good relations with the papacy were all in favour of him rather than his brother. As early as 872 Pope Hadrian II sent a secret message to the king of the western Franks to the effect that 'he himself, the clergy, the people and the nobility of the entire world and of this city' desired to have him 'not only as head and king, but also as patrician, emperor and defender of the Church'.

Hadrian's successor, John VIII, shared this point of view. In his eyes, Charles the Bald was the only king capable of effectively carrying out the tasks he expected of an emperor: the protection of the Roman Church against the lay aristocracy, whose tendency to secularize the Papal State had only been restrained with some difficulty by Louis II, and against the Moslems, who had remained dangerously on the offensive in spite of the victory at Bari. He had accordingly made up his mind to promote the king of the western Franks to the empire. It is worth following the way in which he carried out his plan, for it illustrates the facts set out above concerning the transformations undergone by the idea of empire.

After the death of Louis II (August 875), the pope promptly took the initiative, wisely making certain of support from the Roman aristocracy. He based his action upon the *Ordinatio Imperii*, which, it will be recalled, had required that in the event of Lothair's family dying out, the emperor should be appointed by election under the Church's control. He most cleverly dissociated the imperial dignity from the kingship of Italy, which he left temporarily vacant. This separation enabled him to disregard the hesitations of the notables of the realm assembled at Pavia, who were divided between Charles the Bald and a son of Louis the German, Carloman by name, to whom Engelberga declared Louis II to have bequeathed the Italian kingdom on his deathbed. Thus Charles the Bald's election to the empire was an exclusively Roman affair. It was no doubt effected by a synod including the laity, in which the pope acted as principal elector by interpreting the will of God, whom he declared to have foreseen and foreordained Charles as emperor. At his invitation those present 'elected' the king of the western Franks, that is to say, they expressed by acclamation the choice that had been divinely decreed.

Meanwhile the king had set out by way of the Great St Bernard, and on 29 September he reached Pavia. He succeeded in dispersing a troop of warriors sent against him by Louis the German, and then negotiated with Carloman in person, promising him to leave the eventual fate of Italy for the time being in suspense. Although

aware that Louis the German had invaded France, and had penetrated as far as Attigny, Charles pressed on to Rome and arrived
there on 17 December. And there, on Christmas Day, three
quarters of a century after his grandfather, he was anointed and
crowned emperor by Pope John VIII. For the first time, the
accession rites seem to have had constitutive force: the pope, in
the fullest sense of the term, created the emperor. In these circumstances, it was perfectly natural for Charles to have to make important concessions to his consecrator. In particular, he renewed
the privileges of the Roman Church granted by Charlemagne to
Hadrian I (in the form, no doubt apocryphal, that has come down
to us). He even increased his grandfather's gifts of land, adding
to them certain places in the Campagna for whose defence John
VIII was at the time responsible. Did he go still further, and re-
nounce the *Constitutio Romana* of 824? We cannot know for certain, but such a renunciation would have been very much in keeping with the atmosphere surrounding this fifth imperial accession.
The essential element, however, was the oath taken to John VIII
by Charles to be the faithful defender of the Roman Church.

It remained only to obtain the support of the kingdoms of Italy
and France for what had just been accomplished in Rome. On 5
January 876 Charles the Bald arrived at Pavia, where a general
assembly had been summoned. Those present were few in number
(only about ten counts and a few bishops); but they proceeded to
the imperial election by acclamation of the *Laudes*, took the oath
to Charles, and elected him 'protector, lord and defender'. These
are thoroughly characteristic expressions, making it clear that the
notables did not elect Charles king; for coming after an imperial
election, this would have been unthinkable. The Italian aristocracy recognised in the emperor their lord (in the feudal sense of
the term), their protector and defender, in that his functions as
advocate of the papacy also concerned the kingdom of Italy.

The same procedure was repeated in almost the same form at
the assembly held at Ponthion in western Francia in June and
July, though not, it seems, without some difficulty. Charles the
Bald's imperial title met with some opposition, and notably from
Archbishop Hincmar, who thought that imperial politics were a
thing of the past, and was afraid that a return to them might distract
the emperor from the urgent tasks that lay before him in France.
The acts of the Diet of Pavia were read out, after which a new

text was drawn up, with considerable help from the Italian model. The bishops of Lorraine and Francia—and they alone on this occasion—declared Charles to be elected and confirmed, as he had been elected and consecrated by the pope in Rome and elected by the notables in Italy. We do not know whether there was any fresh taking of an oath. At all events on the final day Charles the Bald came before the assembly, robed in his purple chlamys and wearing the diadem; and as at Pavia, he was greeted with the *Laudes*, which were the assembly's means of solemnly affirming that they recognised their sovereign to be invested with the supreme dignity.

Thus Charlemagne's empire seemed to have been revived by the union of the kingdoms of Francia and Italy under the one prince who had been consecrated emperor by the pope. Very significantly, the bull Charles the Bald had been using ever since his coronation bore the device *Renovatio Imperii Romani et Francorum*, a combination of Charlemagne's first imperial device and his successor's. But would the new empire comprise all the territories that had constituted the empire of the year 800? There was certainly no such idea in Charles the Bald's mind, for Germania proper did not interest him. On the other hand it is possible that he intended to round off his empire by the inclusion of Provence, the whole of the Low Countries, and especially the lands between the Meuse and the Rhine. This would explain why, as soon as he heard the news of Louis the German's death in August 876, he invaded the part of Lorraine he had had to cede to his brother under the treaty of Meersen. He behaved with full sovereign power, rejected a proposal to negotiate put forward by his nephew Louis the Young, who ruled over Franconia, Thuringia and Saxony, and sought to decide the issue by force of arms. But on 8 October he was utterly defeated at Andernach.

This reverse marks 'the beginning of the end' of Charles the Bald's empire. In Italy, there was a rapid change in the situation: the adherents of the German Carolingians raised their heads; whilst in France, the Norman invasions prevented the emperor from going south of the Alps to carry out his duties as defender, as the pope kept exhorting him to do. The Saracens had taken possession of Latium, and were encamped only a few leagues from Rome. It looked, moreover, as if Charles considered that the favourable situation established at Rome, Pavia and Ponthion was not very permanent, and as if he was afraid of an increasingly strong opposition among the aristocracies, which was then beginning to make itself felt. Was this why he induced John VIII to call together at Ravenna in 877 a fresh assembly of one hundred and thirty bishops, to whom he justified his choice of Charles the Bald as emperor? Listening to the pope's words, one would have gathered that his hand had not been forced by Charles, but that Charles had merely accepted the pope's invitation 'to defend religion and protect the servants of Christ. . . . God himself has appointed him saviour of the world.' John VIII had only carried out the divine will in his capacity as leader of the Roman Church, the mother and head of the Church universal. And he therefore begged the bishops to ratify his action. The pope succeeded in obtaining their consent, and strengthened by their approval, he threatened with excommunication any who should oppose the power he had created. The council's proceedings reached Charles the Bald in the course of his second journey to Italy. In the assembly at Quierzy-sur-Oise he had with great difficulty managed to take steps to ensure order in the kingdom during his absence. He met John VIII in September at Vercelli, and they made their way together to Pavia. But at this point news reached them that Carloman had appeared on the scene with a powerful army. Charles's troops were inferior in number, and he did not receive the help he was relying upon from his own kingdom. He therefore decided to separate from the pope, and retire across the Alps. Worn out by illness, he died in the Maurienne valley on 6 October 877.

The lessons to be drawn from Charles the Bald's imperial adventure are many in number. In the first place, it illustrates the strength of the imperial idea in the second half of the ninth century, and the spell cast by the image of Charlemagne on his grandson. His defeat is primarily attributable to the difficulties he encountered in his poorly consolidated kingdom, invaded as it was by the Normans, and shaken by profound changes in its structure. This explains the lack of any means of attempting some more effective reconstruction, if not of the whole Carolingian monarchy, at least of a large part of it. But there is more to it still. Since the middle of the ninth century, there had been a profound change in the content of the imperial concept. The imperial mission had been, so to speak, absorbed by the papacy in the time of

Nicholas I and John VIII; and the supreme power no longer appeared to be more than a function conferred by the pope upon a prince of his choice, to whom he entrusted tasks that were of high importance to him. This function, which necessarily drew the emperor south of the Alps, seemed in France to be incompatible with the duties incumbent upon the king within his realm at home. Since about 850, Hincmar had come round to the idea of a 'national' royalty; and the great lay lords were so busy establishing their power over enormous tracts of territory that they failed to appear at the assembly of Quierzy-sur-Oise. Both of these parties were hostile or indifferent to the policy of empire, which seemed to them a completely foreign idea. Thus the imperial conception fell out of favour in France, and continued so over a long period. It was outside the kingdom of France that the empire now took root. Once only was there a return to the boundaries of the year 800, when the last son of Louis the German, Charles the Fat, united under his imperial authority almost the whole of the former Carolingian monarchy, during the years 881–7. But after this last attempt at regrouping, France settled down to live its own life within the reduced limits set by the treaty of Verdun.

Nevertheless, France contrived to preserve the great emperor's memory so strongly and continuously that it soon became the kingdom of Charlemagne *par excellence*. Sometimes in the twelfth and thirteenth centuries, when its German neighbours spoke of it, they would call it *Kärlingen*, the kingdom of Charlemagne, just as they called the former kingdom of Lothair II Lothringen.

And now, in order to complete our study, it remains only to examine this fundamental reality.

✧ XII ✧

Conclusion:
The king of France as
Charlemagne's successor

After the collapse of Charles the Fat's empire, the history of the kingdom of France seemed for a long time to contradict the true situation we have just outlined.

From the breakdown of the Carolingian entity there arose, apart from France, five kingdoms: Germania (with the boundaries set by the treaty of Verdun), Lorraine, Upper Burgundy (on both sides of the Jura), Lower Burgundy (Provence and Viennois), and Italy, which continued to carry imperial status until the year 924. After ceasing to exist at this point, the empire was restored in 962 under the most powerful western sovereign, Otto I, king of Germania. Belonging to a family originating in Saxony, which in 919 had taken the place in Germany of the Carolingian line, extinct since 911, he had brought Lorraine and Italy under his authority; and in 1033 one of his successors became master of the Burgundian kingdom, which at that time included the whole of the Jura, the Rhône and Provence territories. The new 'Roman Empire' was thus built up from a union of Lothair I's former *Francia Media* with the kingdom of Louis the German, then in process of growth to the east; and up to about the middle of the thirteenth century, it remained the most important territorial and political grouping in Europe. From that time onwards it began to disintegrate; yet it continued to exist in a reduced form until 1806. Now it must at once be emphasised that the kingdom of France, though confronting this empire, always kept its independence, even through the tenth century when the crisis it was

209

then undergoing gave Otto I several chances for intervening among the various parties who called on him to settle their disputes.

This crisis has a number of aspects. After the death of Charles the Fat, when it came to choosing a king, the aristocracy rejected the last of the surviving grandsons of Charles the Bald, also called Charles, because he was too young, and elected the head of a powerful line, Eudes, the son of Robert the Strong, who had distinguished himself in the struggle with the Normans. It was he who had led the heroic defence of Paris against the invaders in the year 885. And so for the time being the Carolingian dynasty was set aside. But an even more serious fact was the internal disruption of the kingdom. There were various great men who had collected counties, abbeys and commanding positions, and they tended to build up territorial principalities around themselves. As yet, these were only rough groupings, constantly reforming, disintegrating and changing, and did not for the most part reach the stage of consolidation until the eleventh century. But whatever their form might be, these territories were more or less independent, and bound to the royal house only by the oath of vassalhood taken to the king by their leaders, the dukes and the counts. The feudal order thus saved France from total disintegration.

While this process was developing, the forefront of the political scene was occupied by the rivalry between the Carolingians and the Robertians, who may already be called the Capetians. Eudes was succeeded by Charles the Simple (898); but a revolt among the notables led to his imprisonment, and to the election of Eudes's brother, Robert I (922-3), soon to be succeeded by his brother-in-law, Raoul of Burgundy. When the latter died in 936, the most powerful person in the kingdom was Robert I's son, Hugh, known as Hugh the Great. He did not however want the crown for himself, but recalled from England, where he had taken refuge, Charles the Simple's son, Louis IV, known as Louis d'Outremer. During the whole of his reign (936-54) the real power belonged to Hugh the Great, who exercised supreme military command in northern France, and succeeded for the time being in extending it to Aquitaine and Burgundy. He was likewise instrumental in causing Louis IV's son, Lothair, to be elected king; Lothair was succeeded in 986 by his son, Louis V. But the latter died prematurely the following year, leaving no son to succeed him. At that moment the only other representative of the Carolingian dynasty in the direct line was Charles, a brother of Lothair, whom the Emperor Otto II had made duke of Lower Lorraine. He was however set aside by the notables, who elected Hugh the Great's son, Hugh Capet (987), whose successors continued to reign over France till 1328.

Although, on the surface, this long crisis in the royal line reminds us of the one described at the beginning of this book—for no reader can have failed to see Hugh the Great as successor to the Mayors of the Palace, one who held the actual power and was much more powerful than the king himself—it would nevertheless be completely wrong to compare the last Carolingians with the decadent period of the Merovingians. Charles the Bald's successors could never have been classed as 'rois fainéants'—far from it. They all did their utmost to resist the disintegration of the kingdom and to save the royal line. Charles III, who has been unjustly given the pejorative nickname of 'the Simple', undoubtedly did much for his country's future by adopting the title *Rex Francorum* (king of the Franks), to be borne by his successors up to the time of Philip Augustus, when it was changed to *Rex Franciae* (king of France). It should be realised that in calling himself 'king of the Franks', Charles the Simple was affirming that the kingdom he ruled was undoubtedly the kingdom of Pepin and Charlemagne. This fact is all the more significant in that at this period the title 'king of the Franks' had disappeared from the protocol of the acts of other sovereigns reigning over the succession states of the former empire, except in Germania, where it reappeared from time to time. Thus the royal title served as a reminder of the continuity between the kingdom of France and the imperial glories of the past.

On the other hand, as the process of disintegration spread increasingly from south to north, the Carolingian kings concentrated their resistance more particularly in the lands between the middle Seine[1] and the Meuse. Unfortunately for them, the royal demesne had melted away as a result of the extensive alienations they were forced to allow in order to keep supporters and gain new ones. By the middle of the tenth century, a few palaces like

---

[1] It must be remembered that the lower Seine regions had been given up to the Normans by Charles the Simple in 911. From the end of the tenth century, a strongly organised Normandy became the most powerful territorial unit in the kingdom.

Compiègne and Attigny, together with the town of Laon, were the only bases left to the king. This poverty explains the two attempts made during the tenth century by the last Carolingians to recapture Lorraine, in order that they might have at their disposal, in the original home of their ancestors, the resources that they urgently needed.

In this operation Charles the Simple was successful, and he became king of Lorraine from 911 up to the time of his captivity. Lothair was less fortunate: a military expedition took him as far as Aachen in 978, but he was compelled to retreat and could not prevent Otto II's punitive expedition into his kingdom. But in 985 he took advantage of the difficulties in Germany arising from Otto III's minority to capture Verdun. This active policy was disturbing enough to the imperial court to make it, at least to all appearances, support the conspiracy initiated by Adalbero, archbishop of Rheims, who, on Louis V's death, contrived to raise to the throne not the late king's uncle but Hugh Capet, who had no designs upon Lorraine.

In this way the Capetians supplanted the Carolingians. For the official interpretation of the facts we can turn to the *History* of the chronicler Richer of Rheims and Aimo of Fleury's *Miracles of St Benedict*, both of which use more or less the same arguments, without any possibility of their having copied from one another. We are told that the Capetian was elected because Louis V had died childless, and because Charles of Lorraine served a foreign king. His accession could not be thought illegal; his ancestors had never attempted to usurp the throne; they had all been completely loyal to the old dynasty; and it was Hugh the Great who had made possible the return of Louis d'Outremer. The authors even assert that Eudes was made king by Charles the Simple. For their part, Hugh Capet and his son Robert the Pious, whom he promptly associated with himself as king, as well as their successors, were intent upon being considered the true heirs of the Carolingians; and their diplomas proclaimed them to be carrying on the work of Charlemagne and Louis the Pious.

But just as the official version was taking shape, an opposite view appeared. It is difficult to know whether this arose from a kind of sentimental attachment to the old dynasty; more probably,

22 *Two pictures of Charlemagne at the close of the Middle Ages* (see also
overleaf)

Charlemagne as one of the nine worthies

A picture of the mid-fifteenth century in the Petit Armorial équestre de
la Toison d'Or (Bibl. nat., Coll. Clairambault, vol. 1312).

The emperor in fifteenth-century armour, and on horseback, with the
helmet's visor raised, is flourishing a sword with one hand and in the
other holds the banner and buckler, both bearing the arms of the empire
and France.

The Holy Emperor

An oil painting, about 1460–70, in the Aachen Cathedral Treasury. Charlemagne was canonised at Aachen on 29 December 1165 at the instance of the Emperor Frederick I, and became the object of a liturgical cult in numerous churches of France and the empire.

Here he is represented in armour with his cloak thrown back over his shoulders; on his head he is wearing a high enclosed (imperial) crown surrounded by a double aura; in one hand he holds the short sceptre crowned with a fleur-de-lys, in the other a model of the church at Aachen which he founded.

its aim was to embarrass the Capetians by presenting them as usurpers. We get evidence of this opposition, for instance, from Aquitaine about the year 990, where the dating of certain charters runs as follows: 'Under the rule of Jesus Christ, Hugh Capet having, contrary to right, usurped the kingdom of France.' Such evidence comes particularly from Sens, where a clerk of the cathedral composed towards the end of the tenth century a *History of the Franks*, in which the events of 987 are presented in a knowingly and deliberately distorted manner. The last French Carolingian, Charles of Lorraine, was not—this author asserts—Louis V's uncle, but his brother; Hugh Capet had risen against him and, after imprisoning him, had procured his own election as king in his place. This interpretation is nothing less than a political pamphlet, no doubt inspired by Archbishop Seguin of Sens, who had had no part in Hugh Capet's election; it would perhaps have been forgotten if—as F. Werner has shown—historians of the eleventh and twelfth centuries such as Sigebert of Gembloux, Hugh of Fleury and Orderic Vitalis, wishing to include in their chronicles a summary of recent Frankish history, had not drawn upon the material provided by Sens. Thus it was easy to make the Capetian accession seem an outrageous usurpation.

However, as this opinion gradually spread, it provoked replies aimed at saving the new dynasty's legitimacy. The most interesting effort of this kind comes down to us in the so-called prophecy of St Valéry. Though composed towards the middle of the eleventh century, it referred to events that were then a hundred years old. Hugh Capet, while still Duke of the Franks, had given back to the abbeys of Saint-Riquier and Saint-Valéry the relics of their patron saints seized by Count Arnold of Flanders in 952. Recalling this restitution, our account represents St Valéry as appearing to Hugh Capet in person, urging him to return his mortal remains to the monks, and assuring him at the same time that this action will later on win him the throne, though his descendants will preserve the line only for seven generations. In the mind of the monk who composed this strange story, the St Valéry oracle was no doubt intended to incite Hugh Capet's successors to exorcise the fate that lay in store for them by granting new favours to the abbey. All the same, it is striking that the limit of seven generations of Capetians should have been so literally accepted by those to whom Hugh Capet's legitimacy was suspect. When writing his chronicle about the year 1130, Orderic Vitalis remarked that the fifth generation had already been reached, and that the time allotted to the Capetians was fast running out.

Whilst there were thus beginning to be some doubts about the dynasty's future, a new argument made its appearance, calculated both to legitimise it and endow it with magical prestige—namely the link between the Capetians and the Carolingians through the female line. The matter was all the easier in that, except for Anne of Kiev, Henry I's wife, all the Capetian kings' spouses were more or less distantly descended from Charlemagne. This fact had long been known, but it was only intermittently remembered, and its implications were not noticed. But there was a change of outlook about the middle of the twelfth century, under the influence of a fundamentally important legal change, which established the right of women in feudal law to pass on the inheritance of a kingdom. Thus it was admitted that the heiress of a family descended from Charlemagne could pass on all the rights of the ancient dynasty to children born of her marriage with the king of France; this made it possible to speak of the kingdom returning to the great emperor's line, *reditus regni Francorum ad stirpem Karoli*. In consequence, Philip Augustus, being the son of Louis VII and Adela of Champagne, and thus descended from Charlemagne, could now be reckoned as a 'carolid'. Support for the Capetians grew even stronger after he married Isabella of Hainault, whose membership of the *stirps Karoli* had been duly established. The child of this union, Louis VIII, was both the seventh descendant of Hugh Capet and, through his mother, one of the posterity of the great emperor. And so St Valéry's prediction seemed to have come true, though without involving the extinction of the Capetian line. The kingdom had come back to the dynasty of Charlemagne, and after a break of several centuries, the Carolingians once again occupied the throne of France.

But this was not an unprepared victory, for well before this realisation had come about, the Carolingians, and Charlemagne in particular, were already enthroned in the collective memory of their one-time subjects.

The memory of Charlemagne had indeed been preserved by the power of the national epic, the *Chansons de Geste* or *Chansons d'Histoire*, which critics nowadays have come to see as a continuous creation beginning at the time of the events they relate. The excellent work of R. Menendez Pidal has made this very clear, particularly by bringing out the notion of a people's heroic age 'in which poetry and history become identified . . . and historical persons may become idealised . . . and the people creates its heroes. . . . The heroic age is that of a nation at the first stage in the development of its culture.' This corresponds to the early Middle Ages, and stretches over the whole of the Carolingian period when the Franks were building the empire and defending Christianity. Now during the heroic age there existed side by side a written history in Latin, restricted to a clerical minority, and a poetic history, not fixed by any written form, and so constantly being transformed with the passage of time, following the changing ethos, and becoming increasingly imbued with miraculous elements as its historical content diminished. This legendary development, however, did not prevent numerous cross-fertilisations between the oral and the written traditions. Thus the result of patient research into the intermediate links between the (supposed) actual events of the battle of Roncevalles and our *Chanson de Roland* in its oldest written form (about 1100), thanks mostly to notes contained in annals scattered through the years of the ninth to the eleventh centuries, has revealed a whole series of successive recastings and enrichments of the original *Roland* (such as the feigned submission of Saragossa to Charlemagne, the handing over of a great treasure to the Frankish king, the miracle of the sun stopped in its course by Charlemagne, as by a new Joshua, the twelve peers, and the friendship between Roland and Olivier). As sung by the *jongleurs*, the poem was already reaching a wide audience by the end of the tenth century. For proof of this, we have only to note the astonishing spread of the name Olivier, often in association with Roland, in southern France and the central western districts, particularly Anjou. Nor should it be forgotten that at the battle of Hastings, which gave England into the hands of the Normans in 1066, the *jongleur* Taillefer spurred on the courage of William the Conqueror's warriors by singing to them of Roland and of Olivier.

This insight into the development of the *Chanson de Roland* may also be applied to the other epics. In a study with the significant title 'L'épopée française est carolingienne', R. Louis has drawn up a list of fourteen important moments in Carolingian history, all corresponding to critical hours in the history of the monarchy and recalled to memory in the *Chansons de Geste*. His highly instructive picture stretches from Charles Martel's victory over Chilperic (716), a theme embodied in *Berthe aux grands pieds*, *Mainet* and *Basin*, to the victory over the Normans won by Charles the Bald's grandson, Louis III, at Saucourt in 881, to be found in *Gormond et Isembart*. And his survey includes Charlemagne's expeditions to Italy (*Chevalerie d'Ogier*), to Saxony (*Chanson des Saisnes*), to Spain (*Roland*), the battles between Guillaume de Toulouse and the Saracens (*Chanson de Guillaume*, *Aliscans*), the revolt of Louis the Pious's sons against their father, who was defended by Guillaume's sons (*Couronnement Louis*), Charles the Bald's subjection of Girard of Vienne (*Girard de Roussillon*), and a number of others.

But by the end of the ninth century the heroic age had come to an end, and with it the songs telling of current events. From the tenth century onwards, as R. Louis observes, there were no more direct memories preserved, except perhaps the intervention of Louis d'Outremer in *Raoul de Cambrai*. A period of decadence had begun, and nothing was any longer worth the telling—in strong contrast to the greatness of the reigns of Charlemagne and his immediate successors.

These *chansons* were the collective result of a succession of creations and remodellings, each the work of several poets, and written down from the end of the eleventh century onwards. In the twelfth they were enriched and multiplied, and regrouped in cycles before being later adapted as historical prose romances. There was no abatement of interest in the great epics until the close of the Middle Ages. In their ruggedness, their cult of the heroic, their individualism often showing the vassal in conflict with the king, their robust and ardent faith, they reflect the early feudal age in which they acquired their definitive character. The portrait they paint of Charlemagne is extremely varied. In the *Couronnement Louis*, the emperor, who 'no longer wished to lead this life nor bear this crown', appears to have reached his decline. In other poems, perhaps built up around some great feudal figure, there are traces of the conflict between the aristocracy and royalty; as for instance when Charlemagne is represented as an extravagant and choleric king reduced to the level of a mere tool in the hands of his vassals. But these discordant echoes are of small consequence in comparison with the glorious image of the emperor which shines forth from the majority of the *chansons*, and especially from the *Chanson de Roland*, the finest and noblest flower of all this extraordinary efflorescence.

Charles li Reis, nostre emperere magne, restorer of the empire, guardian of 'the holy Christian faith', is the supreme lord of the vassals who are personally bound to him, and hold from him their fiefs and their honours. It is first and foremost for him, and only incidentally for the Christian peoples he governs, that Roland gives his life. This sentiment is an authentic part of the Carolingian age and could not be a reflection of the crusading age, when the defence of Christianity was the all-important consideration. Charlemagne is portrayed as the Elect of God, who works countless great miracles on his behalf. He fights the good fight for God—*combien peineuse est ma vie*—subjecting the heathen to his law, and never forgetting to baptise them once they have been reduced to submission—a very close reflection of the actual historical facts. And finally, within the vast extent of the empire, there is one privileged section where Charlemagne's royalty seems as it were to have taken root, the country stretching from 'Saint-Michel du Péril to Sens, and from Besançon to Wissant', the former Romance-speaking Neustria, with its capital at Laon. We must pay particular heed to this geographical extension of France, for it more or less corresponds to the *Francia* of the later Carolingians. Does this not look like a recasting of the ancient poem carried out about the year 1000 'perhaps for purposes of political propaganda or dynastic interests'? Be that as it may, the authors of this poem display a sober and touching love for the area, which is their *Dolce France*, their *Terra majour*, their fatherland exalted by the great deeds of Charlemagne, and remembered by all its heroes when they come to die.

There is no need to press the point. The *Chansons de Geste*, especially the *Chanson de Roland*, kept Charlemagne and his times ever present in the collective memory. They preserved a vivid recollection of the glories of days gone by; and by portraying the gap between the present and the past, they also served as an invitation to restore the greatness of olden times.

The Carolingian tradition was thus a considerable, though rather diffuse, influence. Yet it found in the abbey of Saint-Denis a centre where it was cultivated out of self-interest before it radiated forth over the king himself. The abbey had a long and glorious past; ever since its foundation in the seventh century it had had close connections with royalty, the holy martyr whose name it bore being considered the patron saint of the Frankish monarchy. It played a considerable part in politics under the Carolingians through abbots like Fulrad and Hilduin. Custom had given it two particular privileges which raised it to an unrivalled position: it became the royal burial-place, and at the same time a sort of repository for the insignia of dead kings.

At the end of the eleventh century there are the first signs of a closer link between the abbey and Charlemagne. In its desire to authenticate the relics of the Passion in its keeping, it drew up— certainly between 1080 and 1095—a circumstantial account of a supposed pilgrimage by the emperor to Jerusalem and Constantinople, in the course of which he acquired these precious relics, transferring them subsequently to his chapel at Aachen, whence Charles the Bald brought them to Saint-Denis. This is the first rough outline of the theme of 'Charlemagne, king of Saint-Denis' popularised in the *Chansons de Geste*. It took more definite shape in the reign of Louis VI, who had close links with the monastery, especially during the abbacy of Suger (1122–51), who aimed not only at making his house a great artistic and cultural centre, but also at restoring the political role it had played in Carolingian times. The king himself urged it on in this direction. As early as 1120, a diploma of Louis VI had proclaimed St Denis as the *dux et protector* of the kingdom. Four years later, when faced with the danger of an invasion of France by the Emperor Henry V, the king came to the monastery before assuming command of the royal host, and there, in a memorable ceremony, he set up the saint's banner above the altar, in his capacity as Count of the Vexin and standard-bearer (*signifer*) of the abbey. In so doing, the king acknowledged himself to be the vassal of St Denis. The memory of that time was never forgotten, and seems to have contributed to the production of documents calculated to give the monastery greater prestige and a further increased authority, both being derived from the protection of Charlemagne.

First we have a Latin account, written between 1140 and 1150, of the liberation of Spain and Galicia by the great emperor, put into the mouth of Archbishop Turpin of Rheims, and popularised by the *Chanson de Roland*. It is generally agreed that this *Pseudo-Turpin* was composed by an author from the south-west, probably a Cluniac, but strongly influenced by Saint-Denis. It had a tremendous success—witness the several hundred manuscript versions of the story that have come down to us, not as a rule on its own, but forming part of a compilation intended to glorify the Apostle St James and the pilgrimage to Compostella, the so-called *liber sancti Jacobi*. The influence of Saint-Denis is specially evident in one of the later chapters of the *Pseudo-Turpin*, relating amongst other things that Charlemagne handed over the whole of France to the holy martyr, specifying that no king or bishop should be ordained without his advice. Furthermore, every landowner was to pay four *deniers* towards the fabric of the abbey church; and serfs who had paid this sum were exempted from all further servitude and became 'free men of St Denis'. Setting on one side this last clause, which seems to have been dictated by the need to restore the abbey under Suger, the historical background of the first arrangements, that are supposed to have been made by Charlemagne, is not very clear. The author's intention—or rather the intention of his inspirer—was no doubt to put back to Charlemagne's day the actual situation in which the abbey found itself under Louis VI, who had proclaimed it in a document of 1124 to be *caput regni*, the capital of the kingdom. As for the Saint's indispensable presence at royal ordination, it is perhaps a reflection of the monastery's ambition, since it possessed the royal insignia, to play a part in the anointing and coronation of the king. The central role occupied by Suger in the accession ceremonies of Louis VII, which did indeed take place in 1131 in the abbey church, was perhaps the origin of the singular prescriptive right attributed to Charlemagne.

But the abbey was not content with this position. At some uncertain time, but probably after Suger's death and between 1160 and 1165, a diploma was forged under the name of Charlemagne whose clauses provided an amplification and a partial transformation of the account contained in the *Pseudo-Turpin*. The abbey was here placed at the head of all the churches in the kingdom, and its abbot raised to the level of primate, with considerable privileges attached to that office. This was perhaps an echo of the exceptional position occupied by Suger during Louis VII's crusade, where he had been in effect regent of the kingdom for the space of three years. As regards the royal accession, the diploma follows the line of the *Pseudo-Turpin*, and reinforces what it affirms. It represents Charlemagne as saying: 'We forbid our successors, the kings of France, to be crowned anywhere but in the church of St Denis.' For that was indeed—as the compiler goes on to say, making Charlemagne speak in the first person—where the emperor had placed his diadem upon the altar, a gesture which handed over to the saint the *regale dominium* over the whole kingdom. The tax *(cens)* mentioned in the *Pseudo-Turpin* is changed by our forger into a nominal tax *(cens récognitif)* owed by the kings themselves to St Denis, as a sign that their power is derived solely from God and the holy martyr. 'From God alone and from thee, St Denis'—so Charlemagne is represented as proclaiming—'do I hold the realm of France.' He therefore offers four gold pieces on the saint's altar, and his successors will do the same, 'bearing the tax on their head', as though it were a real *chevage*, indicating by this gesture that they are the vassals of God alone. But as such, they would be exempt from all other dependence. The notables, for their part, were to pay four *deniers* toward the upkeep of the fabric; likewise the serfs, who would then be considered free. Finally, Charlemagne proclaims the complete independence of the kingdom, and even changes its earlier name, *Gallia*, into *Francia*, as a clear indication that it is free, that is exempt from all dependence upon any man whatsoever.

Such are the chief terms of this forged diploma, whose exact intentions are still a puzzle to historians. Was the purpose to fix by law and for all time the position acquired by the abbey half-way through the twelfth century? Or was it simply a scholastic exercise? At all events it is interesting to note that the abbey saw the fulfilment of some of the claims put forward by our document, though not in the extreme form in which they had been couched. The abbot of Saint-Denis assisted the archbishop of Rheims at Philip Augustus's anointing in 1179, and for the second time placed the royal crown on the son of Louis VII in the abbey church in 1180. We see St Louis, moreover, paying to the monastery, after returning from the crusade, the tax *(cens)* prescribed by the forged diploma, and entrusting to the care of Saint-Denis the guardianship of the ceremonial robes and the royal crowns. The ritual for the anointing composed during his reign lays it down that the abbot of Saint-Denis shall bring to Rheims, at each coronation, the various royal insignia, and shall take them back to the monastery immediately after the ceremony. The abbey thus became the guardian of the emblems of sovereignty for the reigning monarch, and not merely a museum for the insignia of dead kings. But there was more to it than this. Not only did the author of this forgery exploit the tradition of Charlemagne for private and particular ends; he also made use of it at the national level. For he turned this famous emperor into the patron of France, and the protector of its independence against any other power. This tendency had already been noticeable in the celebrated account given by Abbot Suger of the events of 1124. It came out more strongly still towards 1160, this time directed against the Holy Roman Emperor, Frederick I Barbarossa, who revived the idea of universal dominion, and who also drew his inspiration from Charlemagne. Thus Frederick's claim of *dominium mundi* was opposed by the ideas of complete exemption for the French *regnum* and of the complete sovereignty of the king of France. Both ideas derived from Charlemagne, and the two-fold concept soon became the essential element in French political thought.

Sustained by the *Chansons de Geste* and firmly anchored to the abbey of Saint-Denis, the Carolingian tradition finally cast an aura over the king himself. It was during Philip Augustus's reign that this victory took definitive shape, so much so that one of the latest historians of our medieval kings, P. E. Schramm, speaks of a *Renovatio Imperii Karoli Magni* as the characteristic of the great Capetian's reign; and there are countless signs of this renaissance.

First there was the reappearance of the name Charles in the dynasty. Philip Augustus called one of his illegitimate sons Pierre Karlot; and one of his grandsons was Charles of Anjou, who was followed by many other princes bearing the illustrious name, from Philip the Fair's brother, Charles of Valois, to the series of kings during the fourteenth and fifteenth centuries. But we must pause a moment at Philip Augustus, and note that there was still a group of political writers round the sovereign exalting the memory of Charlemagne and drawing a number of lessons from it. About 1200 Gilles de Paris, canon of Saint-Marcel, composed for the heir apparent, the future Louis VIII, a long didactic poem, the *Carolinus*, in which the emperor was held up as a moral ideal for his imitation. The author invited his reader to follow his glorious predecessor's attitude towards the Church, that is, to preserve and validate his prerogatives as the Church's defender. With even greater enthusiasm Guillaume le Breton, in the twelfth book of his *Philippide*, celebrates the reappearance of Carolingian virtue (*virtus rediviva*) incarnate *par excellence* in the king, in which all Frenchmen also have a share. It is to this that the king owes his great triumphs; in particular the victory of Bouvines, won over John Lackland's allies, especially the Emperor Otto IV, was interpreted by Guillaume le Breton as a new triumph for the Carolingian Franks over their old enemies, the Saxons. We hear Philip Augustus addressing his warriors as 'companions and heirs of Roland and Olivier'; and we also see him blessing his army before the battle in the manner of Charlemagne, whom the *Chanson de Roland* described as giving absolution to Ganelon before sending him to Marsile. Philip Augustus's heir, the 'Carolid' Louis VIII, is expressly invited to cross the Pyrenees and in a general way to reconquer all the lands belonging to him by the *Jus patrum* (the rights of his ancestors). There is perhaps no better expression of this rediscovered presence of Charlemagne than the association of certain emblems of royalty with his person, which began to take shape just about this time. We seem to feel the hand of the monks of Saint-Denis at work in this, with their preservation of precious objects. From 1181 onwards the royal standard, the very one set up by Louis VI in the abbey church in 1124, became identified with the oriflamme of the *Chanson de Roland*; and not long afterwards the ceremonial sword carried in front of the king at the ceremony of anointing was held to be the great sword 'Joyeuse'. From then on, there was to be no stopping this movement.

The contribution of the Carolingian tradition to the French monarchy from the thirteenth century on was substantial. There can be no doubt in the first place that it harmonised readily with the intrinsic features of the institution. The king of France was anointed, and this 'eighth sacrament', which he received at Rheims on his accession, gave him an exceptional prestige, since he alone among kings was anointed with the 'heavenly' oil from the *Sainte Ampoule*; he cured the sick by virtue of a thaumaturgic power recognised since early times as belonging to royal lines, and accepted by the Church, which gave it a Christian interpretation and derived it from the act of unction. He was God's lieutenant, the inspired of God, the Most Christian King. Thus we may say that the Carolingian tradition was, in a sense, the external manifestation of the prestige attributed to the French monarchy. The *Chanson de Roland* celebrated in Charlemagne the champion of the faith; the legend of the emperor's pilgrimage to Jerusalem made him the prototype of the crusader, as much as any of the actions for which his successors were given the credit. The memory of Charlemagne thus reinforced the theme of the *Rex Christianissimus*.

But it is above all from a political point of view that the Carolingian tradition was to establish a force of the first order for the monarchy. It guaranteed in effect its absolute independence, as also that of the kingdom, from the temporal standpoint. We have seen the proclamation of this idea about the middle of the twelfth century. The idea did not cease to develop and grow thereafter, and its effects can be observed at several levels.

In relation to the Holy Roman Empire, in the first place, the Carolingian tradition preserved in the collective consciousness the bond between the idea of the empire and that of the kingdom of France (*Charles li reis, nostre emperere magne*), and it could appear logical for the Carolids to claim for themselves the supreme power in Christendom. Some in fact considered that the acquisition of the imperial crown by the king of France would consecrate the total fulfilment of this *Renovatio Imperii Karoli Magni*. It is striking that the idea should have appeared for the first time in Philip Augustus's reign. At the height of the civil war tearing Germany apart at the beginning of the thirteenth century, the suggestion was several times made, though rather hesitantly, that the French king should be called to the imperial throne. But Philip Augustus turned a deaf ear to them, and confined himself to playing his own game between the contending parties. He was content to claim quasi-imperial rank, as his final name suggests, for Augustus is not a Christian name, but a title borrowed from the imperial titulary (*Philippus semper Augustus Francorum rex*). In so styling himself, the king exalted himself to the plane traditionally occupied by the emperor alone. Nevertheless, the question of the French candidature had definitely been raised; and ever since the middle of the thirteenth century a prophecy, later much elaborated, repeatedly announced the accession to supreme power of the

French king, the descendant of Charlemagne. This explains why after 1250 a number of French kings tried to take advantage of the empire's disintegration to have themselves elected king of the Romans,[1] and so obtain the imperial diadem by making use of their good relations with the papacy. Thus in 1273 Philip III induced his uncle Charles of Anjou to put him forward as a candidate. Charles was king of Sicily and master of a part of Italy, and perhaps had visions of a universal monarchy for the Capetian dynasty. But the attempt of that year was a failure, because Gregory X did not come out in support. The pope was intent upon maintaining a certain balance in the west, and not at all anxious to have a French emperor. But the idea did not completely perish. It came to life again in the pontificate of Martin IV (1281–5), who was entirely devoted to French interests, and then in Philip the Fair's reign, when we see the author Pierre Dubois urging the king to assume the imperial power in order that he may thus rule over all Christendom, which is conceived as a federation of sovereign states whose disputes would be submitted to a permanent court of justice presided over by the emperor. In 1308 there was some question for a certain time of putting forward as a candidate the king's brother, Charles of Valois, and in 1324 King Charles IV. This was accordingly a latent idea which never came to fulfilment, because at the last moment the German Electors refused to take the decisive step. Yet the idea came up again several times, for example in 1519, when Francis I was the unsuccessful rival of Charles of Spain, and in 1657, when Mazarin tried to put forward Louis XIV as a rival to Leopold I. It was briefly realised only when Napoleon I became emperor and spoke of Charlemagne as his 'august predecessor'.

Quite apart from the candidature of the French kings for the empire as the heirs of Charlemagne, the Carolingian tradition was responsible for a considerable strengthening of the royal power by raising the king of France in his own kingdom to an equality with the emperor. On this level, we are dealing with something that was both an instinctive reaction and the result of a long juridical development.

Its starting-point was the idea that the king of France enjoyed

[1] Title borne from the eleventh century by the kings of Germany after their election; by this they became candidates for the imperial coronation which made them Roman emperors.

exemption from any authority superior to his own; this was linked with the conception that the people of the kingdom were independent. The former notion was fully developed by the middle of the twelfth century; the latter seems to have become popularised not so much through *Pseudo-Turpin* or the forged Saint-Denis diploma as through the very old legend of the Franks' Trojan origin, which we saw arising in the middle of the Merovingian period. According to this legend, the Romans were not the Trojans' only descendants; the Franks were too, and after the fall of Troy were thought to have settled in Pannonia, where they formed the kingdom of the Sicumbri before their conquest of the Gauls. To be sure, this idea was used not only in France: it was often put forward by certain German historians and political doctrinaires, in whose eyes Germania formed part of the ancient Frankish state. But the contemporaries of Philip Augustus, in particular Raoul Rigord and Guillaume le Breton, were the people who drew the essential political inferences of the theory. They maintained that the Franks, descended from the ancient Trojans and brothers of the Romans, had always contrived to preserve their independence of the Roman empire, and had always affirmed themselves to be the free people *par excellence*. And so, within the common ideal of independence and freedom, bonds of solidarity were forged between the king and the nation.

It is possible to follow up a few further stages of the development undergone by the theme of the king's full sovereignty, which became ever closer to that of the emperor.

As early as 1204, Pope Innocent III, deliberately breaking away from the doctrine of the emperor's general supremacy in the world, declared that 'by common knowledge, the king of France did not recognise any authority in the temporal sphere superior to his own'. This formula, as yet stating a fact rather than laying down a legal right, was the origin of intense juridical consideration throughout the thirteenth century, marked in the first place by the great canonists' compilations, then by the work of the French feudists and jurists. Thus in a commentary on the first collection of Innocent III's Decretals, Alan of Bologna laid it down as a matter of principle that since the formation of the kingdoms that had succeeded the Roman empire, each independent king or prince had as much power in his own state as the emperor in the empire. The commentator thus seems to combine

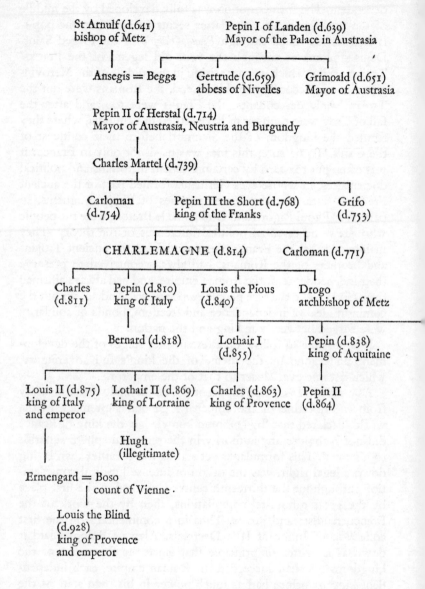

St Arnulf (d.641)
bishop of Metz

Pepin I of Landen (d.639)
Mayor of the Palace in Austrasia

Ansegis = Begga

Gertrude (d.659)
abbess of Nivelles

Grimoald (d.651)
Mayor of Austrasia

Pepin II of Herstal (d.714)
Mayor of Austrasia, Neustria and Burgundy

Charles Martel (d.739)

Carloman
(d.754)

Pepin III the Short (d.768)
king of the Franks

Grifo
(d.753)

CHARLEMAGNE (d.814)

Carloman (d.771)

Charles
(d.811)

Pepin (d.810)
king of Italy

Louis the Pious
(d.840)

Drogo
archbishop of Metz

Bernard (d.818)

Lothair I
(d.855)

Pepin (d.838)
king of Aquitaine

Louis II (d.875)
king of Italy
and emperor

Lothair II (d.869)
king of Lorraine

Charles (d.863)
king of Provence

Pepin II
(d.864)

Hugh
(illegitimate)

Ermengard = Boso
count of Vienne ·

Louis the Blind
(d.928)
king of Provence
and emperor

Simplified genealogical table of the Carolingians

Capetian line

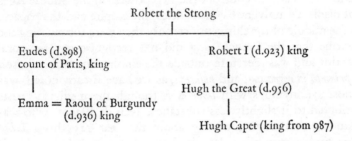

Robert the Strong

Eudes (d.898)
count of Paris, king

Emma = Raoul of Burgundy
(d.936) king

Robert I (d.923) king

Hugh the Great (d.956)

Hugh Capet (king from 987)

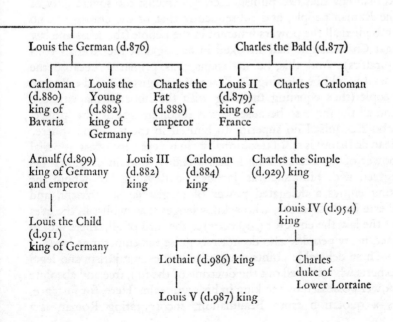

Louis the German (d.876)

Charles the Bald (d.877)

Carloman
(d.880)
king of
Bavaria

Louis the
Young
(d.882)
king of
Germany

Charles the
Fat
(d.888)
emperor

Louis II
(d.879)
king of
France

Charles

Carloman

Arnulf (d.899)
king of Germany
and emperor

Louis III
(d.882)
king

Carloman
(d.884)
king

Charles the Simple
(d.929) king

Louis the Child
(d.911)
king of Germany

Louis IV (d.954)
king

Lothair (d.986) king

Charles
duke of
Lower Lorraine

Louis V (d.987) king

the aspiration towards full sovereignty on the part of the kings in their own countries with the existence of an empire expressing universalist tendencies, though without considering how these two notions could be reconciled.

The conclusions of Alan of Bologna were taken up by French jurists, who applied them exclusively to the king of France. Roman law, which they were gradually rediscovering and applying to the full, enabled them to give the monarchy the imperial status and the authority both to impose its will in every part of the kingdom and to confront the two powers in the Middle Ages that displayed universalist tendencies, the empire and the papacy. By the middle of the thirteenth century they were formulating the doctrine that the French king did not recognise any temporal superior and was therefore outside the empire, and to be classed as *princeps in regno suo*; and *princeps*, as we have already noted, was almost synonymous with *imperator*, though the medieval jurists attributed to it slightly less substance. Jean de Blanot, who was a student at Bologna, writing about the year 1255 his *Libellus super titulo institutionum*, lays it down that a vassal who rebels against the king at once comes under the law of *maiestas*, the Roman law that had punished crimes against the sovereignty of the Roman people, and subsequently that of the emperor, who embodied all the powers inherent in the people (the self-same law that Charlemagne had invoked in 800 against the Roman conspirators). And this, he maintains, was primarily because the vassal would be plotting the death of a magistrate of the Roman people (thus equating the king with the imperial magistrates), and all the more so because he was revolting against the 'prince' who recognised no superior to himself in the temporal sphere. Jean de Blanot is still a traditionalist: in his eyes, the quasi-imperial power of the French king is still a reality. Certain other writers agreed with him, such as Jacques de Révigny, for whom the king enjoys a delegated power of magistracy as *princeps*, and Pierre de Belleperche, who acknowledges that, whilst in the eyes of the law the emperor (*imperator*) is the lord of all, 'there are, in fact, many peoples who do not recognise the emperor as lord'.

These debatable points were raised by crown jurists and legal experts who worked out the doctrine of the full, free and absolute power possessed by the king in his own realm. Here, for instance, is a quotation from Beaumanoir, incorporating Roman law among the sources of common law, and applying it to the king in the following famous adage: 'What pleases the prince has the force of law.' Bishop Guillaume Durant of Mende, the illustrious canonist and liturgist, writes that the king of France is *princeps* in his kingdom; but though he writes *princeps*, he is already thinking in terms of *imperator*. It was in Philip the Fair's time that the decisive step was taken. To read the words of Thomas de Pouilly is the best possible way of realising the force of the assimilation established between the king of France's power and the emperor's:

> As the king in his kingdom possesses all the power
> [*imperium*] that the emperor possesses in the empire, and as
> he has no temporal superior in the whole world, one may
> say the same of him as of the emperor, namely that all the
> rights, and primarily those that concern his kingdom, are
> contained within his heart. Of him, his actions and his
> conscience, what is written of the emperor is likewise true:
> the king of France is emperor, and occupies the place of the
> emperor in his own kingdom.

It was the even more definite formula of Guillaume de Plaisians that gained general acceptance: 'The king, our Lord, is emperor in his own kingdom.'

But let there be no mistake upon this matter. This strongly affirmed equivalence between the king, as emperor in his home territories, and the titular emperor, which destroys the earlier doctrine of imperial universalism, was not intended to urge on the French king to claim an unrealisable *dominium mundi*. Its only object was to assure the king the full extent of public power as set forth in Roman law, and to proclaim the supremacy of his authority. This authority was no longer, as it had been during the feudal period, derived from a contract: it was now treated as the indispensable instrument of the welfare of society. It marked royalty with the impress of imperial absolutism; a new age had begun; the state was reborn, incarnate in the king-emperor, drawing the nation into unity around his person. The sovereign state emerged victorious under Philip the Fair from the conflict with Boniface VIII, the last authority that still claimed to limit royal powers. In the end, this equivalence of king and emperor became one of the essential arguments in the theory of monarchy.

The political theorists of Charles V's reign, and particularly the author of the *Songe du verger*, further emphasised it by insisting on the supremacy of the royal title and thus minimising France's loss of the imperial title. It was both the cause and the consequence of the strengthening of the great Capetians' power during the thirteenth century. In the last analysis, it goes back well beyond the rediscovery of Roman law to the living tradition of *Charles li reis, nostre emperere magne.*

Far from trying to revive a bygone past, but able to discern the lessons of greatness and glory taught by the past, this tradition in France has always been forward-looking; in a word, it has always been an element of progress in the nation's life.

That certainly is why the most impressive moment in the great emperor's history, the moment when the western empire was reborn, deserves to be numbered among the 'days which made France'.

Appendix

Selected texts relating to the coronation of Charlemagne

I The excellence of the Frankish royalty

A *Laudes Regiae*
(796–800)

I Christ conquers, Christ reigns, Christ is emperor [thrice]

II Hear us, O Christ   *R.* Long life to Leo, supreme Pope and universal pontiff

III	Saviour of the world	help him
	St Peter	help him
	St Paul	help him
	St Andrew	help him
	St Clement	help him
	St Sixtus	help him
	Hear us, O Christ	Long life and victory to Charles, the most excellent, crowned of God, mighty and peaceful, king of the Franks and Lombards, patrician of the Romans
	Redeemer of the world	help him
	St Mary	help him
	St Michael	help him
	St Gabriel	help him
	St Raphael	help him
	St John	help him
	St Stephen	help him

Hear us, O Christ	Long life to the most noble family of kings
Holy Virgin of Virgins	help them
St Silvester	help them
St Laurence	help them
St Pancras	help them
St Nazarius	help them
St Anastasia	help them
St Genevieve	help them
St Columba	help them
Hear us, O Christ	Long life and victory to all the judges and all the army of the Franks
St Hilary	help them
St Martin	help them
St Maurice	help them
St Denis	help them
St Crispin	help them
St Crispinian	help them
St Gereon	help them

IV   Christ conquers, Christ reigns, Christ is emperor

V	King of kings	*R.* Christ conquers
	Our king	Christ conquers
	Our hope	Christ conquers
	Our glory	Christ conquers
	Our mercy	Christ conquers
	Our help	Christ conquers
	Our strength	Christ conquers
	Our liberation and redemption	Christ conquers
	Our victory	Christ conquers
	Our most invincible arms	Christ conquers
	Our impregnable fortress	Christ conquers
	Our defence and exaltation	Christ conquers
	Our light, our way, our life	Christ conquers

VI   To him alone empire, glory and power for ever and ever, world without end. Amen.

To him alone strength, might and victory through all ages, for ever and ever. Amen.

To him alone honour, glory and praise through endless years, for ever and ever. Amen.

VII   Hear us, O Christ [thrice]

VIII Good fortune [thrice]
      Prosperity [thrice]
      For many years
      Amen

Laudes Regiae, ed. E. H. Kantorowicz (University of California Press, 1968), pp. 15–16.

B   Davidic royalty in the view of Alcuin

Extracts from two letters from Alcuin to Charlemagne

1   No. 44, written in 794 or 795, after the Council of Frankfurt

Happy, said the Psalmist, is the nation whose lord is God, happy the people raised up by a leader and upheld by a preacher of the faith whose right hand wields the sword of triumph, whose mouth sounds the trumpet of catholic truth. Thus was it that in former days David, picked by God to be king of the nation that was then his chosen people . . . by his victorious sword subjected to Israel the nations round about and preached the law of God to his own people. From the noble descent of Israel there came forth for the salvation of the world the 'flower of the fields and valleys', the Christ to whom the people that he has made his own owe the new David. Under the same name, inspired by the same virtue and the same faith, he is now our leader and our guide, a leader in whose shadow the Christian nation is at peace, who on all sides fills pagan peoples with terror, a guide whose devotion and steadfastness in the gospel do not cease to inspire the catholic faith against heretics and schismatics, ever watchful lest anything contrary to the teaching of the apostles enter anywhere, ever busy to make the catholic faith shine everywhere in the light of the grace of heaven.

2   No. 177, written in July 799

[After begging Charlemagne to show wisdom in handling the case of Leo III, Alcuin reminds him of his mission to the world in the following terms.]
It is to govern the realms, dispense justice, renew the churches, correct the people, guarantee their rights to all people and all ranks, to defend the oppressed, to give laws, to comfort pilgrims, to show to all and in all places the way of justice and of heavenly life, so that all may be comforted by your holy coming, and that the most illustrious sons of

your line may benefit, thanks to your good works, from an abundant blessing. . . . Just as we read that through the holiness of your namesake David, the beloved of God, the power of the royal throne was preserved for all his descendants, so shall we see the growth of the might of your sons, prosperity in the realm, wellbeing among the people, plenteousness of harvests, and joy in all that is good; and for you there will be the bliss of the heavenly kingdom that God-in-Christ, dearest David, will bring to its perfection in days of eternity.

Monumenta Germaniae Historica, Epistolae, IV: *Karolini Aevi* II.

II The imperial coronation

The Royal Annals

796 Pope Hadrian died, and Leo, on his succession, sent ambassadors with gifts to the king. He also delivered to him the keys to the Confession of St Peter and the standard of the city of Rome.[1]

799 The Romans seized Pope Leo during the major litany, blinded him and took out his tongue.[2] He was placed under a strong guard but managed to escape during the night. Joining the envoys of the lord king at the basilica of St Peter, he was taken to Spoleto.

The lord king set out for Saxony, crossed the Rhine, made his way up the Lippe and reached the place called Paderborn. There he stayed and divided his army into two groups. His son Charles was sent with half the troops to the Bardengau to meet the Slavs and to receive the Saxons coming from Nordalbingia. Charlemagne kept the other half of the army with him, and at Paderborn he received Pope Leo with the greatest honours. There he awaited the return of his son, and he sent the pope back with honours equal to those with which he had been welcomed. The pope set off at once for Rome, and the king returned to his palace at Aachen.

800 At the beginning of the month of August the king came to Mainz and gave orders to march into Italy. When his army had reached Ravenna, he ordained an expedition against Benevento. After seven days he resumed his march on Rome and sent the army under his son

---

[1] The version of the Royal Annals inaccurately known as Einhard's recension adds that an invitation was sent by Leo to Charlemagne to despatch one of his nobles to Rome to 'strengthen by means of oaths the allegiance and subjection of the Romans to him'.

[2] The same source prudently adds at this point, 'as some thought'.

Pepin to ravage the territory of Benevento. Pope Leo came out to meet him in company with a group of Romans, and humbly received the king with the highest honours at Nomentum [Mentana] at the twelfth milestone from the city. After eating with the king, he returned at once to Rome in order to be there on the king's arrival. The next day he sent the standards of the city to be presented to Charlemagne on the way, and placed groups of citizens and foreigners on the route to sing the *Laudes* as the king passed. The pope took his place on the steps leading up to St Peter's, and there, in the midst of the bishops and the clergy, he received the king, who dismounted from his horse and climbed the steps. The pope recited a prayer and led him into the basilica of the blessed apostle Peter while all sang psalms. This took place on 24 November.

After a week the king summoned an assembly to which he explained why he had come; and from then on he gave all his efforts every day to settling the business for which he had undertaken the journey. The most important and difficult of these tasks, already begun elsewhere, was to discuss the crimes with which the pope was charged. As no witness was found to give evidence in support of the accusations made against him, the pope in the presence of all the people assembled in the basilica of the apostle Peter mounted the pulpit holding the Gospel, called on the name of the Trinity, and by an oath purged himself of the crimes of which he was accused.

The king celebrated the birth of the Lord in Rome. The year was now 801. On the most sacred day of Christmas, when the king was rising after his prayer at the Confession of the blessed apostle, Pope Leo placed a crown on his head, and all the Romans cried out, 'To Charles Augustus, crowned by God, mighty and peaceful emperor of the Romans, life and victory'. After the *Laudes* he was adored by the apostolic lord in the manner of the ancient emperors, and, having laid down the title of patrician, he was hailed by all as emperor and Augustus.

After several days he summoned *those who the year before had overthrown the pope*. They were arraigned under Roman law and they were convicted of the crime of *majestas* and sentenced to death. Inspired by holy thoughts, the pope interceded for them with the emperor. Accordingly they were not killed or mutilated, but because of the enormity of their crime they were condemned to exile. The leaders of this faction were the *nomenclator* Pascal, the *sacellarius* Campulus, and numerous other Roman nobles, against whom the same sentence was pronounced.

Having then set aright the affairs, public, ecclesiastical and private, of the city of Rome, of the pope, and of Italy as a whole, and having indeed given the whole of the winter to this work, the emperor sent another force against Benevento under his son Pepin, left Rome on 25 April after Easter, and came to Spoleto.

Scriptores Rerum Germanicarum, ed. F. Kurze (1895), pp. 98–114.

B   *The annals of Lorsch*

799   The lord king once again celebrated Easter at his palace at Aachen. Prompted by the devil, the Romans attacked the apostolic Lord Leo during the litany of 25 April. They took out his tongue and would have blinded him and put him to death. But by God's will they could not complete the evil they had begun. The same year the king entered Saxony and established his residence at Paderborn. There he was joined by the apostolic lord, whom the Romans had wished to kill. The king received him with honour, conferred on him numerous gifts and manifold tokens of respect, and then sent him back to his own residence in peace and with great dignity. *Missi* of the king formed his guard of honour, and they brought back to the king those who had plotted the death of the pope. . . .

800   During the summer season Charles called his nobles and his faithful to the city of Mainz, and when he had learned that peace reigned in all his lands, he recalled the wrong done to the apostolic lord Leo by the Romans. He took the decision to go to Rome and put it into effect at once.

There he held a great assembly of the bishops and abbots, together with the deacons, the counts and the rest of the Christian people, and there appeared before it those who had wished to condemn the pope. When the king understood that their wish to condemn him sprang not from considerations of justice but from hatred, it seemed good to the most pious prince[1] Charles, and to all the bishops and holy fathers who comprised the assembly, that if such was his will and his request, the pope should exculpate himself not by any judgment passed on him by the assembly, but of his own free will. This was done. The oath was pronounced, and the holy bishops together with all the clergy, the prince Charles himself and the devout Christian people intoned the hymn *Te Deum laudamus, Te Dominum confitemur.* When it was finished, the king and all the faithful people gave thanks to God that they had been worthy to keep the apostolic lord Leo intact in body and unharmed in his soul. The king spent the winter in Rome.

[1] 'Prince' serves as a general translation of *princeps,* a word drawn from the vocabulary of the empire. The annalist perhaps wished to imply that Charlemagne was here exercising quasi-imperial powers.

801 As the imperial title was vacant among the Greeks and the powers of the emperor were being exercised by a woman, Pope Leo himself, and all the holy fathers present at the council, and all the Christian people thought it fitting to bestow the name of emperor on Charles, king of the Franks, in whose power lay the city of Rome, the traditional imperial residence, together with the other places of residence in Italy, Gaul and Germany. Almighty God had been pleased to place them all under his authority, and they thought it right that, with the help of God and conforming to the request of all the Christian people, he too should bear the name of emperor. King Charles, unwilling to meet this request with a refusal, submitted humbly to God and to the desire of the priests and the Christian people, and on Christmas Day received the title of emperor and the consecration of Pope Leo. Forthwith he restored peace and harmony in the holy Church of Rome, ending the discord that had raged among its members. There too he celebrated Easter. At the approach of summer he set off for Ravenna, restoring peace and justice everywhere. From there he returned to his residence in Francia.

Monumenta Germaniae Historica, Scriptores, I, ed. G. Pertz, pp. 37–8.

C *Liber Pontificalis*

1 The assault

[The biographer gives a circumstantial account which, as we have seen, omits the essential point. Leo III was attacked near the Church of SS Stephen and Silvester by a group of conspirators instigated by the *primicerius* Pascal and the *sacellarius* Campulus. He was thrown to the ground, and an attempt was made to gouge out his eyes and cut out his tongue. He was then dragged into the church, where the brutal treatment continued. The pope was shut up in a cell of the monastery, and during the night was moved to the Greek monastery of St Erasmus. There he miraculously recovered his sight and speech. He was then brought by faithful followers to St Peter's, and thence taken by Duke Winichis to Spoleto.]

2 At the court of Charlemagne

When it was known that Leo III had arrived, the most Christian, orthodox, and merciful king sent out to meet him his chaplain, Archbishop Hildebald, Count Anschaire, his own son the most excellent king Pepin, and other counts, who brought him to the place where the great king awaited him. The king received him as the Vicar of the blessed apostle Peter, with honour and respect amidst hymns and sacred canticles. They embraced and wept. The pope chanted the *Gloria in excelsis,* which was taken up by the clergy, and said a prayer for the people. As to the lord Charles, the great King, he gave thanks to God that, at the bidding of the princes of the apostles, Peter and Paul, he had wrought so great a miracle for his servant and brought to nothing the men of evil.

While the pope stayed for a time with the serene king, the wicked prelates[1] and sons of Satan, after the great conflagration they had kindled in the domain of St Peter, strove, though God was against them, to spread false accusations against the holy pontiff and to make the king take cognisance of them. But they could not provide proof of what they said. Meanwhile archbishops, bishops and priests assembled from all quarters about the great and merciful king, and with the approval of the great and most pious king they sent the pope back to the apostolic seat with great honours.

3 The pope's return to Rome

In each city he was received as though he were the apostle himself. The Romans welcomed their shepherd with immense joy on St Andrew's eve, crowding onto the Milvian bridge with all the banners unfurled. There were gathered there the leaders of the clergy with all their clerics, the nobility, the senate and the armed forces, the entire people of Rome, together with the nuns, deaconesses, both noble and of common birth, together with the colonies of foreigners, Franks, Frisians, Saxons and Lombards. All these received the pope with sacred hymns, and took him to St Peter's, where he celebrated mass and all shared in the Body and Blood of our Lord Jesus Christ.

The next day, St Andrew's day, the pope entered the *patriarchium* of the Lateran. After some days, the faithful *missi* who had accompanied him, that is, the most reverend Archbishops Hildebald [of Cologne] and Arno [of Salzburg], the most reverend and holy Bishops Cunibert [see unknown], Bernard [of Worms], Atto [of Freising] and Jesse [of Amiens], Bishop-elect Erflair, the most glorious Counts Helmgaud, Rotchaire and Germaire, established themselves in the *triclinium* of Pope Leo[2] and for more than a week questioned the evil-minded criminals on the malicious charges they brought against the pope. As they could say nothing against him, the *missi* arrested them and sent them to Francia.

---

[1] i.e. the officials of the papal palace who had stirred up the conspiracy.

[2] The great reception hall of the Lateran Palace, site of the famous mosaic discussed in chapter VIII.

4 Charlemagne in Rome

[(a) The council and exculpation of Leo III: the text of the *Liber Pontificalis* is included in chapter IX, p. 137.]

(b) After this, all met once again in the basilica of St Peter to celebrate Christmas. Then, with his own hands, the venerable and august pontiff crowned the king with a most precious crown. Then the faithful Romans, seeing the great love he bore to the Roman Church and its Vicar (whose defence he had assured), at the command of God and of the blessed Peter who guards the gates of the kingdom of heaven, cried out with one accord, 'To Charles, most holy Augustus, crowned by God, mighty and peaceful emperor, life and victory.' This acclamation was uttered three times before the Confession of the blessed Peter. Numerous saints were invoked, and he was made emperor by all the people. Immediately afterwards the most holy bishop and pope anointed with holy oil Charles, the most excellent son of the emperor, on the same day of the Nativity of the Lord.

Liber Pontificalis, ed. L. Duchesne (Paris, 1886–92), vol. 2, pp. 4–8.

D Einhard: *The Life of Charlemagne*

§28 There were, besides, other reasons for Charles's last visit to Rome. The Romans had violently assaulted Pope Leo—putting out his eyes and cutting out his tongue—so that he was obliged to seek the help of the king. Charles thus came to Rome to restore the position of the Church, which had been shaken by these events, and eventually spent the whole winter there. Now it was that he received the title of emperor and Augustus. At first, this was not his intention at all; he said that he would have refused to enter the church that day, although it was a major festival, had he been aware of the pope's plans. Yet he endured with great forbearance the jealousy of the Roman emperors who were furious at the title he had taken. Thanks to the high-mindedness which was so much nobler than theirs, he finally succeeded in overcoming their resistance by sending them frequent messengers and addressing them as 'brothers' in his letters.

E Theophanes: *Chronography*

Another event in this year (797*) took place at Rome. The relatives of Pope Adrian of blessed memory combined in inciting a popular demonstration against Pope Leo whom they overcame and blinded. They were not however able to put out his eyes completely because of

* The demonstration against Leo occurred in 799—Theophanes' date of 797 is wrong (R.D.S.).

the humanity of those who carried out the deed who spared him. Leo then fled to Charles, king of the Franks, who severely punished Leo's enemies and restored him to his throne; for Rome was at the time under the sway of the Franks. In return Leo crowned Charles emperor of the Romans on 25 December of the ninth indiction (800) in the church of St Peter the Apostle, where he anointed Charles with oil from head to foot and placed the imperial vestments and crown on him.

Ed. C. de Boor (1883), pp. 472-3, trans. R. D. Scott.

III   The negotiations with Constantinople and the coronation of Louis the Pious

A   Theophanes: *Chronography*

800   On 25 December of this year [800] in the ninth indiction Charles, king of the Franks, was crowned by Pope Leo. Charles changed his plans for an expedition against Sicily, preferring to secure a marriage with Irene, and so in the following year in the tenth indiction sent ambassadors to her for this purpose.

801-2   The ambassadors who had been sent by Charles and Pope Leo arrived and begged the most pious Irene to marry Charles and so unite East and West. She would have agreed had she not been prevented by Aetios (the one I have mentioned frequently) who had enormous influence and was plotting to gain the throne for his brother.

802   [At end of account of Irene's fall.] Nicephorus granted Irene her wish and immediately banished her to the monastery which she had founded on the island of Principos. Charles's ambassadors were still in Constantinople and saw what happened.

811   At sunrise on Thursday 2 October of this year [811] of the fifth indiction, Michael the most pious commander of the palace guards was proclaimed in the Hippodrome as emperor of the Romans by the entire senate and by the army.

811   The Emperor Michael also made overtures to Charles, king of the Franks, about arranging peace and a marriage for his son Theophylact. Nicephorus, the most holy patriarch, posted his synodical letter to Leo, most holy pope of Rome, which earlier he had been prevented from doing by the Emperor Nicephorus. On Thursday 25 December of the fifth indiction the most serene Michael had his son Theophylact crowned emperor by the patriarch Nicephorus in the ambo of the great church.

Ed. C. de Boor (1883), pp. 475, 478, 493, 494, trans. R. D. Scott.

B *The Royal Annals*

802 [Irene], empress of Constantinople, sent an ambassador, the *spatharius* Leo, to establish peace between the Franks and the Greeks. When his mission was completed, the emperor gave him his leave, and in his turn sent to Constantinople Jesse, bishop of Amiens, and Count Helmgaud to establish peace with the empress.

803 The envoys of the lord emperor returned from Constantinople bringing with them the envoys of the Emperor Nicephorus, who then governed the state. [Irene] had in fact been deposed after the arrival of the Frankish mission. They met the emperor on the river Saal in Germany at the place called Salz, and from him received a written project for a treaty of peace. They were then sent back with a letter from the emperor and reached Constantinople by way of Rome.

[Negotiations broken off and war declared.]

812 After winning many great victories in Moesia, the emperor Nicephorus died fighting the Bulgars. His son-in-law and successor as emperor, Michael, received in Constantinople the envoys that the lord emperor Charles had sent to Nicephorus. He then sent them back together with his own ambassadors, Bishop Michael and the *protospatharii* Arsaphus and Theognostus, and through their agency confirmed the peace already outlined by Nicephorus. They presented themselves to the emperor at Aachen, and in the church they received from him the treaty written out according to their custom, that is, in the Greek language. They then acclaimed him and hailed him as emperor and *basileus*. Passing through Rome, they received from Pope Leo in the church of the apostle St Peter another copy of the same treaty.

813 The emperor spent the winter at Aachen, and at the beginning of spring sent to Constantinople Bishop Amalaire of Trier and Peter, abbot of the monastery of Nonantula, to confirm peace with the Emperor Michael.

He then held a general assembly and placed the crown on the head of his son Louis, king of Aquitaine, whom he had summoned to his presence, and associated him with himself in the imperial title. He placed his grandson Bernard, son of Pepin, at the head of Italy and commanded that he should be called king.

Scriptores Rerum Germanicarum, ed. F. Kurze (1895), pp. 117–18 and 136–8.

C   Letter from Charlemagne to Emperor Michael I

In the name of the Father, the Son, and the Holy Spirit.

Charles, by the abundance of divine grace Emperor Augustus, King of the Franks and Lombards, to his well-loved and honourable brother Michael, glorious Emperor Augustus, eternal salvation in Our Lord Jesus Christ.

We bless the Lord Jesus Christ, our true God, and we give him hearty thanks with such strength and skill as we possess that by the ineffable gift of his good will he has heaped upon us his benefits and in our day has thought fit to establish the peace long sought and always desired between the eastern and the western empires; has thought fit also in our time to unite and set at peace his holy and spotless catholic Church that is spread throughout all the world. We say that all this is almost accomplished because we have done all that needed to be done on our side. We do not doubt that for your part you too wished to do this.

Ardent in our desire to bring to its definite conclusion the task we have begun, we have sent to your glorious and well-loved fraternal presence the ambassadors that you have before you, Amalaire, the venerable bishop of Trier, and Peter, the devout abbot of the monastery of the Holy Apostles [of Nonantula]. Just as our well-loved brother's faithful ambassadors, the venerable metropolitan Michael and the glorious *protospatharii* Arsaphus and Theognostus, have received from us the written text of the treaty of peace, completed by our signature and those of our bishops and our nobles, so do we wish that our envoys may receive from your hands, which will have taken it from the holy altar, the text of the treaty that you will on your side have caused to be written and confirmed by the signatures of your bishops, your patricians and your nobles. This treaty they will bring us forthwith. It was our opinion, and it accorded with the judgment of your ambassadors, that reason required us, after their departure, as soon as the first moment came to undertake the voyage, to send our own ambassadors to your glorious and well-loved fraternal presence to receive the text of the treaty from you and bring it to us.

For this reason we entreat our well-loved and glorious brother, if the text that we have settled and sent to you pleases you, graciously to give our envoys a like document, written in Greek and confirmed in the manner that we have mentioned. Furthermore, when they have come to you and been received with kindness (for we have full confidence in your charity), we entreat you to give them their leave without needless delay, so that we may be able to rejoice in their return and in the treaty, if that be the will of God. And may God, the giver of all good things, give back to you as your just reward all that you have given in the service of peace, showing that you love and will strengthen that peace which he has commanded shall reign among his people. Farewell.

Monumenta Germaniae Historica, Epistolae, IV, p. 556.

D Einhard: *The Life of Charlemagne*

§16 Furthermore, Charles received many messengers from Nicephorus, Michael and Leo, emperors of Constantinople, who spontaneously sought his friendship and alliance. But, since he had taken the title of emperor, they suspected him of wishing to wrest the empire from them; he therefore concluded a firm treaty with them so as to eliminate any cause of conflict. But the Romans and Greeks were still uneasy about the power of the Franks, as the Greek proverb shows: 'If you are friendly with a Frank, he is certainly not your neighbour.'

§30 At the end of his life, when he was bowed down by sickness and old age, he called to him [Louis the Pious] king of Aquitaine, the only surviving son of his marriage to Hildegard, and in the presence of all the Frankish leaders at a general assembly, with their agreement he nominated him to share in the government of the entire kingdom and to be heir to the imperial title. Then, placing the crown upon his head, he decreed that henceforward he should be addressed as emperor and Augustus. This decision was warmly welcomed by the assembly, as it appeared to be inspired by God for the good of the kingdom.

IV The religious tone of the imperial idea at the close of Charlemagne's reign

The words of the *missi* to the peoples (a document of the period 801–12):

Beloved brethren, hear the admonition that our master, the Emperor Charles, addresses to you through us. We have been sent here for your eternal salvation, and it is our duty to admonish you to live virtuously according to the law of God and justly according to the law of the world. We would have you know first of all that you must believe in a single God, Father, Son and Holy Spirit, truly a Trinity and together One. . . . Believe that there is but one Church, the society of all pious men on earth, and that only those will be saved who are steadfast to the end in the faith and the communion of this Church. . . . Love God with all your hearts. Love your neighbours as yourselves. Give alms to the poor according to your means. Welcome travellers to your homes. Visit the sick. Have mercy on those in prison. Forgive each other your debts as you wish that God may forgive your sins. Ransom captives, give help to the oppressed, defend widows and orphans. . . . May the dukes, counts and other public officials give justice to the people and be merciful to the poor. May money not turn them aside from righteousness. . . . Nothing is hidden from God. . . . Life is short, and none can foretell the moment of death. Let us be always ready.

Monumenta Germaniae Historica, Capitularies, I, p. 239.

Chronological table

I The reign of Pepin the Short

751 Pepin comes to the throne

754 Discussions between Pepin and Pope Stephen II at Ponthion and Saint-Denis. The Quierzy Assembly. The promise of donation made to the pope by the king of the Franks.

754 or 755 Pepin's first expedition to Italy.

755 Council of the Frankish bishops at the palace of Ver.

756 Pepin's second Italian expedition; the formation of the Papal State.

757 Tassilo, duke of Bavaria, pays homage to Pepin and takes a solemn oath to be his vassal.

759 Capture of Narbonne; conquest of Septimania.

760–768 Submission of Aquitaine.

763 Duke Tassilo gains his independence.

767 Council of Gentilly.

768 Pepin divides the Frankish kingdom between his sons Charles (Charlemagne) and Carloman. Death of the king, 24 September.

II The reign of Charlemagne

768 Charlemagne elected king 9 October at Noyon. Reigns first in association with his brother Carloman, proclaimed king on the same day at Soissons.

769 Rebellion of Hunaud of Aquitaine.

771 Death of Carloman. Charlemagne becomes sole king of the Franks.

772 Beginning of the Saxon wars.

773 Charlemagne's first expedition to Italy in response to Pope Hadrian I's appeal.

774 Charlemagne's first stay in Rome (April); renewal of Pepin's donation. Capitulation of Pavia (June). Charlemagne becomes king of the Lombards. Peter of Pisa arrives at the Frankish court.

775 Renewal of the Saxon campaigns.

776	Charlemagne's second Italian expedition. The suppression of the revolt of Hruodgaud, duke of Friuli.
777	Assembly of Paderborn: first mass baptism of the Saxons. The Frankish king is summoned to Spain by the governor of Saragossa for assistance against the emir of Cordova.
778	Spanish expedition; Roncevalles (15 August); disturbances in Aquitaine call for a firmer assertion of Frankish dominion. Insurrection of part of the Saxons under Widukind.
779	The king's first authentic capitulary (the Herstal capitulary) in March. Vigorous renewal of the Saxon campaigns, which continued annually.
781	Charlemagne's third expedition to Italy; his second stay in Rome; establishment of Italy and Aquitaine as kingdoms. Betrothal of Rotrud, Charlemagne's daughter, to the young Emperor Constantine VI. First meeting between Alcuin and the Frankish king.
782	Frankish defeat in the Süntel massif, Saxony, followed by the massacre of Verden.
783	Paul the Deacon at the king's court.
785	Widukind's submission and baptism; promulgation of the capitulary *de partibus Saxoniae*; Saxony apparently subjugated. Franks take Gerona.
786	Alcuin at the palace.
787	Fourth Italian expedition; third stay in Rome; siege of Capua; negotiations with Arichis, duke of Benevento. Rotrud's betrothal broken off. Ecumenical Council of Nicaea.
788	Byzantine offensive in southern Italy. Charlemagne appoints the new duke of Benevento. Bavaria submits and becomes part of the Frankish state.
789	A general circular (*Admonitio generalis*) addressed by the king to all ranks of the Church's hierarchy and all lay dignitaries.
790 onwards	The Palace of Aachen becomes the king's principal residence.
791	Beginning of campaigns against the Avars. Conquest of Istria.
791 or 792	Composition of the *Libri Carolini*.
792	Conspiracy of Pepin the Hunchback.
793	Fresh revolt of the Saxons; Saracen offensive north of the Pyrenees.
794	Council and General Assembly of Frankfurt.

795 Defeat of the Avars. Resumption of conquest of the Spanish March. Election of Pope Leo III in Rome, 26 December.

Between 794 and 800 The circular *De litteris colendis.*

796 Alcuin appointed abbot of Saint-Martin de Tours.

797 Submission of the greater part of Saxony; promulgation of a new capitulary. Embassy sent to Bagdad. In Constantinople, imperial power seized by Irene, mother of Constantine VI.

798 Embassy sent by Irene to the Frankish court to treat for peace.

799 25 April: Romans' attempt on the life of Leo III. Summer: meeting between the pope and the king at Paderborn.

800 24 November: Charlemagne arrives in Rome; from 1 December onwards, examination of the case against Leo III; 23 December: the pope takes an oath of compurgation and exonerates himself; the assembly of Romans and Franks before whom this procedure has taken place expresses a wish that the empire should be re-established, with Charlemagne as its head; an embassy from the Holy Land arrives in Rome; 25 December: Charlemagne crowned as emperor by the Pope.

801 Capture of Barcelona: exchange of embassies between Charles and Irene.

802 Aachen: spring and autumn assemblies, marked by a great effort to put the empire in order, continued in the following years. General taking of an oath of loyalty to the Emperor.

803 Promulgation of the *Capitulare legibus additum.* Arrival at Salz of an embassy sent by the Emperor Nicephorus; relations between Charlemagne and Constantinople broken.

804 Submission of the last Saxon rebels in Wihmode and Nordalbingia. Death of Alcuin.

805 The double capitulary of Thionville: measures on behalf of internal peace. Conquest of Byzantine Venetia by King Pepin of Italy.

806 *Divisio Regnorum.* Reconquest of Venetia and Dalmatia by the Byzantines.

807 Arrival of monks from the Holy Land at the court of Aachen.

809 Byzantine fleet attacks Comacchio. Council of Aachen.

810 Pepin king of Italy takes Venice. Towards the end of the year, arrival of an ambassador from Nicephorus at Aachen.

811	Envoys from Charlemagne set out for Constantinople.
812	Emperor Michael I, successor to Nicephorus, sends an embassy to Aachen. Peace between the two empires.
813	Five regional councils meet simultaneously. September: General Assembly at Aachen; Louis the Pious crowned emperor.
814	Death of Charlemagne (28 January).

III   Crisis in the empire

814	27 February: Louis the Pious arrives at Aachen
816	Beginning of ecclesiastical reforms; meeting between the emperor and Pope Stephen IV at Rheims.
817	January: imperial privilege for Pope Pascal I. July: *Ordinatio Imperii.*
818	Bernard of Italy's revolt suppressed. Death of the empress Ermengard.
819	Louis the Pious marries Judith of Welf.
822	Public confession of the emperor at Attigny.
823	Lothair I, Louis the Pious's eldest son, associate emperor from 817, is anointed and crowned emperor by Pascal I in Rome. Birth of Charles the Bald.
824	*Constitutio Romana*
825	The name of Lothair appears in the imperial acts alongside his father's. Revolt of the Spanish March; victory of Bernard, count of Barcelona.
829	Four councils put forward addresses to the emperor.
829	The Act of Worms: Charles the Bald is allotted territory in the empire. Palace revolution, disgrace of Lothair.
830	Revolt by Lothair and his brothers Pepin and Louis the German against their father.
831	Louis the Pious resumes power and sides with his two younger sons against Lothair.
833	Second rebellion of the three brothers; intervention by Pope Gregory IV; June: the Field of Lies (Lugenfeld); deposition of the emperor. October: public penance by Louis at Saint-Médard de Soissons.
834	Louis the Pious restored by Pepin and Louis the German.
837–8	Louis the Pious makes over important territories to Charles the Bald.
840	Death of Louis the Pious. Lothair claims the whole Empire.

841	Charles the Bald and Louis the German join together and defeat their elder brother at Fontenoy-en-Puisaye.
842	The oaths of Strasbourg.
843	The treaty of Verdun.

Bibliography

Original documents

1 J. F. Böhmer and E. Mühlbacher, *Die Regesten des Kaiserreichs unter den Karolingern,* 2nd ed., Weimar, 1908.
2 W. Wattenbach, W. Levison and H. Löwe, *Deutschlands Geschichtsquellen im Mittelalter,* 3 vols, Weimar, 1952–7.

General works on the period

3 F. Lot, C. Pfister and F. L. Ganshof, *Les Destinées de l'Empire en Occident de 395 à 888* (vol. 1 of *Le Moyen Âge,* ed. G. Glotz), 2nd ed., Paris, 1941.
4 F. Lot, *La Naissance de la France,* Paris, 1948.
5 A. Kleinclausz, *L'Empire carolingien, ses origines et ses transformations,* Paris, 1902.
6 L. Halphen, *Charlemagne et l'Empire carolingien,* Paris, 1947.
7 H. Fichtenau (trans. P. Munz), *The Carolingian Empire,* Oxford, 1957.

To these works, of which the last three are concerned mainly with politics and institutions, the following are added for the social, economic and religious framework:

8 H. Pirenne (trans. B. Miall), *Mohammed and Charlemagne,* London, 1939.
9 R. Boutrouche, *Seigneurie et féodalité,* vol. 1, Paris, 1959.
10a R. Latouche (trans. E. M. Wilkinson), *The Birth of Western Economy,* London, 1961.
10b G. Duby (trans. C. Postan), *Rural Economy and Country Life in the Mediaeval West,* London, 1968.
11 E. Amann, *L'Époque carolingienne* (vol. 6 of *Histoire de l'Église,* ed. A. Fliche and V. Martin), Paris, 1936–7.
12 H. von Schubert, *Geschichte der christlichen Kirche im Frühmittelalter,* Tübingen, 1921.
13 G. Schnürer, *Kirche and Kultur im Mittelalter,* 3 vols, Paderborn, 1929–36.

and on the great currents of civilisation:

14 L. Génicot (trans. L. and R. Wood), *Contours of the Middle Ages,* Routledge & Kegan Paul, 1967.

Charlemagne: Monographs

15 L. Halphen, *Études critiques sur l'histoire de Charlemagne*, Paris, 1921.
16 A. Kleinclausz, *Charlemagne*, Paris, 1934.
17 J. L. A. Calmette, *Charlemagne, sa vie et son œuvre*, Paris, 1945.
18a F. Ganshof, 'Charlemagne', *Speculum*, 24, 1949; excellent survey of the reign.

On the legend of the emperor

18b R. Folz, *Le Souvenir et la légende de Charlemagne dans l'Empire germanique médiéval*, Paris, 1950.
18c R. Folz, *Études sue le culte liturgique de Charlemagne dans les églises de l'Empire*, Paris, 1951.
18d Council of Europe, *Charlemagne: Oeuvre, rayonnement et survivances*, Aix-la-Chapelle, 1965 (catalogue of exhibition setting out all aspects of the carolingian reign and civilisation).

The Frankish royalty at the time of Pepin and Charlemagne

Institutions (in addition to nos 3, 4 and 6)

19 Fustel de Coulanges, *Histoire des institutions politiques de l'ancienne France*, Paris, 1888–92, especially vols III (*La Monarchie franque*) and VI (*Les Transformations de la royauté pendant l'époque carolingienne*).
20 F. L. Ganshof, 'L'immunité dans la monarchie franque' in *Recueils de la Société Jean Bodin*, 1, 2nd ed., 1958.
21 F. L. Ganshof, *Recherches sur les Capitulaires*, Paris, 1958.
22 F. L. Ganshof, 'Charlemagne et l'usage de l'écrit en matière administrative', *Le Moyen Âge*, 57, 1956.

Feudal background (in addition to no. 9)

23 Marc Bloch (trans. L. A. Manyon), *Feudal Society*, Routledge & Kegan Paul, 1961.
24 F. L. Ganshof (trans. P. Grierson), *Feudalism*, London, 3rd ed., 1964.
25 H. Mitteis, *Lehnrecht und Staatsgewalt*, Weimar, 1933.

The oath

26 A. Dumas, 'Le serment de fidélité et la conception du pouvoir du Ier au IXe siècle', *Revue historique de droit français et étranger*, 1931.

27 A. Dumas, 'Le serment de fidélité à l'époque franque', *Revue belge de Philologie et d'Histoire*, 14, 1935.

28 F. L. Ganshof, 'Charlemagne et le serment' in *Mélanges d'Histoire du moyen-âge dédiés à la mémoire de Louis Halphen*, Paris, 1951.

29 H. Helbig, 'Fideles Dei et regis', *Arch. für Kulturgeschichte*, 33, 1951.

30 Ch. E. Odegaard, 'The concept of royal power in Carolingian oaths of fidelity', *Speculum*, 20, 1945.

Relations between royalty and the Church

31 D. Delaruelle, 'Charlemagne et l'Église', *Revue d'Histoire de l'Église de France*, 39, 1953.

32 F. L. Ganshof, 'L'Église et le pouvoir royal dans la monarchie franque sous Pépin III et Charlemagne', *Settimane di studio sull'alto Medioevo*, Spoleto, 7, 1960.

33 F. L. Ganshof, 'Observations sur le synode de Francfort de 794' in *Miscellanea historica in honorem A. de Mayer*, Louvain, 1946.

Political and religious ideas

34 H. X. Arquillière, *L'Augustinisme politique*, Paris, 1934.

35 R. Bonnaud-Delamare, *L'Idée de paix à l'époque carolingienne*, Paris, 1939.

36 E. Ewig, 'Zum christlichen Königsgedanken im Frühmittelalter' in *Das Königtum* (*Vorträge und Forschungen*, vol. 3), Lindau, 1956.

37 L. Halphen, 'L'idée d'état sous les Carolingiens', *Revue historique*, 185, 1939.

38 E. H. Kantorowicz, *Laudes Regiae*, Berkeley, Calif., 1946.

The atmosphere at the end of Charlemagne's reign

39 F. L. Ganshof, 'L'échec de Charlemagne', *Comptes Rendus de l'Académie des Inscriptions et des Belles-Lettres*, 1947.

40 F. L. Ganshof, 'La fin du règne de Charlemagne, une décomposition', *Revue suisse d'Histoire*, 28, 1948.

The Carolingian renaissance[1]

41 P. Riché, *Éducation et culture dans l'Occident barbare, VIe-VIIIe siècles*, Paris, 1962; mainly valuable for the period preceding Charlemagne.

[1] In this volume will be found reference to important works concerning culture in general (nos 41–48b), two important personalities of the renaissance (nos 49–51), and architecture (to place Aachen).

On the renaissance of scholarship and letters, the following may be consulted in addition to nos 2, 7, 11, 12, 13, 14:

42 J. de Ghellinck, *La Littérature latine du Moyen Âge*, vol. 1, Paris, 1939.

43 M. L. W. Laistner, *Thought and Letters in Western Europe*, London and Ithaca, 1931.

44 E. Lesne, *Histoire de la propriété ecclésiastique en France*, vol. 4 (*Les Livres, scriptoria et bibliothèques du commencement du VIIIe à la fin du XIe siècle*), Lille, 1938.

45 E. Lesne, 'Contribution des églises et monastères de l'ancienne Gaule au sauvetage des Lettres antiques', *Revue d'Histoire de l'Église de France*, 23, 1937.

46 W. Levison, *England and the Continent in the Eighth Century*, Oxford, 1946.

47 P. Lehmann, 'Die karolingische Renaissance', *Settimane di studio sull'alto Medioevo*, Spoleto, 1, 1954.

48a A. Monteverdi, 'Rinascimento carolino', ibid.

48b J. Fleckenstein, *Die Bildungsreform Karls des Grossen*, Freiburg i. Br., 1953.

49 A. Kleinclausz, 'Alcuin', *Annales de l'Université de Lyon*, 3rd series, E. 15, 1948.

50a L. Wallach, *Alcuin and Charlemagne*, Cornell Studies in Classical Philology, vol. 32, Ithaca, 1959.

50b F. C. Scheibe, 'Alcuin und die Admonitio generalis', *Deutsches Archiv*, 14, 1958.

51 F. L. Ganshof, *Eginhard biographe de Charlemagne* (Bibliothèque d'Humanisme et Renaissance, vol. 13), 1951.

52 K. J. Conant, *Carolingian and Romanesque Architecture, 800 to 1200*, Penguin Books, 1959.

53 A. Grabar, *Martyrium*, 2 vols, Paris, 1946.

54 J. Hubert, *L'Art pré-roman*, Paris, 1938.

55 R. Lantier and J. Hubert, *Les Origines de l'art français*, Paris, 1947.

56 R. Krautheimer, 'The carolingian revival of early Christian architecture', *Art Bulletin*, 24, 1942.

57 E. Lehmann, *Der frühe deutsche Kirchenbau*, Berlin, 1938.

58 J. Ramackers, 'Das Grab Karls des Grossen und die Frage nach dem Ursprung des Aachener Oktogons', *Historisches Jahrbuch*, 75, 1956; see also no. 83.

The papacy and Italy in the second half of the eighth
and the ninth century (In addition to nos 5, 6, 11 and 12)

59 E. Caspar, 'Das Papsttum unter fränkischer Herrschaft, *Zeitschrift für Kirchengeschichte*, 54, 1935.
60 L. Duchesne (trans. A. H. Mathew), *The Beginnings of the Temporal Sovereignty of the Popes, AD 754-1073*, Kegan Paul, Trench, Trübner, 1908.
61 J. Haller, *Das Papsttum: Idee und Wirklichkeit*, vols 1 and 2, 2nd ed., Basle, 1950, 1953.
62 L. M. Hartmann, *Geschichte Italiens*, vol. 2, Leipzig, 1897–1914.
63 A. Lapôtre, *L'Europe et le Saint-Siège à l'époque carolingienne*, vol. 1: *Le Pape Jean VIII*, Paris, 1895.
64 L. Levillain, *L'Avènement de la dynastie carolingienne et les origines de l'État Pontificial* (Bibliothèque de l'École des Chartes), Paris, 1933.
65 C. G. Mor, *L'Età feodale (Storia politica d'Italia*, vol. 1), Milan, 1952.
66 L. Saltet, 'Les prétendues Promesses de Quierzy (754) et de Rome (774) dans le *Liber Pontificalis*', *Bulletin de Littérature ecclésiastique* (Institut catholique de Toulouse), 1940–1.
67 P. E. Schramm, *Kaiser, Rom und Renovatio*, 2 vols, Berlin, 1929.
68 W. Ullmann, *The Growth of Papal Government in the Middle Ages*, London, 1955.

The idea of empire in general

69 L. Bréhier, *Le Monde byzantin*, vol. 2, Paris, 1948.
70 E. Eichmann, *Die Kaiserkrönung im Abendland*, 2 vols, Würzburg, 1942.
71 C. Erdmann, *Forschungen zur politischen Ideenwelt des Frühmittelalters*, 1951.
72 E. Ewig, 'Das Bild Constantins des Grossen in den ersten Jahren des abendländischen Mittelalters', *Historisches Jahrbuch*, 75, 1956.
    See also nos 7 and 67 and the works in the next section.
73 R. Folz (trans. S. A. Ogilvie), *The Concept of Empire in Western Europe from the Fifth to the Fourteenth Century*, London, 1969.
74 O. Treitinger, *Die oströmische Kaiser und Reichsidee*, Jena, 1938.

The coronation of Charlemagne

In addition to nos 3–7, 11, 12, 15, 16, 36, 38, 59, 61, 62, 68, 70–3, where the problem is raised, see the following special studies, in order of original publication:

75 K. Heldmann, *Das Kaisertum Karls des Grossen. Theorien und Wirklichkeit,* Weimar, 1928.

76 L. Levillain, 'Le couronnement impérial de Charlemagne', *Revue d'Histoire de l'Église de France,* 18, 1932.

77 H. Löwe, 'Die karolingische Reichsgründung und der Südosten', *Forschungen zur Kirchen und Geistesgeschichte,* 13, 1937.

78 E. Rota, 'La consecrazione imperiale di Carlo Magno' in *Studi di storia e diritto in onore di E. Besta,* Milan, 1939.

79 F. Dölger, 'Europas Gestaltung im Spiegel der fränkisch-byzantinischen Auseinandersetzung des IX Jahrhunderts' in *Der Vertrag von Verdun* (a symposium), Leipzig, 1943 (see no. 99).

80 F. L. Ganshof, *La Révision de la Bible par Alcuin* (Bibliothèque d'Humanisme et Renaissance, vol. 9), 1947.

81 W. Ohnsorge, *Das Zweikaiserproblem im früheren Mittelalter,* Hildesheim, 1947.

82 F. L. Ganshof, *The Imperial Coronation of Charlemagne: Theories and Facts,* Glasgow, 1949.

83 H. Fichtenau, 'Byzanz und die Pfalz zu Aachen', *Mitteilungen der Instituts für österreichische Geschichte,* 59, 1951.

84 P. E. Schramm, 'Die Anerkennung Karls des Grossen als Kaiser', *Historische Zeitschrift,* 172, 1951.

85 H. Fichtenau, 'Karl der Grosse und das Kaisertum', *Mitteilungen I.ö.G.,* 61, 1953.

86 H. Fichtenau, 'Naissance de l'Empire médiéval', *Diogène,* 1953.

87a H. Fichtenau, 'Il concetto imperiale di Carlo Magno', *Settimane di studio sull'alto Medioevo,* Spoleto, 1, 1954.

87b L. Wallach, 'The genuine and the forged oath of pope Leo III', *Traditio,* 11, 1955.

87c L. Wallach, 'The Roman synod of December 800 and the alleged trial of Leo III', *Harvard Theological Review,* 49, 1956.

88 I. Déer, 'Die Vorrechte der Kaisers in Rom', *Schweizer Beiträge zur allgemeinen Geschichte,* 15, 1957.

89 H. Beumann, 'Nomen imperatoris: Studien zur Kaiseridee Karls des Grossen', *Historische Zeitschrift,* 185, 1958.

90 R. E. Sullivan (ed.), *The Coronation of Charlemagne,* London, 1959.

91 P. Munz, *The Origin of the Carolingian Empire,* Otago, 1960.

92a W. Mohr, 'Karl der Grosse, Leo III und der römische Aufstand', *Bulletin du Cange,* 30, 1960.

92b H. Zimmermann, 'Papstabsetzungen des Mittelalters. I: Die Zeit der Karolinger', *Mitteilungen I.ö.G.,* 69, 1961.

92c H. Beumann, 'Die Kaiserfrage in den Paderborner Verhandlungen von 799' in *Das erste Jahrtausend,* vol. 1, Bonn, 1962.

Iconography of Charlemagne

93 P. E. Schramm, *Die zeitgenössischen Bildnisse Karls des Grossen,*
Leipzig, 1928.
94 P. E. Schramm, *Die deutschen Kaiser und Könige in Bildern ihrer Zeit,*
Leipzig, 1928.
95 P. E. Schramm, *Herrschaftszeichen und Staatssymbolik,* vols 1 and
2, Stuttgart, 1954, 1955.

The evolution of the Empire in the ninth century

*In addition to nos 3–7, 11–12, 24–7, 30, 34–5, 38, 60–3, 65, 67–8, 70–1, 73
see the following:*

96a F. L. Ganshof, 'Louis the Pious reconsidered', *History,* 42, 1957.
96b W. Mohr, *Die karolingische Reichsidee,* Munster, 1962.
97 J. Reviron, *Les Idées politico-religieuses d'un évêque du IXe siècle:
Jonas d'Orléans et son 'De Institutione regia',* Paris, 1930.
98 E. Delaruelle, 'En relisant le *De Institutione regia* de Jonas d'Orléans' in *Mélanges L. Halphen,* Paris, 1951.
99 Th. Mayer (ed.), *Der Vertrag von Verdun,* Leipzig, 1943.
100 F. L. Ganshof, 'Zur Entstehungsgeschichte und Bedeutung des
Vertrages von Verdun', *Deutsches Archiv,* 12, 1956.
101 J. L. A. Calmette, *L'Effondrement d'un Empire et la naissance
d'une Europe,* Paris, 1941.
102 J. L. A. Calmette, *La Diplomatie carolingienne du traité de Verdun
à la mort de Charles le Chauve* (Bibliothèque de l'École des Hautes
Études, Sciences historiques, vol. 135), Paris, 1901.
103 J. Dhondt, *Études sur la naissance des principautés territoriales en
France,* Bruges, 1943.
104 P. Zumthor, *Charles le Chauve,* Paris, 1957 (see also no. 105).

French medieval royalty
(problems raised in the last chapter)

105 P. E. Schramm, *Der König von Frankreich,* 2 vols, 2nd ed., Darm-
stadt, 1960; a fundamental work.

See also the following:

106 A. Adler, 'The "pelerinage de Charlemagne" in a new light', *Speculum*, 22, 1947.

107 A. Barroux, 'L'abbé Suger et la vassalité du Vexin en 1124', *Le Moyen Âge*, 1958.

108 Marc Bloch, *The Royal Touch*, Routledge & Kegan Paul, 1973.

109 F. Calasso, *I Glossatori e la dottrina della sovranità*, Milan, 1957.

110 M. delle Piane, *Vecchio e nuovo nelle idee politiche di Pietro Dubois*, Florence, 1959.

111 Ercole, 'L'origine francese di una nota formula bartoliana', *Archivio storico italiano*, 1915.

112 E. H. Kantorowicz, *The King's Two Bodies*, Princeton, 1957.

113 C. van de Kieft, 'Deux diplômes faux de Charlemagne pour Saint-Denis du XIIe siècle', *Le Moyen Âge*, 1958.

114 W. Kienast, *Deutschland und Frankreich in der Kaiserzeit*, Leipzig, 1943.

115 R. Lejeune, *Recherches sur le thème des Chansons de Geste et l'Histoire*, Liège, 1948.

116 R. Louis, *De l'Histoire à la légende*, 3 vols, Auxerre, 1946-7.

117 R. Louis, 'L'épopée française est carolingienne' in *Coloquios de Roncesvalles*, 1956.

118 M. Lugge, *'Gallia' und 'Francia' im Mittelalter*, Bonn, 1960.

119 R. Menendez Pidal, *La Chanson de Roland et la tradition épique des Francs*, Paris, 1960.

120 S. Mochi-Onory, *Fonti canonistiche dell'idea moderna dello stato*, Milan, 1951.

121 J. de Pange, *Le Roi très chrétien*, Paris, 1949.

122 H. Pinoteau, 'Quelques réflexions sur l'œuvre de Jean du Tillet et la symbolique royale française', *Archives héraldiques suisses*, 1956.

123 W. Ullmann, *Medieval Papalism in the Political Theories of the Medieval Canonists*, London, 1949.

124 W. Ullmann, *Principles of Government and Politics in the Middle Ages*, London, 1961.

125 K. F. Werner, 'Die Legitimität der Kapetinger und die Entstehung des Reditus Regni Francorum ad stirpem Karoli', *Die Welt als Geschichte*, 12, 1952.

126 G. Zeller, 'Les rois de France candidats à l'Empire', *Revue historique*, 1934.

Index